CRUNCH!

Crunch!

A History of the Great American Potato Chip

DIRK BURHANS

THE UNIVERSITY OF WISCONSIN PRESS

The University of Wisconsin Press
1930 Monroe Street, 3rd Floor
Madison, Wisconsin 53711-2059
www.wisc.edu/wisconsinpress

3 Henrietta Street
London WC2E 8LU, England
eurospanbookstore.com

Printed in the United States of America

This book may be available in a digital edition.

Library of Congress Cataloging-in-Publication Data

Burhans, Dirk E., 1955–
Crunch!: a history of the great American potato chip / Dirk Burhans.
p.   cm.
Includes bibliographical references and index.
ISBN 978-0-299-22770-8 (cloth: alk. paper)
1. Potato chips—United States—History.
2. Potato chip industry—United States—History.   I. Title.
HD9235.P82U434   2008
338.4′766480521—dc22
2008011962

ISBN 978-0-299-22774-6 (pbk.: alk. paper)

This paperback edition is dedicated to the memory of
DONALD NOSS.

It's amazing how happy you can make someone by giving them a twenty-cent bag of chips. I've often said that I'm glad we don't make screwdrivers and wrenches. You're not going to give someone a screwdriver and have them say, "Oh, that's wonderful."

Bob Jones,
president, Jones Potato Chip Company

Contents

Illustrations

Preface

When I approached people in the potato chip industry for interviews for this book, I heard one response over and over again. Occasionally the wording was altered slightly, but most of the time it was phrased, word for word, exactly as follows: "Why would anyone want to write a book about potato chips?"

Amazing—the plant managers, marketing reps, vice presidents, and company owners who spent their whole lives in the industry didn't see the fascinating story right in front of them. With a plethora of trade books in the past fifteen years about American popular foods— Coca-Cola, beer, doughnuts, candy, hamburgers, pizza, oysters, "road food"—the question that I kept asking myself was a different one. My question was: "Why is it that up to now, no one has written a book about potato chips?"

How could I be so lucky?

The second question that I heard repeatedly, and continue to hear, is: "How did you become so interested in potato chips?"

Other than twice-yearly family visits, I never had much reason to spend time in my hometown after leaving for college and career at age eighteen, until I returned to Ohio in the late 1990s to take care of my elderly parents' affairs. One day, while shopping for my father at the local Kroger's supermarket, I noticed an entire aisle of shelves stocked with quirky little potato chip brands—Conn's from Zanesville, Mike-sell's from Dayton, Herr's of Pennsylvania (but made in nearby Chillicothe, Ohio), and Mister Bee—a chip from just across the river in Parkersburg, West Virginia, featuring an odd, antiquated logo of a bumblebee wearing a tuxedo and top hat. As I sampled the brands, I was surprised at how varied they were. Conn's and Mister Bee's were different from each other but had a family similarity—both were thin, light blond chips that almost melted in my mouth. Mike-sell's, on the other hand, was thick and golden in color—a hearty, aggressive, salty chip, the type that goes really well with beer, devoured before-you-know-it while watching a baseball game.

Reflecting on the differences, I realized that I had never tried chips like some of these. My mom hadn't bought Conn's or Mister Bee when I was a kid, and I never knew that a potato chip could be such a subtle, delicate experience. The more I thought about it, the more I realized I had mostly experienced just one type of potato chip, one that was somewhere in the middle, of medium weight, moderately salty, somewhat oily, but certainly tasty—like the standard Lay's and Wise chips with which most of us are familiar. I wondered why there didn't seem to be chip companies like these in the other states and cities I had lived in since leaving home in the 1970s. Why hadn't I encountered such diverse, colorful, oddball little potato chip companies outside of southeastern Ohio? Had comparable regional chip companies ever existed in other parts of the country? If so, why did they disappear?

This book began as an attempt to understand those questions. In the process, it has probably evolved into something else, but there is one thing that I hope this book is not. I truly hope that it is more than a nostalgic feel-good tome to be sold at factory outlet stores next to the decorator gift tins. Without question, much of what attracts us to snack foods to begin with is the happy, colorful mystery about their behind-the-scenes operations. As with Willy Wonka's factory, we long to know what goes into that cornucopia of tastes and textures in the shiny package. While I hope that this volume conveys the merriment inherent in America's most popular snack, there is ever so much more to the story of potato chips than fun-filled facts that make up a junk food junkie's dream.

Finally, I note here several pertinent updates to the 2017 paperback edition of *Crunch!*, originally published in 2007. The first is that we can now move the origin of the potato chip back at least four years, from 1853, as mentioned here in chapter 2, to 1849. Exhaustive work by David Mitchell, an engineer, historian, and former director of the Brookside Museum in Saratoga County, has uncovered a *New York Herald* article from August 1849 documenting potato chips at the Loomis Lake House (the property that later became Moon's Lake House, where George Crum and Katie Wicks worked). Although the stories of Crum and Wicks from chapter 2 of this book are engaging ones, the take-home point remains that while we can't yet credit any single individual with the "creation" of the potato chip, we can still reliably credit Saratoga Springs as the place of the potato chip's development as America's great snack. One can find David Mitchell's articles at http://chipscrumsandspecks ofsaratogacountyhistory.com.

Also worthy of mention is that Saratoga Springs, as the birthplace of the potato chip, has begun an annual summer Chip Festival, organized and sponsored by the Lion's Club, open to both the general public and industry participants. Saratoga Springs–based potato chip enthusiast and collector Alan Richer, also instrumental in the festival, estimates that the debut 2016 show had 2,500 paying attendees out of about 5,500 total visitors. Richer himself has accumulated much in the way of chip history and artifacts, regularly gives talks about potato chips for historical societies and libraries, and has posted extensive images, company histories, and potato chip blogs at http://togachipguy.com.

June 2017

Acknowledgments

This book permitted me to indulge in one of my very favorite activities: interviewing old men about their life's work (and, of course, interviewing women and men of other ages too). Some people interviewed for this project confided nearly their entire life stories. To produce a succinct and readable product, in many cases I could not include all, or even some, of their stories. Whether in print or not, all of my sources were invaluable in informing my perspective for what I hope is an accurate and rounded account of the history of potato chips. To all of them, I am extremely grateful. I especially thank Bob Jones, Don Noss, Ken Potter, and the Rider family, who showed not only great patience but true friendliness during my prolonged research for this book.

Vince Waldron, Jeffrey Cohen, and David Tager all encouraged me to pursue this book when it was just an idea. Lisa Silverman and Ibtisam Barakat provided helpful input on earlier versions.

I thank my editor at University of Wisconsin Press, Raphael Kadushin, whose patience and support for this book over several drafts yielded a greatly improved final product. I also thank Maggie Hilliard, Les Chappell, Diana Cook, and Adam Mehring for their help throughout the submission and editing processes.

In addition to the interviewees, the following people directly or indirectly helped at some time in some way or another: Molly Baker, Andrea Brown, Terry Buchheit, Brian Butko, Samantha Clemens, Michael DeSantis, Gordon Flagg, Linda Gorham, Melinda Hemmelgarn, Tim Hollis, Joy Houle, Megan Johns, the Kansas City Public Library, the Lancaster Mennonite Historical Society, Phil Langdon, Kim LaVoie, Tim McCook, George Neiderer, Lois Noss, Mary Jane and Charlie Pike, Robert Skitol, Kerig Taylor, Dale Ann Thomas, Vince Waldron, Steve Watkins, Mike Wolfinger, and Kathleen Edwards at the Freedom of Information Center at the University of Missouri. Bob Jones, Tim Hollis, Ed and Betty Rider, Kevin Fritsche, and two anonymous reviewers provided helpful critiques of earlier drafts and individual chapters. I am very grateful to Betsy Collins for her help with the manuscript. And as much as I might wish to take credit myself, I must acknowledge Vince Waldron's excellent suggestion for the book's title. I am grateful to Barbara Smith, my daughter Shawna Cady Burhans, and the many loyal friends to whom I did not reveal the nature of this project for their patience and moral support over several years.

CRUNCH!

1

The Great American Vegetable

The houses were all stocked with maize, beans and truffles, spherical roots which are sown and produce a stem with its branches and leaves, and some flowers, although few, of a soft purple colour; and to the roots of this same plant, which is about three palms high, they are attached under the earth, and the size of an egg more or less, some round and some elongated; they are white and purple and yellow, floury roots of good flavour, a delicacy to the Indians and a dainty dish even for the Spaniards.

Juan de Castellanos, 1601

A man surveys an undulating green field that stretches almost as far as the eye can see—a carpet of eighteen-inch-high plants. A little farther away, the pattern is broken by a different variety of plant, this one dotted with millions of tiny snow-white flowers. The man has fluffy white hair and eyes that are the color of baby-blue marbles. Over six feet tall, he is solidly built. He has the body of a working man—a truck driver, a mechanic, a farmer.

A potato farmer. Like his father and grandfather, Don Ramseyer has grown chipping potatoes his entire life. For three generations, the Ramseyer potato farm, an oasis of green on a rolling plain wedged between the suburbanizing towns of Wooster and Smithville, Ohio, has produced potatoes for potato chip factories. Now it is one of the last chipping potato farms left in Ohio.

Chipping potatoes are different from potatoes used for baking and salads. Because potatoes are mostly water, the act of frying them in hot oil leaves little potato matter when the water evaporates. In the early days, potato chip makers (called "chippers" in the business) tried the same varieties that we use for cooking at home—Russets, Katahdins, Irish Cobblers. But many of these yielded poorly, sometimes as little as 22 percent—twenty-two pounds of chips from one hundred pounds of raw potatoes. Today, chippers use modern varieties that can yield 30 percent or higher. These varieties have what chippers call high specific gravity—high dry-matter content.

Ramseyer grows two of the these varieties. One variety, Snowden—the one with white flowers in his field—is grown specifically for winter storage. Storage is important for the chip industry because fresh potatoes simply cannot be found from November to March. Chip factories—especially large ones like those of Frito-Lay, Wise, Herr's, and Utz—demand a product that is consistent the year round, a chip that tastes and looks the same all the time. Ramseyer makes his living from potatoes that chippers can use during the winter months.

"A problem we have with the Snowdens," says Ramseyer, "is stem end discoloration. The ideal thing is for them to die naturally, and then the chip quality is just excellent. If they're still green and growing and you're running out of time; you have to chemically kill them. But sometimes near the stem end there's a deposit of sugar that hasn't naturally tapped out, and it stays there—and when you chip 'em, there's a brown spot from the sugar."

Stem end discoloration is only one of many vagaries that potato growers and chippers have to deal with. Heat, internal necrosis, greening, sunscald, vascular browning, pressure bruises from storage, scabs, late blight, tuber rot, ring rot, mechanical injury, hollow heart, freezing . . . the list goes on and on.

A major consideration in the quality of storage potatoes like Snowdens is heat. By winter, Ramseyer's winter storage barn will be loaded almost to the ceiling with four-foot-square wooden crates full of Snowdens. If the temperature is too low, the starch in the potatoes turns to sugar, yielding a brown chip. But if the temperature is too high, depending on the maturity of potatoes when harvested, sugars can also accumulate, resulting in a brown chip. Either temperature extreme results in what consumers like you and me usually call a "burnt" potato chip.

"Ideally, you keep it at fifty degrees," Ramseyer says. "One way to disperse that brown buildup on the Snowdens is to increase the heat in the storage barn." But when that happens, the potatoes will start to sprout, and Ramseyer will be forced to use a sprout inhibitor.

"Once we cranked it to sixty-five, and it took three or four weeks before the chip quality came around. But then you're under the gun to get the things outta here—when it's that warm they're gonna try to sprout no matter what, even with the sprout inhibitor."

Ramseyer goes to no small effort to make sure his potatoes are ripe for chipping, as he should; if a shipment arrives with more than 15 percent defects, it can be returned by the chipper, at Ramseyer's expense.

"If it's rejected"—here Ramseyer pauses, not quite sighing—"it comes back to me, and I pay for the freight down and back."

In 2003 Ramseyer dumped twenty-five semi-loads of potatoes because of sprouting. At least, if he dumps the potatoes, all he has to pay is the dumping charge. For potatoes that go far, say, to North Carolina, it's actually easier for Ramseyer to find a farm there that will take them for cattle feed, so that he doesn't have to

Don Ramseyer digs young Reba potatoes. (courtesy of Don Ramseyer)

pay the freight back. Ideally, Ramseyer says, perfect weather would be rain once every two weeks, with dry weather three to four weeks before harvest. If the potatoes are drier toward the end, the chips will be better.

"But if it's too dry," he says, "you get a poor yield. So dry conditions get that starch content up. But we never get that all just right. Never."

Irrigation could solve some of Ramseyer's problems but is economically unfeasible, even though it has led to the awkward situation in which he finds himself today.

"There's a Frito-Lay plant right here in Wooster," says Ramseyer. "For us it was maybe a four- or five-mile trip."

The Frito-Lay plant had been the Ramseyers' main buyer since 1946, when it was owned by a chipper called New Era. After Frito-Lay acquired New Era, it eventually bought 75 percent of the Ramseyer potatoes. On a given day, the chipping potatoes of Ramseyer and other local growers were as good as any, but without irrigation the Ohio farmers found it hard to meet the consistency level increasingly demanded by Frito-Lay. Frito dropped the Ohio potato farmers in 1990, changing to growers in Michigan and North Dakota who relied on irrigation for a uniform product. Ramseyer says those growers now ship their potatoes all the way from Michigan and North Dakota to Frito-Lay's Wooster plant, which is an hour's walk from the Ramseyer farm. (Frito-Lay spokesman Jared Dougherty says that Frito-Lay obtains chipping potatoes from "all over the country," not just Michigan and North Dakota, including trademarked chipping potato varieties grown especially for Frito-Lay.)

"We understood why that happened," says Ramseyer, "it was understandable. They wanted to go for a consistent crop every year. But we're so close."

After 1990, the Ramseyer farm—and the rest of the Ohio potato farms that had arisen to serve the Frito-Lay plant—had to look elsewhere for contracts. Where Ramseyer once served the nearby plant almost exclusively, it now supplies faraway chip companies like Wise in Pennsylvania through potato brokers.

On the day of my visit, Ramseyer is building a water storage pit for a potato washing operation. At this point, it is just a wedge-shaped hole cut into the ground, about five feet deep by ten feet wide, tapering to perhaps thirty feet in length. In the past, chippers washed the potatoes themselves; but recently some have placed the burden of washing back on the growers. Small chip plants don't like washed potatoes because it may take them as long as a week to go through a load, and wet potatoes are easily bruised. But for large plants that go through a lot of potatoes quickly, washing by the grower reduces the plant's labor and processing time. Potato washing is something new for Ramseyer and other growers. There are no places to buy the equipment, no designs for such a contraption, no blueprints—it is something that Ramseyer and other potato growers will have to come up with on their own.

Fresh Springtime Potatoes: Florida

While Ramseyer is harvesting and washing potatoes in October and November, growers in Florida are negotiating contracts for next year. In January, while Ramseyer's ground is frozen and he ships Snowdens from his heated barn, Florida growers will be planting fresh seed potatoes.

Each April there's a moment of mild anxiety in the chip industry: just as the winter storage potatoes from people like Ramseyer are running out, fresh Atlantic potatoes from Florida are coming on. If the two events don't dovetail—if there's a shortage in Florida due to a weather event or bad growing season, or if the winter storage potatoes don't last—big money players can tie up uncontracted, open-market Florida potatoes. Sarah Cohen, president of Route 11 Potato Chips in Middletown, Virginia, recalled a year when such an event occurred.

"There was a year when Rob from E. K. Bare [Pennsylvania potato broker] said, 'Sarah, I don't know what to tell you, but I can't [guarantee potato shipments].' It was right at cusp where they were running out of stored potatoes, waiting for April potatoes. They told us that plants were closing down. There's that two-week-to-a-month window when Florida's here; it's a small supply, but they were the only fresh potatoes anywhere."

A former chipping potato farmer from Florida, who wished to remain anonymous for this book, remembered the previous decade or so as a good period for Florida potato farmers—she and her husband were able to partially retire from the money they made during those times. Yet she also noted the leverage big chip plants had in the situation.

"In the late '80s and early '90s they [large buyers] would tie up as much of the market potatoes as they could. They had no feeling at all for the smaller chip plants. They could afford to pay, and didn't hesitate to do so. In '87 we got seventeen to eighteen dollars per hundred-weight [one hundred pounds]. In '93, we got twenty-five dollars per hundredweight."

Florida has one of the highest costs per-acre for potato farming—the soil is sandy and requires chemicals; the weather is warm, so there are bug problems. Like their Ohio counterparts, Florida farmers have recently had to assume the expense of potato washing. And Florida's heat, even in early spring, can be a disaster for chipping potatoes, especially if they're wet.

"In Florida, heat will decimate potatoes," said the anonymous Florida farmer. "Atlantics have almost no skin. You can rub the skin off with your fingers. If they're wet—if the truck is delayed—you have a real problem."

"I carried a load of wet potatoes once, and you didn't get a hundred miles from the farm that you could smell that load of potatoes cooking. The juice runs out the bottom of the trailer," recalled Ira Rider, a retired potato buyer from Wooster, Ohio—almost next door to the Ramseyer farm. His daughter-in-law, Betty, has seen wet potatoes melt down in storage boxes "almost like ice cream."

Growers suggest too that the standards for white, unblemished potatoes increasingly demanded by Frito-Lay and other large chip plants are a sometimes arbitrary and fickle standard.

"A good friend once said to me that a blind man wouldn't know if he's eating a green potato chip; it tastes the same," said the anonymous Florida grower. "Once they found out that the average person doesn't care, they decided it doesn't matter. But they use blemishes as an excuse to drive down market prices paid to growers, even though the market research says it doesn't matter. It became a standard that the big buyers wanted to put in the grower's minds—that you have failed somehow."

"If you bruise them up, they won't take 'em," echoed Ed Rider, a potato buyer from Wooster, Ohio, and son of Ira. "The restrictions on the potato grower nowadays are ten times what it used to be. [It's because of] competition to have a white chip with no marks."

As with Ohio, increasingly stringent demands from large potato buyers, unpredictable weather events, and increasing costs of fuel, insurance, and chemicals have combined to make costs prohibitive for all but the largest Florida farmers. In an average year today, Florida growers may be getting two to three dollars per hundredweight compared to hundredweights in the teens in the 1980s and early 1990s. The anonymous Florida grower estimated that fifteen years ago there were some three hundred potato farms in her region of northern Florida compared to forty or fifty today, and that most of these are now in larger farms. Her family opted out of the business several years ago and now they grow cantaloupes and watermelons where they once grew potatoes.

"We always absorbed the added costs, but it got to a point where we couldn't," she said. "In the '80s it was good; in the early '90s it was good, but it got to a point where the contract price was not going up enough. After forty years in this we could no longer make a living."

As more and more Florida potato farms are lost to development, recent events in potato breeding may reduce chippers' dependence on early Florida potatoes. At the time of this writing, new varieties, such as Dakota Pearl and Glacier Chips, have been successfully stored into June, well past the April date when storage potatoes are usually giving out. According to some, these varieties will be able to tolerate storage temperature fluctuations as great as ten to twenty degrees without turning to sugar, chipping white the whole time.

New potato varieties like those could provide a big boost to Ohio potato farmers like Ramseyer, who need all the help they can get. With increased burdens such as irrigation and washing, Ramseyer estimates that where there used to be thirty to forty thousand acres of potato farms in Ohio, there now may be five to six thousand acres, with only half of that in chipping potatoes. Ramseyer's neighbors have added corn mazes, pumpkins, and hayrides to diversify sources of income as the market for chipping potatoes wanes. Other neighbors have said that if they have to start washing potatoes on top of everything else, they're finished.

Don Ramseyer doesn't share that viewpoint.

"You have to keep up with the times," he says. "That's what this is all about here," he adds, pointing to the hole in the ground that is to become a potato washer. "If you don't upgrade, and keep up with what they want, well . . ."

At the moment, Ramseyer sells most of his potatoes to Wise, which has chip plants in Pennsylvania and Tennessee. Selling to Wise seems to work out for both the Ramseyers and for Wise. It gives Ramseyer an advantage compared with the faraway Michigan farmers—no small advantage, considering the price of gas today.

"That's about the only advantage we have anymore. We don't irrigate; we have to depend on the weather, and the weather pretty much dictates the quality of your potato."

Irrigation versus drought; washing versus bruising; natural vine death versus chemical death; chemical death versus stem end discoloration; stem end discoloration versus cold storage; cold storage versus heated storage; sprout inhibitors versus sprouts.

Good chipping potatoes, versus paying the dumping charge in North Carolina, and dumping the whole load for cattle feed.

It's a long row to hoe for an Ohio chipping potato farmer.

Origins

If Florida is almost too hot for potatoes, it's because the vegetable is no stranger to cool places like the Ramseyer barn. Its entire history as a food product—from South American prehistory to the present—is intimately intertwined with temperature.

Within the nightshade family there are almost one thousand members of the potato's genus, *Solanum*, worldwide. The tuberous *Solanums*—the species having the fleshy underground stems, or tubers, that we eat—all originated in the Americas. While most tuberous *Solanum* species are South American, many are Central American or Mexican, and some are found as far north as Colorado, Utah, and even Nebraska. Although we are tempted to think of these locations as hot, within these regions potatoes are adapted to grow at cool altitudes—an adaptation key to the cultivated potato's later success in temperate climates like Maine and Ireland, as well as their persistence during the cool months in the Ramseyer barn. While elsewhere on the American continent, the great civilizations of the Maya, Aztecs, and Pueblo were built on maize, the high altitudes of the Andes were too cold. At altitudes over eleven thousand feet, maize grew stunted, and at over twelve thousand feet, it grew not at all. Manioc, a staple in the South American forest regions, did not grow in the highlands either.

But the locally adapted ancestors of the potato were a different story. Some tuber-bearing members of *Solanum* could be found as high as fifteen thousand feet—almost at the snow line. Although neither the harsh altitudes nor the depauperate *Solanum* species growing there were particularly suitable for humans, certain other tuberous *Solanums* grew at more hospitable altitudes around eleven thousand feet.

It is one of these hardy and frost-hardy tuber-bearing *Solanums* that was the ancestor of our modern cultivated potato, and it was cultivated in the Andes—a ribbon of mountains draped on the west coast of South America, running north from Colombia, through Ecuador, Peru, and Bolivia. John Gregory Hawkes, the world authority on evolution of the domestic potato, believes that the potato was domesticated between seven and ten thousand years ago, on the basis of radiocarbon dating of remains. In a region straddling the Andes across modern-day Peru and Bolivia, Hawkes believes, the potato originated from a wild species called *Solanum leptophyes*, and that the domestication of the potato began with *Solanum stenotomum*, a species still grown in this part of Peru and Bolivia. The best evidence for the potato's antiquity in South America comes from ceramics made by early South American peoples. Unfortunately, the climate best for growing potatoes—the cool, moist Andes—is the climate least hospitable for archaeological preservation, while the climate best for preservation—in this case the hot, dry northern Peruvian Pacific coast—was the climate least hospitable for potato growth. The cultures that produced the earliest known pottery with images of the potato were peoples of the Peruvian coast, who likely obtained their potatoes by trade with the Andean cultures.

But other archaeological evidence for the antiquity of the potato goes back even further. Some ancient food remains of "chuño"—potatoes in which the water is removed and the rest freeze-dried for preservation—are thought to date to about 5000 BC, while very early remains of wild potatoes used by Andean peoples in southern Chile may date to about 10,000 to 11,000 BC. Chuño is still made to this day by Andean peoples, for frost hardy though they may be, stored potatoes cannot tolerate repeated hard freezing in a climate that is cold much of the year. The chuño can be ground into potato flour, or it can be used whole. According to Salaman's 1949 book, "No chupa, or stew was, or is today thinkable without it, nor is a journey undertaken without carrying a supply of it."

By the 1500s, the Incas ruled over the entire Andean range, with an empire surpassing in length even that of the Romans. In 1532 the cultural trajectory of South America changed forever when Francisco Pizarro arrived in Tumbes with a small force of soldiers. Torn by internal civil war in the early 1500s, the Incas were easily conquered by Pizarro. Subsequent Spanish administrations utilized potatoes as food resources in maintaining the overall system of exploitation. Salaman quotes early sources documenting use of chuño to maintain the slave miners of Potosí in Bolivia, notorious as a place of cruelty where thousands of slaves perished.

Back to the New World

Although edible potatoes were strictly a New World vegetable and potato chips are a definitively American snack, it was a roundabout path that led the tuber of the Andes back to the hemisphere of its birth.

No one seems to know exactly when the potato arrived in Europe or who introduced it there, but it is thought to have appeared in Spain sometime around 1570. Slow to spread, it reached most of the rest of western Europe by 1600. It appears initially to have been a novelty plant of interest only to botanists, and had difficulty gaining acceptance as a food. In T*he Potato: How the Humble Spud Rescued the Western World*, historian Larry Zuckerman documents the considerable prejudice that accompanied the potato on its rise to acceptance in Europe — a rise that took centuries, and prejudice that continues today. The berries resembled deadly nightshade, and, like the poisonous members of solanaceae, potatoes contain alkaloids that can be harmful in large amounts. Because propagation was by mysterious underground tubers rather than seeds, potatoes were suspect in matters of sexual and sensual concerns that are bewildering by twenty-first-century standards. Potatoes were said to stimulate women to menstruate or lactate and to prompt men to produce sperm; herbalists said potatoes produced lust. Some of these characteristics were also attributed to underground crops such as radishes, onions, and turnips. Most of all, potatoes needed little tending or maintenance, and prospered in places where other crops struggled. Because they offered relief from hunger in otherwise tiny and inhospitable plots and required little work, "lazy" potatoes were usually associated with the poor.

Antoine Parmentier of France survived on potatoes as a frequent prisoner during the Seven Years' War with Prussia (1756–63). When he returned to France, he worked tirelessly to promote the potato, even persuading the court of Louis XVI to wear potato flowers on their apparel. In a well-known legend that, from all accounts, appears to have actually happened, Parmentier persuaded the king to give him a plot of the worst possible land to grow potatoes. The plot, on the outskirts of Paris, was guarded by a soldier during the day, but left unguarded at night. Aroused by the conspicuous daytime guards, peasants broke in by night to steal the tubers, thus helping spread the gospel of the potato to the rest of the population.

While the productivity of the potato led to its becoming a staple food of poor people in much of Europe, most countries were not entirely dependent upon it. Not so Ireland. Continuous warfare and conflict in the sixteenth and seventeenth centuries subjected a poor Irish population to constant disruption and ravaged crops. Absentee landowners sublet small tracts to middlemen, who in turn broke the lots into smaller and smaller parcels that were farmed by tenant peasants; tenant farmers then further subdivided the parcels among their offspring, sometimes resulting in tracts smaller than one acre. The situation was ripe for rescue by the potato, which produced more food per acre than any other crop, and whose underground habitat made it somewhat immune to raiding by marauding troops. High yields and inadequate land supply "rendered the cultivation of the potato almost obligatory" to Ireland — in the words of potato scholar W. G. Burton.

But all crops are subject to failure, via drought, flooding, or diseases like "curl" that affected the plants. Irish famines between 1800–1801 and 1817 resulted in deaths estimated at forty to sixty thousand people each. In August 1845 a new potato blight struck. Within a matter of weeks, the blight was prevalent throughout Europe, killing all potatoes, including storage potatoes, of all varieties. Fields could be ruined within a day, the potatoes turning black, going soft, and leaving a stench in their wake.

The famine was most serious in Ireland, where the enormous peasant population was almost totally dependent upon potatoes. Striking repeatedly in 1846, 1848, and 1849, the blight brought accompanying diseases like typhus and dysentery, as water supplies and living conditions were disrupted and populations were forced from homes. Accounts of Ireland of the time speak of emptied houses, roads jammed with the migrating poor, and living skeletons huddled in the remaining habitations. From an estimated 8.2 million prior to the famine, Ireland's population fell to 4.4 million by 1911—much of the reduction due to emigration, but much also to starvation and disease.

Records of potatoes "returning" to be grown in the New World—of course, they never left, but were brought to northern latitudes by colonists—date to 1685. William Penn described potatoes in a list of vegetables grown in his colony. Zuckerman, the potato historian, says that potatoes were grown throughout the northern colonies by the early eighteenth century. Readily accepted in North America, they were a dietary standby by the time of the Revolutionary War, when they were part of the troops' daily rations. By the 1800s potatoes could be found at the everyday dinner table of average Americans, comprising the "meat and potatoes" sensibility that came to dominate the all-American diet.

Once ensconced in the United States, it was probably only a matter of time before some inventive and enterprising American would stumble upon the concept of deep-frying thin potato slices in hot oil.

2

Creation Myths

Hm hm, that's good. That's a good accident. We'll have plenty
of these.

attributed to George Crum

In the summer of 1853, George Crum was a chef at Moon's Lake House
of Saratoga Springs, New York.

The Adirondacks were full of summer hotels catering to middle-
class and wealthy New Yorkers, but Saratoga Springs was prime. Located on the southeast edge of the Adirondacks, Saratoga Springs, if
you could afford it, was the closest and swankiest location for New
Yorkers looking to escape the summer heat and humidity in the days
before air-conditioning. Crum, an American Indian, but apparently
with some African American ancestry, was reputedly a colorful character. Legend has it that he was a guide in the Adirondacks for a time; he
was also a former hunter, fisherman, and trapper who supplied the fancy
upstate hotels with fresh game. They say he had several wives—perhaps
as many as five. In the summer of 1853, he was chef at this upscale lodge,
in this most upscale New York summer spot.

Crum was a respected chef and not a man to be trifled with. Known
for his cranky temperament, he did not bow to anyone. Patrons of his
cooking included former presidents, governors, and robber-baron mil-
lionaires of the times, but even these upstanding citizens were treated
just like everyone else. Legend has it that Crum once made both
William Vanderbilt and Jay Gould, two of the era's wealthiest entrepreneurs, wait well over an hour just to be seated for dinner—taking

their turn along with wage earners. Crum bragged that he could take any food and make it into a dish "fit for a king"—but if someone ever did complain, he was rewarded with "the most indigestible substitutes Crum could contrive."

So it was, they say, that one day in the summer of '53, a wealthy customer—often purported to be Cornelius Vanderbilt—returned some fried potatoes to the chef, protesting that they were not crunchy enough. Some sources say that the patron complained they were not salty enough, or that the potatoes were too thick. Whatever the exact complaint, there is unanimity about Crum's alleged response: he sliced additional potatoes into paper-thin wafers, deep-fried and vigorously salted them, and returned them to the peevish customer. Expecting a reaction of disdain, Crum was surprised when the patron not only devoured the potatoes but asked for more. So it is, the legend goes, that the potato chip was born.

The story about George Crum and the creation of the potato chip is nearly ubiquitous in modern industry lore. Almost any Web site or written treatment about potato chip history will repeat the Crum legend, including many histories in the promotions from potato chip companies themselves. Some will repeat the exact words from another source; others will alter the wording a bit, impugning motives or feelings to the characters; some will mention Cornelius Vanderbilt as the dissatisfied customer, some won't. For a long time, snack food industry associations included the Crum legend in their promotional materials.

But while the legend about George Crum returning razor-thin fried potatoes to a fastidious customer at Moon's Lake House is a compelling story and is the most oft-cited potato chip creation myth, there is better evidence that someone else actually created the chip—although Crum clearly had something to do with it. Potato chips are not even mentioned in Crum's 1914 obituary; an obituary in a yearbook only scantly mentions "Saratoga chips," devoting much more discussion to Crum's vaunted culinary skills, and the Crum version of the story does not find its way into other printed records until the 1940s. But like the child's game of telephone, the story becomes embellished with each retelling. By the late 1970s, the fussy customer who returned Crum's fried potatoes became Cornelius Vanderbilt—a permutation that later created no small amount of acrimony in Saratoga Springs.

George Crum in front of his restaurant at Saratoga Lake. (collection of Brookside Museum, Saratoga County Historical Society)

Certain parts of the Crum legend are in agreement: Crum was born in Ballston Spa, New York, to Abraham and Catherine Speck. Abraham Speck was described as from Kentucky, and his wife was variously described as a "Stockbridge Indian" or as an Indian from "the St. Regis tribe." But conflicting stories abound about even such a simple thing as Crum's name. The simplest explanation is that Crum simply took his name from his father, who while a jockey used the name Crum instead of Speck. A more imaginative version is that Commodore Cornelius Vanderbilt confused the concepts *crumb* and *speck* when trying to recall the chef's name and called him Crum, although that provokes the question of why the name wasn't then spelled the usual way (Crumb).

The Vanderbilt name is linked to Crum's in more ways than one. There seems to be no dispute that Crum's appreciative customers, whether at Moon's Lake House or Crum's own later restaurant, included important citizens like presidents Chester A. Arthur, Grover Cleveland, a string of New York governors, and wealthy individuals like tobacco magnate Pierre Lorillard. A well-known local story relates that William H. Vanderbilt, son of the Commodore, loved canvasback ducks but was unhappy with the way local hotels cooked them. Vanderbilt brought two canvasbacks to Crum, who boasted he could cook anything. Crum kept the ducks over hot coals exactly nineteen minutes, until "the blood followed the knife," and Vanderbilt liked the ducks so much that he "sent Crum many customers from all over the country."

An entertaining and enlightening analysis of the Crum legend by Skidmore College sociologists William Fox and Mae Banner reveals that the Crum version, although present for decades, became dominant sometime after a 1973 advertising campaign by the St. Regis Paper Company, and the Vanderbilt variant gained prominence soon thereafter. St. Regis ran full-page ads in magazines like *Time* with a photo of Crum, describing the potato chip/fussy customer incident.

In August 1977 Mary Lou Whitney, wife of Cornelius Vanderbilt "Sonny" Whitney, the great-great-grandson of the Commodore, and a well-to-do summer resident of Saratoga Springs, hosted a "potato chip party" for the publication of her *Potato Chip Cookbook*. Before the party, representatives of Mrs. Whitney contacted Saratoga County historian Violet B. Dunn for information about the potato chip's origins. None of the information that Dunn supplied mentioned Cornelius Vanderbilt. Yet the cover of the Whitney cookbook stated, "In honor of the 124th Birthday of the potato chip and its founder Commodore Cornelius Vanderbilt"—and nowhere mentioned George Crum.

A year later, Dunn stated on local television that, after extensive research, she had found no evidence that Cornelius Vanderbilt was the fussy patron who sent the potatoes back; a newscaster then reported that Dunn impugned Mrs. Whitney as an "opportunist who merely seized upon the potato chip story as a theme for one of her parties." Although Mrs. Whitney did not take well to these criticisms, the quality of her responses suggests her promulgation of the Commodore part of the myth was an innocent—if obtuse and poorly thought out— promotional effort based on the information she may have obtained from a newspaper clipping.

After Mrs. Whitney threatened to take her high-profile socialite parties elsewhere, Saratoga city officials met, some suggesting that historian Dunn had harmed the city of Saratoga, that Mrs. Whitney might sue the county, and that Dunn should apologize. A city official reportedly warned Dunn, "Saratoga Springs isn't going to forget this," to which she replied, "I hope they won't." The chairman of the board of supervisors personally apologized to Whitney, as did the president of the city's major bank, who expressed that "the rich and famous" were "entitled" to come to Saratoga, "free from harassment over trivia," and hoped Mrs. Whitney would continue to spend summers there. Newspaper editorials and letters sections rang hot with commentary on both sides, most supporting Dunn as a year-round resident of Saratoga who was not obligated to rewrite history to suit the whims of a moneyed summer resident. As the whole affair simmered, Mrs. Whitney and Mrs. Dunn made peace, with Mrs. Whitney even inviting Mrs. Dunn to her parties, to which the latter accepted.

The Whitney *Potato Chip Cookbook* occasionally surfaces in Ebay auctions. It is a small-format, sixty-page spiral-bound booklet, entirely handwritten in pen and marker. The following text is on page 8 of the book under the heading Potatoes: "In Ireland, during the famine of 1845–46, potatoes were plentiful and the Irish were eating potatoes at every meal. There were two varieties, Stelk and Colcannon."

And that's all it says about the famine and the potato in Ireland.

Whitney's book goes on to list recipes for chip dips, seafood dishes with crushed potato chips, vegetable dishes with crushed potato chips, and meat dishes with crushed potato chips.

If she truly believed the Vanderbilt variant on the potato chip creation myth to be correct, Whitney must have obtained the information from materials related to the Snack Food Association's 1976 meeting in Saratoga Springs, reportedly from a newspaper clipping. According to Fox and Banner, the likely promoter of the Vanderbilt variant was the Snack Food Association's publicity agency at the time. In doing its own research, the agency relied upon an account from a popular Saratoga history book that left the fussy customer unnamed, but added Vanderbilt's name because he had long been thought to be the customer in chip industry folklore. The latter point is hard to validate, but it appears likely that there was an existing oral tradition within the industry naming Vanderbilt as the customer. When asked about the Vanderbilt story, some industry veterans express certainty that the alleged interaction between Vanderbilt and Crum took place; others know of the story but don't venture to comment on its veracity.

While all evidence indicates that Saratoga Springs was the birthplace of the potato chip and that members of the Crum family had something to do with it, the best information points to Crum's sister as its creator. Crum, who by all accounts was not a modest man, never claimed invention of the chip, while Katie Wicks, his sister, did take credit in an 1899 interview that came out while Crum was alive. David Mitchell, former director of the Brookside Museum in Saratoga County, said that "never in his life did Crumm/Speck take credit for it," and that had he invented it "he would have said so, because he was not a humble man." First-person interviews conducted in a 1980 oral history project with Saratogans old enough to have known Crum show that most of them did not hear the Crum version of the story until the 1930s. An 1893 history of Saratoga County, published well before Crum's death in 1914, makes no mention of chips but focuses on his cooking, farm, and hunting dogs.

The most credible version is that Katie Speck Wicks invented the chip in an accident not dissimilar to the culinary misfire in which the brownie was born (from a mix-up of cake and fudge). "Aunt Katie," who also worked at Moon's Lake House, was frying crullers and peeling potatoes at the same time. A thin slice of potato found its way into the frying oil for the crullers, and Katie fished it out. Noticing the chip, Crum tasted it and said, "Hm hm, that's good. How did you make it?" After Katie described the accident, Crum replied, "That's a good accident. We'll have plenty of these." Wick's obituary of 1917 credits her as inventor of the chip, but doesn't mention the accidental nature of the invention.

Another version claims that Katie Wicks learned to make the chips from brother-in-law Peter Francis, a chef with whom she worked at the Sans Souci Hotel in Ballston Spa, near Saratoga Springs; yet another version says that Cary Moon (proprietor of the Lake House where the chips were first served) or his wife invented the chips. Although no one disputes that Moon's promotion of chips helped them skyrocket in regional popularity, there seems to be little support for these versions.

Why has there been no general agreement on any single version of the legend? Perhaps it is important to remember that, at the time of Crum's and Wick's deaths—the 1910s—potato chips were still in a state of infancy and American culture was still a locally focused affair. While the telephone, automobile, and airplane had all been invented, advertising and mass media like radio and television had yet to create the sense of "community" that today crosses local and regional boundaries. By the 1910s, the daily cultural context in which Americans found themselves had a lot more in common with the horse-and-buggy times of the preceding nineteenth century. Although the new food had dispersed nationally by the 1910s, potato chips were still mostly a cottage industry; if they were not produced and consumed solely within the confines of a restaurant, at most they were sold within a few miles from where they were produced. Served from baskets, bins, or in plain paper bags, they had little or nothing in the way of recognizable brand names, publicity, or associated advertising.

In the 1959 *Chronicles of Saratoga*, historian Evelyn Barrett Britten adds that because Francis, Moon, Wicks, and Crum were all associated with one another, it was natural that confusion about the origin of the chip should arise. Research by David Mitchell, the former museum director, supports this view. Indeed, when newspaper and book accounts can't even agree on versions or spellings of Crum's or Wick's names (*Crum, Crumm, Chum, Crumb; Speck, Speke, Wicks, Weeks*), it's no wonder that the subsequent stories about their larger life's work would be so varied.

Perhaps, too, the myriad of myths surrounding the founding of such a simple food contain a larger truth: even if a particular person, such as Crum, didn't personally invent potato chips, he could have. Anyone who ever set foot in a nineteenth-century kitchen could have invented a potato chip; several histories have pointed out that potato chips, as simple as they are, were likely invented and reinvented independently several times. But if the invention went no further than grandma's handwritten recipe book, who would be the wiser? As they say in real estate, it's all location, location, location. In no small part, upscale Saratoga Springs—with its wealthy ambience, chic restaurants, and influential citizenry—was the ideal location from which the great American potato chip could not only start but boldly go where no snack had gone before.

3

Bursting the Seams

Such periods of expansion, a sort of flowering season, have occurred over and over in the history of life among various
groups successively.

George Gaylord Simpson, *Tempo and Mode in Evolution*

As hard as it is to trace the potato chip's origin, it is even more of a challenge to trace its dispersal in the half decade after 1853. We know that
immediately after its invention at Moon's Lake House, "Saratoga chips"
were served there nightly in baskets—or "paper cornucopias"—at tables,
a custom that spread to the other Saratoga hotel restaurants, and then
likely spread farther into surrounding New York State, Pennsylvania,
and New England. In a 1970s interview an executive of a chip company
suggested that a caterer named Fleeper, who supplied box lunches to
excursion boat passengers between Boston and Nahant, was the first to
sell potato chips outside of Saratoga Springs. Without dates this information is hard to verify, but it is also likely that chips simultaneously ra-
diated outward into towns proximate to Saratoga Springs, where they
would also have been served in restaurants at first.

In addition to restaurants, stores dispensed potato chips from barrels
or glass cases and into bags. Stores of the time were not self-service—
that development became widespread only after the Second World
War. In addition to groceries and restaurants, fairs, farmers' markets,
bars, and bakeries were sellers' opportunities. "Each summer, the family
would pack up and set off for the fairs," wrote Leslie C. Mapp in his account of Mike-sell's Potato Chips, Dayton, Ohio. "They lived in a tent

and sold from a glass case filled with potato chips, with the children soon developing an unerring knack for knowing how large a scoopful would fill a five-cent bag." Mose Mesre of Conn's Potato Chips, Zanesville, Ohio, says that Mrs. Conn sold chips in "old beer joints and things like that. And everybody wanted more and more, and she could only give 'em so much, and that's why she did it [sold out to a factory operation]."

At some point, potato chips moved from a humble kitchen-cooked product to factory production, but naming a single creator for mass production of potato chips in the context of late nineteenth-century commerce would be like naming Fats Domino or Bill Haley or Elvis as the single creator of rock 'n' roll. Nonetheless, one person who comes up in any article about early potato chip history is William Tappenden of Cleveland, Ohio. Accounts from the Snack Food Association mention Tappenden and his horse-drawn wagon as "a familiar figure on Cleveland's streets." In 1895 he was among the first to take chips out of the kitchen and into a factory setting, where he "converted a barn at the rear of his house into one of the first potato chip factories."

It is likely that every city in the eastern half of the United States at the turn of the century had its own version of William Tappenden. Part of the reason we know about Tappenden, and not the others, may be his Ohio connection. In 1931 a loose group of Ohio chippers united as the Ohio Chip Association under the charismatic leadership of Harvey Noss, sales manager of Noss Pretzel and Cone company. Today known as the Snack Food Association (SFA), the group at first was laden with Ohio chippers, many of whom probably knew Tappenden personally.

And if Ohio was—and is—a place of chip diversity, so was—and is—Pennsylvania. Today, Lancaster County, Pennsylvania, has the greatest density of independent potato chip companies in the United States. One of these, Original Good's Potato Chips—not to be confused with Ralph Good's Potato Chips, a distant family relative in the same county—appears to be the oldest extant chipper in the country. Dating to 1886, Original Good's predates Tappenden in Cleveland by nine years. Until its recent merger, a wall inside Original Good's twelve-thousand-square-foot metal building showcased photos from five generations of Goods, starting with founder Anna Good, in a tinted photo and wearing a Mennonite prayer cap, next to a photo of Lewis and Lynn Good, the present owners. The legend is that Anna Good started cooking potato chips in her kitchen, later moving to a small shed for a factory. From conversations with his grandfather, Lewis Good learned that at least three generations ago, if not earlier, the company delivered to stores via delivery routes, much as modern companies do.

One thing we know for sure is that most early chip companies grew exactly in the manner of Tappenden's and Original Good's: they started literally in the kitchen and moved out of the home as sales volume increased. Often they moved first into an outbuilding, like a shed or a garage, before finding a true factory. Almost every chip company surviving from the first half of the twentieth century tells its history on a package, Web site, or other promotional item. After a while they all start to sound the same:

> Backer's Potato Chip Company was founded in 1931, by Grandpa and Grandma Backer on the bank of Hillers Creek in Callaway County, Missouri. The potatoes were peeled by hand, sliced in a hand crank slicer and cooked in a doughnut kettle a few pounds at a time. Our distribution was a 15 mile radius with the potato chips being delivered with the family car. Today we've moved to town and use the most modern equipment.

> The [Ralph] Good's Potato Chip family, now in their Fourth generation, started making Potato Chips on their kitchen stove in 1928. By 1939 a home made cooking kettle was set up in their garage to meet the growing demands of the popular snack chip. In 1952 the Good's moved into their present facility. In 1966 a continuous cooker was installed to meet the growing demand.

> Wise Snacks came to exist because a young grocer named Earl Wise, Sr. had too many potatoes. Being a frugal businessman, he decided to use the extra potatoes to make potato chips. This was in 1921, so he did all the work by hand and sold the chips in brown paper bags from his store. . . . For over 80 years, from small batches in his mom's kitchen to a remodeled garage to the current state-of-the-art facility, one thing has never changed. Earl Wise, Sr. and the company that bears his name make terrific chips.

One assumes that surviving chip companies make these histories available either because they are proud of them or because customers respond positively to them. The frequency with which supermarket shoppers seem to blithely bypass locally made chips in favor of other snacks, however, suggests that these reverent histories carry little weight with the modern consumer.

Num Num & Noss

When chip industry veterans over the age of seventy get together, the name of Harvey Noss invariably arises. Noss, who organized Ohio chippers into an early industry association, resisted the snack food business at first. A talented amateur magician and a self-taught pianist who played for silent movies part time, Noss was a journalist for the *Cleveland Plain Dealer* and at first had other career plans. But soon enough, he joined the family business, the Noss Pretzel and Cone Company, formerly the Noss Baking Company, to become general manager in 1922.

Don Noss, Harvey's youngest son, lives in Brecksville, Ohio. It is a quiet suburban neighborhood on the outskirts of Cleveland backing up on the Cuyahoga Valley National Park—an enclave of 1950s-era houses, where suburban deer browse backyard bird feeders among spreading sugar maples and towering tulip trees. As the first decade of the twenty-first century approaches a close, Don, in his early eighties, still works as an independent packaging broker for a small Ohio chip company.

The stuffy name of the business in the 1920s—Noss Pretzel and Cone Company—didn't last long, thanks to a toddler. At a family get-together to debate a name change for the company, the elders reached an impasse and couldn't come up with anything. At that point, Don's oldest brother, a toddler nicknamed Speed, wandered through wanting a pretzel, saying "Num num." Don's uncle, an executive in the company, sprang to attention. He asked the toddler to repeat what he'd said.

The toddler said it again: "Num num."

Noss's uncle observed: "You know, that sounds a helluva lot better than Noss Pretzel and Cone Company." The Num Num Food Company was born.

With the mass of Cleveland potato chippers at his disposal, Harvey Noss set about forming a promotional organization. At first called the Ohio Chip Association, in 1931 the group included Clevelanders like Num Num, Restemeier, and Dan Dee, but soon added such other Ohio chippers as Salem, Mike-sell's, and Husman and began recruiting into nearby Michigan. Soon Noss was ready to take it national and in 1937 changed the name to the National Potato Chip Institute.

Don Noss remembers as a child of ten or twelve years old traveling with his father to Pennsylvania to recruit chippers for the fledgling organization. "We'd get in the '38 Buick, and away we'd go to Pennsylvania, looking for steam coming out of the stacks. I'd say, 'There's a chip plant.' Dad would say, 'No, that's a steel plant.' But that's how we found our recruits."

Don Noss explains that they could have searched for chippers in the phone directory, but at that time phone books didn't always list potato chip companies. Father and son knocked on the doors of chip plants unannounced, and as often as not came away with a new member for the institute:

> I can remember one in Altoona, Pennsylvania. Dad said, "Okay, you wait in the car." He came back and said, "Swell, we've got another new member for the chip association." That's when I learned "how do you do, sir," "nice to meet you, sir." I was only twelve years old.
>
> We went in to one [chipper]; he says, "You keep your mouth shut, let me do the talking." "Yes, Dad." After a conversation, he says, "Well, Mr. Noss, what am I gonna get for fifty dollars a year?" "Well, you're gonna get a monthly report of activity in the chip industry, and the machinery industry, and we'll keep you up to date on everything that's going on." "Okay—you want me to write you out a check now?" "No, just send it to my address." And they'd shake hands and he'd walk out. Everything was done with a handshake—can you believe that?
>
> That was 1938, '39. Things are different now. You can't do it with a handshake anymore.

One gets the feeling that the elder Noss stayed up late at night developing his chip organization. The first newsletters were mimeographed, replete with crossed-out words—indicating that the typist, likely not a secretary, changed his mind in mid-sentence. One also gets the feeling that Harvey Noss had his work cut out for him. It's hard to believe now, but at that time there were ongoing problems educating retailers and consumers about just what potato chips were; some merchants thought they were to be used for washing, like soap chips.

Noss had a ripe field of chippers to enlist for his fledgling organization, with hundreds of tiny companies springing up nationwide. With the rise of Prohibition, these chippers got a break; Don's uncle, a vice president at Num Num, recalled the speakeasies: "The bootleg joints— the speakeasies—would serve pretzels, snack sausage sandwiches, and even potato chips," said Carl Noss. "They would give these snacks away free. And anytime you give stuff away, you use a lot of it. They were all over. It wasn't only Cleveland, but the entire country." Leonard Japp Sr., founder of Chicago's Jays Foods, notoriously got his start running chips to Al Capone's speakeasies.

By the 1930s, the Great Depression dampened economic opportunity generally, but may have benefited the chip industry. Many chip companies started during the Depression, when financial circumstances forced men and women to take risks they would not have dreamt of only a few years before. William Backer says that Backer's Potato Chip Company, Fulton, Missouri, began after his father lost his Missouri restaurant to a fire in 1929. He opted to give potato chips a try, although after the fire "he went to doing nothing for about two years. We moved to the country; my mother bought a little place, twelve acres. Two-story log house. It was big. I think the price of the whole damn thing was two hundred dollars. We were living out there without electricity, without gas, water, or a sewer system; it was primitive. And those first chips were primitive."

At Kitchen Cooked in Illinois, which also started during the Depression, "Mrs. Flossie Howard and her family began making potato chips as a way to help supplement the family's income. Their efforts included the tedious process of peeling, slicing and cooking by hand the potatoes in small, cast iron kettles. Their small business located in the front portion of an abandoned church, would also serve as their home in the small Central Illinois community of Farmington."

Charles Seyfert, founder of Seyfert's, later a dominant regional company, and Herman Lay of the country's first nationally distributed potato chip similarly got started when their previous livelihoods went belly-up during the Depression.

But chip making in the 1920s and 1930s could be a scary business for more than economic reasons. At this time, most chippers were making chips in lard, and fire was a daily concern. If the kettles caught, everything might go up. Don Noss said that at the Num Num plant such an event might occur every two or three months. "They had a giant metal

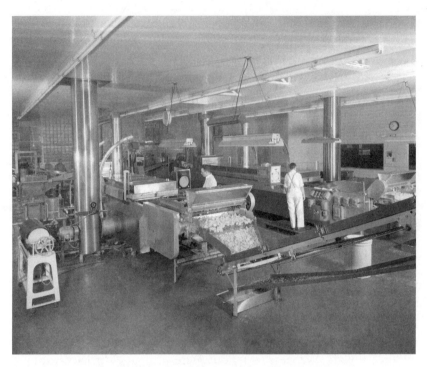

Early Utz continuous cooker. (courtesy of Utz Quality Foods, Inc.)

cone they'd lower with pulleys and chains on the kettle to snuff it out. Of course, it meant shutting everything down. Production would come to a halt for the rest of the day so that the soot could be cleaned. Listen, when that fat catches on fire, it sputters all over the place. You know how your cooking pan sputters in the kitchen?"

Occasionally, such a conflagration might catch an entire plant. In 1951 the Herr plant in Nottingham, Pennsylvania, burned to the ground, forcing it to start from scratch with a new factory. Early fires also destroyed the Wise plant, Mike-sell's of Dayton, and Cain's of Massachusetts. Even into the late 1970s, a continuous cooker at Flaherty's Potato Chips in Akron, Ohio, set the plant on fire: Noss recalls that "Vince Flaherty was coming home from the airport the day it happened. As he got closer to work, he sees fire [in the distance] and says, 'That's a helluva big fire over there.' Then he realizes it's his place! The fire trucks sprayed water on it and spread flaming oil all over the place." Bob Jones, president of Jones Potato Chip Company, Mansfield, Ohio, remembers "driving to Akron with my dad and older brother to look at what used to be a chip factory. By the time we arrived there was nothing but a hole in the ground. Mr. Flaherty was not a young man at the time and he decided that he wouldn't rebuild his factory."

If the economic climate of the 1930s enticed would-be businessmen and businesswomen to invest in potato chipping despite risks like fire, technology had a more complex effect. Even as one development in the 1930s allowed chippers to take off nationwide, another invention was so expensive that the Depression dampened the ability of chippers to take full advantage.

Ferry's Tales Come True

Arthur Ross of the Ross Potato Chip Company in Richland, Pennsylvania, had a problem. He was on the losing end of a special partnership with a pretzel company called Hygrade out of Philadelphia. Ross primarily sold the potato chips he produced, but added Hygrade's pretzels to his sales routes to diversify his product line. Hygrade inverted the process; it primarily sold the pretzels it produced, but enhanced its line by distributing Ross's potato chips on its pretzel routes.

The problem was, Hygrade had the advantage. Hygrade manufactured pretzels by a high-volume continuous process that made pretzels nonstop, whereas Ross — and all the other chippers — produced potato chips by the "batch kettle." Although many chip companies started out with cast iron kettles in the kitchen, by the 1920s and 1930s "kettles" were rectangular cookers with capacities of 40 pounds per hour, 120 pounds per hour at most. By 1929 all potato chips were still made via this batch process, one lot at a time — taking anywhere from five to ten minutes. The only way to increase production was to increase the number of kettles, whereas Hygrade could simply turn on the pretzel machine and crank out pretzels all day.

Ross was more than willing to experiment with an invention brought to him by the J. D. Ferry Company of Harrisburg. The Ferry company had invented a continuous cooker for potato chips, designed by an engineer named McBeth. The cooker allowed uncooked potato slices deposited at one end to be carried downstream in hot oil, via a system of paddles, to the other end in a period of three or four minutes, to emerge hot and cooked via a system of conveyors. No longer did potato chips need to be cooked by the batch; like Henry Ford's cars, they were ready to enter the era of mass production. Early continuous machines could easily produce chips at rates of hundreds of pounds per hour. In the next few years, Ferry continuous cookers were bought by Rainey of Philadelphia, Schuler of Rochester, Stock's Quality Foods of Reading, and Hiland of Iowa.

But Ferry cookers weren't for everyone. They were physically large and prohibitively expensive, and most companies couldn't afford them. The first cookers made by Ferry were so cumbersome that the combustion chambers were bricked onsite at the chip factory, after which the cookers were part of the building and could not be moved. Only later were the heating chambers made an integral part of the machine, so that the units could be shipped from Ferry intact. Even so, in subsequent decades the continuous cookers became the industry standard. New engineering companies arose to meet the demand for the machines. To this day, chippers sometimes call them Ferry cookers in the same way we refer to photocopiers generically as Xerox machines.

Mass production was not the chippers' only limitation in the early part of the twentieth century. Even when chippers could keep up with demand, they could not keep their stock fresh; nor could they distribute chips any appreciable distance from the factory. They were "a dehydrated, salted product that would quickly become rubbery and unappetizing when exposed to high humidity, as after a rain." When chips weren't sold from cases or barrels, the best technologies of the times permitted only bagging in plain paper sacks or unsealed wax bags, to be closed with a clip or a staple.

Mose Mesre recalls that Mrs. Conn "made the chips in that washing-machine type cooker. I can see her now with the basket under arm, with the little bags of chips in wax paper bags, no printing on 'em. Used two clips of the stapler. Of course, in the early days they used bags with a little clip, and that was all right, except when the muggy weather came, you know what happened. . . . You made 'em in the morning and they was almost stale by noon." At Backer's in Missouri, says William Backer, "The way you'd close 'em was with a paper clip. You had your stack of bags over here. The first thing you'd do was separate them; then you'd scoop 'em up with a metal scoop, and you'd have a scale—and you'd get to where you didn't need to weigh them—but you still weighed them on a balance. And then you'd set it in a slot. Later on it got to where you used a stapler." Backer says the staplers had no base: "You'd keep it palmed, never lay it down. The bagger would make one fold, keeping the stapler in one hand the whole time." There was no label or name on the bag. At O.K. Potato Chips of Akron, chips were hand-packaged on tables. Betty Rider, now in her early fifties and a potato buyer with her husband, recalls that she and other women at O.K. hand-filled the bags with a scoop, stapling the bags with a foot pedal. O.K. used staples into the 1970s, after the vast majority of chip companies had gone to automated sealing—thanks in part to a formidable lady who accomplished more on behalf of potato chips than any woman since Katie Wicks.

The Second Lady of Potato Chips

Laura Scudder was trained as a nurse and a lawyer, and was a former restaurant owner. A determined and decisive lady, but benevolent to those under her wing, she cut an imposing and photogenic figure in spectacular wide-brimmed hats.

After starting her own chip company in Monterey Park, California, in 1926, she noticed that customers and grocers had to go to lot of trouble for a bag of chips. The grocer had to open a glass case or barrel, reach inside, and scoop and weigh chips into a paper bag. Chips were bought by the ounce or by the pound, as one might purchase flour or candy.

Scudder set out to bypass bulk display entirely. A woman who had spent her life swimming upstream in the male-dominated world of business, Scudder used female employees for light labor such as packaging, as did many factories of the time. She instructed the women to take the empty bags home at night and iron slips of wax paper inside near the neck of the bags. The next day, after workers filled the bags, all they had to do was iron the top shut; the wax paper, already in place, merged the two layers for an airtight seal. Now chips could be displayed on a shelf in bags, eliminating the need to ladle them out behind a counter. With the airtight wax seal, they stayed fresher.

Scudder's business took off and she went on to add plants in Oakland and Fresno. A tireless public promoter for chips, she visited

Female employees often performed the jobs of bagging and weighing. (courtesy of Golden Flake Snack Foods, Inc.)

women's clubs, schools, and hospitals, and went on the radio twice each week to talk to housewives about cooking, never neglecting to mention recipes with potato chips. By the late 1950s, she was on television—narrating commercials for Scudder-sponsored local programming. Seasonal lows in chip consumption inspired her to add peanut butter and mayonnaise to her production lines, bringing new dimension to Scudder Foods. In 1957 Scudder Foods was sold to an oil company. Soon after, in 1959, the grande dame of potato chips passed away at the age of seventy-seven, but not before becoming a household name throughout California.

A Flowering Season

If Laura Scudder took the first steps to improve chip packaging, others did her concept one better. At about the same time that Scudder

Early Golden Flake display. (courtesy of Golden Flake Snack Foods, Inc.)

discovered wax paper's advantages, engineers elsewhere were experimenting with cellophane. The Dixie Wax Paper Company—makers of the Dixie Cup—finally made a truly sealed bag, the Fresheen bag, using glassine. Apparently, piercing the waxy coating and hard surface of glassine to create the seal was no easy task, but it revolutionized the industry, taking chips off the counter and allowing them to be shipped more than twenty miles from the factory. Opaque printing inks could now be used with the new materials. With nicely printed labels on good packages, the public learned to associate an image or a logo with a certain type of chip. John Morgan, a former executive of Dixico, said that by 1934, when chip companies got the new Fresheen bags, they "just burst out of their seams."

Don Noss has what may be the world's largest collection of potato chip bags, numbering in the hundreds—many donated by Charlie Pike, formerly of Cleveland's Dan Dee potato chips, but many collected by Noss himself. One of them is a glassine Laura Scudder's Bluebird Potato

Chips bag with an image of a bluebird in a red top hat. Another, a five-cent Mike-sell's bag, is not even labeled "potato chips." The front has the Mike-sell's logo, similar to the Mike-sell's bags of today; the back, in small type, reads: "Pretzels—2 ozs or more. Potato chips—1 oz or more. Carmelcrisp—2 ozs or more." Apparently, Mike-sell's used the same bag for whatever snack was coming off the line. Because the product lost mass when settling, the labeling provided some flexibility in weight—hence, "1 oz or more" of potato chips. "They'd put you in jail if you tried that today," Noss says about such labeling.

Other packaging images were entirely regional. On a 1930s Dan Dee bag in Noss's collection, a bullet-nosed "Gee Bee" type plane with pontoons flies before the Terminal Tower, Cleveland's revered 1930s-era skyscraper—air races were a big part of Cleveland's culture of the time. A Seyfert's bag from Columbus has images of thirteen school pennants, with names like Arlington, Bexley, Eastmoor, and Rosary—all schools in the company's central Ohio distribution area.

Perhaps the most unusual bag in Noss's collection is his "Big Tits" bag. Contrary to what one might think upon first hearing the name, Big Tits here appears to refer to a person. Under the Big Tits logo at the top of the bag is a drawing of a happy, well-dressed, rotund man in checked trousers, bowler hat, and cane—presumably Big Tits himself. That someone would actually name an innocent product like potato chips Big Tits says a lot about changing vernacular over the years.

But if packages like these could be mass-produced by the 1930s, the way they were processed and filled at chip plants lagged behind. For the most part, workers still scooped chips into the bags, after which they were sealed by hand. Dan Woodman, a consulting engineer for Lay's, solved the problem by designing a machine in which bags could be dropped, filled, and clipped through openings in a rotating turret. Woodman went on to start his own company to produce packaging machinery for the increasingly automated chip plants, as other engineering companies followed suit.

John Kelley was an engineer for Woodman in the 1940s, right after the war. "My opinion, when I started," says Kelley, "was that most production facilities were antiquated, even for those times." Most machines, other than Woodman's, filled twenty bags a minute, but the average company could produce a thousand pounds of chips an hour. If

Utz production line. (courtesy of Utz Quality Foods, Inc.)

the packaging machinery broke down, the cook was typically called on to repair it. According to Kelley, "He'd have a ball peen hammer and an adjustable wrench, and that's about it. I was appalled."

Kelley's trial by fire as a fresh young engineer was to fly to New Orleans to repair a Woodman packager owned by Bill Dickey of Dickey's Potato Chip Company. Another packaging company had sold Dickey four packaging machines that didn't work, and Dickey was "mad as a wet hen," says Kelley. Woodman talked Dickey into trying a Woodman machine instead, and he ordered two, but Dickey couldn't get the Woodman machines to work either. Dickey made plane reservations for the young engineer and met Kelley at the airport. Kelley recalls:

> Dickey looked at me and said: "Goddamn, I asked Woodman to send me a man, and he sent me a boy." I was young, just out of the Navy— but I did know about mechanics. It was a cold, cold drive from there to the plant. I said to him, "Mr. Dickey, maybe you need to give me a chance to exercise my talents before you criticize me."

I corrected the problem. When the machine was ready, it started bagging at sixty bags a minute. I had Mr. Dickey pull the lever that changed the speed, and told him to pull the lever to speed it up to sixty-five, seventy, and seventy-five bags a minute. Dickey said to me: "It's doing good, but I don't want you to go back yet. Stay here for three days, and I want to see how the machine operates without you feeding it with a bottle every hour." I installed the second Woodman machine. Then I said, "Mr. Dickey, you need a controlled feeding system." I put in a feeding system the next week. I stayed around so long I was about to become a native of New Orleans, but the guy was still hostile to me. He was one mean S.O.B. After all this, I said, "Time for me to go home."

Meanwhile I had instructed an old guy, who was about sixty-five or seventy at that point, in the plant to fix the packaging machine. At night he [Dickey] screwed stuff up to see if the old man could fix it, and the man learned by trial and error. After seeing all would be good, Dickey said, "I want you to go to the hotel, shower and dress, and I'll take you to dinner."

I met him, and he was in a Cadillac with his wife and daughter. Dickey's second wife was a step or two higher than him on the social ladder, so he was very well known. He'd pull out twenty dollars for a one dollar drink. You'd walk into a bar, and every bartender would wait on him. All the doormen at the nice hotels—everyone knew him. We went to a New Orleans restaurant and had a great meal.

After dinner, Dickey took me back to my room. "You've done a good job," he told me, "and when you do a good job, you deserve a feather in your cap. Here's a check for the first machine, and here's a check for the second machine, and here's checks for three more." He paid [Woodman] for five machines total.

Now, that's a feather in your cap!

At the next National Potato Chip Institute convention, Dickey posted himself in a chair in front of the booth of the other packaging company—the one that sold him the four faulty machines to begin with—and told anyone who cared to listen that this company's machines were no good. "Go see John Kelley at Woodman instead," Dickey said.

"I made a friend for life" in Bill Dickey, says John Kelley, "but I didn't like the way he ran his business, the way he chewed out the employees. Otherwise I would have worked there myself."

Never Fear When Harvey's Near

By 1941 Noss and his National Potato Chip Institute were recruiting members nationally, and had a more upscale magazine to go with their ascending status. But in 1942 wartime sanctions took hold; first price regulations, which specified price ceilings for products, and then limits on lard and oil. Even worse, there was talk that production would have to cease because potato chips were not an essential wartime food.

It was here that Harvey Noss made the transition from being the eccentric, energetic, enthusiastic founder of a potato chip organization to becoming a legend. Noss went to Washington, D.C., armed with a document listing thirty-two reasons that potato chips are an essential food, such as, "Potato chips are an economical energy lunch for children," "Potato chips are usually available at army camps," and potato chips are "the only palatable way of eating potatoes cold." By the time the persuasive Noss was finished, potato chip production was allowed to continue, although ongoing struggles for materials such as oil, gasoline, potatoes, and paper continued to plague the industry throughout the war years.

Another wartime casualty, albeit a temporary one, occurred at Japp's Potato Chip Company. Started by Leonard Japp Sr. during the Prohibition era, Chicago-based Japp's grew into a respectable regional . . . and then came the attack on Pearl Harbor. After the start of the war, the family changed the name of the chip to the name it bears today: Jays. Jays potato chip tins are not hard to find on Ebay, and can be successfully bid for in the range of ten to fifteen dollars. But every once in a while, a prewar Japp's tin will appear, and bidding for those invariably climbs into the hundreds of dollars.

During this time—after Noss's victory in Washington—the National Potato Chip Institute's membership roll swelled to include players like Utz, Red Dot, and a company called Lay's of Atlanta. A survey in 1943 revealed 438 chip companies nationwide, of which 114 were institute members. Regarded as the white knight of the industry for saving the chippers and their livelihoods from wartime sanctions, Harvey Noss is still remembered by retired chippers for his legendary trip to Washington. The saying "never fear when Harvey's near" greeted Noss when he entered rooms full of chippers at the conventions.

The yearly conventions, where members of the National Potato Chip Institute held their business meetings, were more than just business. Like other subcultures where contact among professionals is sometimes brief and perfunctory, chippers really knew how to party when released from their routines, as they recalled in interviews.

> *Alan Klein, Mister Bee Potato Chips, West Virginia:* The manufacturers worked all the time. Unlike the big companies today, they were sole proprietors; they did everything. Once in a while they liked to go to a national meeting and let their hair down.

> *Frank Dodd, former executive, John E. Cain Company, Massachusetts:* The entrepreneurs worked eight days a week, sometimes nine when it was busy. When they went out, they partied hardy.

> *John Kelley:* It was one party after another at those conventions. And I don't think anyone ever enjoyed himself more than I did.

> *Alan Klein:* Things that went on were devilish, let me put it that way. I can't mention any names.

According to Don Noss, the chippers spent their money well; big city hotels fought over the right to host the conventions, and Harvey Noss knew how to show people a good time. Noss's experience as an amateur magician was a plus for keeping the troops entertained. Always the prankster, Noss might kick off convention dinners by placing questionable foreign objects in attendees' drinks beforehand. One favorite trick was a large wooden box containing a "wild animal" that he kept in his office to show new clients but also brought to the conventions. Don Noss says:

> My dad had this great big box. It was a wooden box with big red letters that said: "BEWARE: WILD MONGOOSE." It had a metal netted lid. It was partly covered from the top. You could see bread crumbs in there, but otherwise all you could see was a tail. Dad would pull this lever to make the tail twitch. Then he'd say, "Watch out!" and he would push a button and this ball of fur would jump out. He would let that fly. You should have seen them all try to get out through the revolving doors.

The ball of fur, of course, was a fake, but succeeded in clearing the room.

Chippers meeting at Greenbrier, West Virginia, summer 1968. *Left to right:* Harvey Noss Sr., Lois Noss, Don Noss; *far right*, Mrs. Lippold; others unknown. (courtesy of Don Noss)

Photos in a 1949 *Life* magazine article about that year's National Potato Chip Institute convention show hijinks that were typical, likely confirming to Americans exactly what people making such a fun product should look and act like: a branch manager for Jays, naked except for shoes and socks, wears a huge Jays tin strapped around his waist; a gang of chip executives, wearing white baby bonnets, drink milk from nippled bottles for a milk drinking contest; a model hired to play "potato chip queen" for the convention wears a bra made of potato chips. In the early 1960s, on the heels of the Beatles' British Invasion, Noss once placed armfuls of Beatle wigs—blond, brunette, and black—at tables for members to don during dinner. At least one convention saw an impromptu diving contest in a hotel lobby fountain. After-hours parties ran late into the night in private rooms, at which Harvey Noss might play piano or perform magic tricks. Alan Klein remembers hanging out with Sam Snead at the Greenbrier and keynote speeches by David Brinkley, Henry Kissinger, and then-Congressman Gerald Ford.

Large-format photos of the conventions in Noss's collection show men in suits with wives at dining tables in palatial hotels like the Greenbrier of West Virginia, the Palmer House in Chicago, and the Netherlands Plaza in Cincinnati. All the celebrities of the industry were there.

Don Noss: There's Jerry Husman right there. That's Charlie Pike [of Dan Dee]. That's my dad there—and that's Mr. and Mrs. Harold Cregar [of Easton Potato Chip Company]. Boy, look at that handsome guy there! That's me with Herman Lay, in something like in 1948–50. Herman Lay was a super guy. I can't say enough about him. Herman Lay had class. Most of the guys that made it in this chip business had class. The yucks didn't make it, with few exceptions.

Herman Lay was yet another chipper whose circumstances changed with the economy in the late 1920s and early 1930s. When the Depression put Lay out of work as a salesman for Sunshine Biscuits in the early 1930s, he became a distributor—eventually the best distributor—for an Atlanta-based snack producer called Barrett's, who sold Gardner potato chips. When Barrett died and his widow was left with the failing company, Lay raised money to buy Barrett—first two plants, then a third—borrowing cash all the way.

Chippers at 1952 convention, Sherman Hotel, Chicago. (courtesy of Don Noss)

It was a start. Buying up small companies was an expansion method that, up until then, few in the chip business had explored, but it was only one of several strategies that Herman Lay and his company were to use to great advantage.

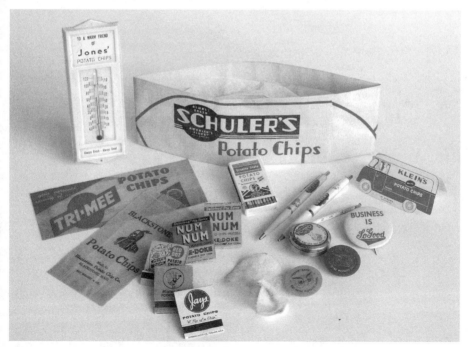

Mike@DeSantisphotography.com

courtesy of Don Noss

courtesy of Don Noss

courtesy of Don Noss

courtesy of Don Noss

courtesy of Don Noss

courtesy of Don Noss

courtesy of Don Noss

courtesy of Don Noss

courtesy of Don Noss

4

Storm Warning

We are very optimistic. We feel we are in the type of business
that will continue to grow.

Herman W. Lay, 1969

The story goes that after moving to Greenville, South Carolina, eleven-
year-old Herman Lay sold Pepsi-Colas from a stand in his family's
front yard, charging a nickel a bottle, while the city baseball park nearby
charged a dime. Not only was he successful enough to open a bank account, he expanded to hire neighborhood kids for the stand and used
the additional proceeds to get himself a bike and start a paper route on
the side.

Other early indications of an entrepreneurial streak include a teen-
age Lay becoming the top peanut salesman at the same ballpark—the
one whose Pepsi sales he had undercut years earlier. Later, after Lay and
a buddy invested one hundred dollars in ice cream to sell along the parade route of the 1928 Democratic Convention in Houston, they were to
see "their investment melted away when the parade was rerouted at the
last minute, leaving them and their ice cream on a deserted street."

Herman Warden Lay was born June 3, 1909, in Charlotte, North
Carolina. The Lay family moved to different southern cities several
times. By the time young Herman left home to find work during the
Depression—acknowledging that his ambition of becoming a professional ballplayer was likely unattainable—he had been a salesman for
Sunshine Biscuit, a laborer in the midwestern wheat harvest, a lumber-
jack in Washington State, a salesman in a novelty jewelry store, and a

43

trainee for a farm machinery company—the type of business his father was in.

A job at Barrett Potato Chip Company in Atlanta did not fall in Lay's lap, nor did he jump at the chance when it was offered. Reportedly, prior to taking it, he had written some two hundred letters to prospective employers. When he heard back from Barrett and was offered a sales route position, he turned it down at first, thinking better of it a week later. He called back at Barrett, where he was offered another sales position because the initial one had been filled.

Within the year, a distributorship at Barrett's Nashville office opened up, and Lay took it. Industry legend has it that from Lay's Model A, he sold potato chips to "road stands, grocery stores, filling stations, soda shops, and anywhere else customers might buy chips, including schools and hospitals." Lay built the Barrett Nashville distributorship to twenty-five employees and added a new warehouse. When Mr. Barrett passed away and his widow was over her head handling the company, it was probably no surprise that Lay was one of the first prospective buyers the family contacted in 1938. Lay borrowed over half the required sixty thousand dollars from friends and a bank, bought the company plants in Atlanta and Memphis, and arranged to pay the rest in preferred stock from his new company. Lay soon added the third Barrett plant in Jacksonville, Florida.

Next, Lay bought the Richmond Potato Chip Company of Virginia, Tas-Tee of Huntington, West Virginia, Halter's of Canton, Ohio, Brooks of Springfield, Missouri, and later and most famously, Red Dot of Madison, Wisconsin. But buying out small chippers was not Lay's only strategy; he also built new plants. "More of a builder than a buyer," Lay built plants in Jackson, Mississippi, Louisville, Kentucky, Greensboro, North Carolina, Chamblee, Georgia, and Washington, D.C.

Doolin's Doin's

At about the same time Lay got his start with potato chips, Elmer Doolin was living in San Antonio, Texas, and trying to run an ice cream company, which was reportedly in the middle of a price war. One day at a small restaurant, he bought a package of corn chips that had been fried in oil. Intrigued, he looked into selling them. The maker of the corn chips turned out to be a Mexican who wanted to sell the business. Doolin "bought the man's recipe, rights to his 19 retail accounts and his production equipment—an old, hand-held potato ricer." Fritos were born.

Which is not to say that corn chips were unknown in Mexico or that other U.S. businesspeople had not also thought about marketing the ethnic food in the Southwest. At about the same time that Doolin started marketing his Fritos, I. J. Filler, also in San Antonio, started to manufacture corn chips based on the Mexican model. Doolin even developed his own production equipment—after starting operations in his mother's kitchen—including a press that was more efficient than the potato ricer for cutting strips of corn flour. Within a year, Doolin moved to the geographically favorable city of Dallas to start his own manufacturing plant. Setting up new accounts in new cities on a shoestring budget, so the story goes, Doolin took a job as a cook one night in St. Louis because he ran out of money while on the road.

At the same time that Lay was buying and building in the Southeast, Doolin was expanding in the Southwest and elsewhere. Frito was adding potato chips to its lineup by buying out existing firms, including Crispie of Stockton, California, Nicolay-Dancey of Detroit, and the Noss family's Num Num of Cleveland. Don Noss recalls that "Lay's [actually Frito] bought out Num Num in '56. Later, they slowly changed the name from Num Num to Lay's. It was called the Num Num Foods Division of Frito-Lay. My cousin said that after they changed the name, they lost 50 percent of the Num Num business, mostly to Dan Dee. Even though they didn't touch the chip, everyone thought the chip was different!"

In 1945 Frito entered into agreement with H. W. Lay & Company, giving Lay exclusive rights to not only distribute but manufacture Fritos in the Southeast. Frito granted franchises to several other small companies, eventually merging them back to become larger. In 1949 a weary Herman Lay, diagnosed with ulcers and exhausted from the nonstop hustle of business, almost sold Lay's but was talked out of it. The mergers undertaken by the two like-minded companies continued toward the inevitable. Lay, interviewed by *Nation's Business* in 1969, put it this way: "We set out with one objective in mind, to become national in operations, distribution, advertising, and marketing. To achieve that we merged Lay's Potato Chips with the Frito Co. in 1962."

Elmer Doolin died in 1959, not living to see the merger, but he had to have seen it coming. A consultant for Lay at the time described it as the "Lay Co. manpower marrying the Frito Co. money," with the smaller but more aggressive Lay taking over the operational side of the company. Decades before computerized marketing research, upon entering a new market, Lay organized his company to canvass the potential of a new region thoroughly, to the tune of seven hundred "supermarkets, superettes, food stores, drug and sundry stores, eating and drinking places, service stations. We also surveyed cafeterias and food stands in hospitals, schools and industrial plants." Especially important was that such surveys be kept secret, lest the competition become aware of Lay's intentions:

> The final report from all this data gathering was enormously detailed, including brand distribution for all types of outlets, recommended allocation of operational routes for sales territories, complete with geographical layout, balanced work load and sales potential; sales potential for Lay's merchandise by types of outlets in dollars and cents per week; estimates as to the number of "new account" trucks and trained "two-man sales teams" required to attain 50 percent distribution in the first week of operation, and for "merchandising service" trucks and personnel; number of trucks operated by competitors; and so on and on. With that kind of thoroughness, the H. W. Lay & Co. seemed to outsiders like some kind of near-irresistible force.

The merger of Frito and Lay resulted in two de facto nationally distributed snacks: Cheetos and Frito's corn chips. However—amazing as it may seem nowadays—there was no nationally distributed brand of potato chip in the United States. Over the course of the next four years, Frito-Lay altered that situation by converting the regional brands it had bought to one uniform potato chip brand: Lay's. By 1965 Lay's chips were on the shelf in every state of the Union.

Given the dedication and aggressiveness inherent in its makeup, Frito-Lay's national brandsmanship would have been accomplished no matter what. But the rapidity and completeness of the conquest were in no small part due to a new advertising medium that had come fully into its own at about the same time. A friend to potato chips from the start, it was to benefit from potato chips as well—an ecologically symbiotic relationship if there ever was one.

Chips, Dips, Clowns, and Kids

Television depends upon people to watch it, and people like to eat while watching TV. Television depends upon advertising for revenue, and snack foods depend upon television for promotion. And snack foods are eaten by television viewers.

What partnership could be better? From early sponsorships of local kiddie shows to the Super Bowl, television and potato chips have been codependent. Noss's Snack Food Association, which today represents manufacturers of pretzels, popcorn, corn chips, and cheese snacks as well as potato chips, observed that, in the early days of TV, when it came time for sustenance in front of the TV, the "biggest beneficiary of this trend was the potato chip." No doubt an early aspect was television's instrumental promotion of dip, a development that widened the appeal of potato chips at the same time that it shifted chip plants' production away from flat-cut chips toward "rippled," "wavy," and "marcelled" chips. The most famous wavy chip of all—Frito-Lay's Ruffles—indirectly got its start in Indiana from Terre Haute's Chesty . . . or perhaps in Ohio from Cleveland's Dan Dee. An advertising image in Don Noss's collection shows a bizarre-looking man, face cratered like the Fantastic Four's comic book character the Thing, brandishing a banner with "Potato Ruffles" next to the words: "DAN DEE—THE ARISTOCRAT OF CHIPS."

Some believe that Dan Dee sold the Ruffles name to Frito-Lay. But the Snack Food Association's fiftieth anniversary book reproduced an old promotion of the blond Chesty Boy, proudly puffing out the chest of his striped shirt with the letter *C*, with the text: "Come in and taste the NEW SENSATIONAL 'CHESTY' POTATO RUFFLES. 'The food it's fun to eat.' A new kind of potato chip—attractive waffle slice—drier—crispier—perfect for parties. Large introductory package . . . 25 cents." The book mentions only "Chesty, the first to produce the 'Ruffles' product (the patent for which was later sold to Frito-Lay)." In *Hi There, Boys and Girls!,* pop culture critic Tim Hollis tells of a Cape Girardeau, Missouri, station for which a Dwayne Kirby suited up as Ruffles the Clown, sponsored by Chesty, and that Chesty used Ruffles the Clown in other television markets as well.

In any case, the wavy cut, by that time under varying names by

Jones billboard, 1958. (courtesy of Jones Potato Chip Company)

numerous chippers, lessened breakage, as chips were employed like little front-end loaders to pick up heavy, cream-based dips.

The SFA's list of food companies making advertising tie-ins with chips indicates that chippers and food makers missed hardly any cooperative opportunities. It includes the Canned Salmon Institute (casserole), Campbell's soup (soup and chips), Gulden's mustard (mustard-based dips), Kraft Foods (cream cheese dips), French National Cognac Producers (cognac-based dip), Underwood hams (ham dips), and Star-Kist Tuna (casserole, tuna on chips). The recipe for tuna and potato chip casserole—the quintessential '50s and '60s modern TV-age dinner in its economy of both ingredients and appearance—is often credited to Eugenia Japp, wife of Jays Potato Chips originator Leonard Japp.

But the big beneficiary of dip was Lipton. Lipton sponsored Arthur Godfrey's *Talent Scouts* program, mounting a massive promotion for its dried onion soup. Mixed in sour cream or cream cheese it became a chip dip. As in many other commercials from the early days of television, Godfrey, the show's host, participated in the commercial. The SFA history describes one program where Godfrey gave a demonstration to novice snackers wanting to get with the trend, showing them how to

The better the oil,
the better the chip

Swift & Company oils are custom-refined for frying potato chips. They are completely bland to preserve the good potato flavor, and assure a chip of guaranteed customer satisfaction.

Call your Swift salesman today. Ask him about our branded oils, or our custom blending service.

Swift Oils

Swift & Company, General Refinery Division, Chicago, Ill.

OUR 108TH YEAR

Advertisement from an early 1960s issue of *Potato Chipper*. (courtesy of the Snack Food Association, all rights reserved) make dip on camera, emptying the soup packet into a bowl of cream: "Brother, I can't think of anything less expensive for 'horse drawers'— 25 cents worth of potato chips . . . dip the chips . . . sensational!"

Almost every television market had commercials featuring a regional chip brand, often involving a local celebrity or media personality. Where I grew up in southeastern Ohio, it was Sam Slater on Parkersburg, West Virginia's WTAP. Slater was WTAP's gregarious late-night sportscaster, who had reportedly covered the 1936 Berlin Olympics. In the late 1960s, still an era when announcers introduced and augmented commercials, Slater did a spot for Mister Bee potato chips nightly. Alan Klein, owner of Mister Bee Potato Chips in Parkersburg, West Virginia, recalls the commercials: "The thing I used to love about Sam Slater was that they'd yell 'commercial,' so he'd pick up a bag [of Mister Bee potato chips] and talk about Mister Bee. It was supposed to be thirty seconds, and it would end up being two minutes and forty-five seconds. They'd be yelling 'Sam, Sam—go back to the show!'"

Interspersed within Slater's talk was a short animated commercial of the bee doing a choppily animated dance to the song. Over thirty-five years later, I can still remember the melody and lyrics: "Our potato chips are crisp delight / In every tasty, crunchy bite."

Mister Bee's motto, "200 miles fresher," appeared in billboard and print advertisements. It came about when Klein's father observed how a Lexington, Kentucky, bread company's motto, "50 miles fresher," obliquely denigrated the shelf life of the competition in Louisville, a little over fifty miles away. "My dad realized that the chip companies we competed with were from Pennsylvania or Cleveland," says Klein, "so he came up with '200 miles fresher.'" Years later when they expanded, the motto got Mister Bee in trouble when a competitor threatened a lawsuit, alleging that Mister Bee was now within 140 miles—not 200 miles—of the nearest competition. A lawyer told the unnamed competitor that to win his case, the competitor would have to demonstrate that Mister Bee's competitive radius was exactly 140 miles, or less, for its entire distribution range. "He dropped the lawsuit," says Klein, "but not before cussing me out." Klein acknowledges that "140 miles fresher" just didn't quite have the ring of "200 miles fresher."

Just outside of Mister Bee's range and a couple of decades later, in Columbus, Ohio, Richard Downey wanted to advertise his Conn's chips on the *Wheel of Fortune* TV show. Conn's, based in Zanesville, was trying to break into the Columbus market. Downey recruited Mose Mesre, the company's amiable, avuncular, middle-aged production manager. Mesre had no background in broadcasting but Downey wanted him to host the commercials. As Mesre recalls:

> Unfortunately, Downey said, "You're gonna be in 'em." I said, "That's not my bag," and he said, "Yes, it is."
>
> Anyway, we made the commercial, and the kids were asking me for potato chips, and this and that; first night it was on the air, this lady called and said, "You're encouraging kids to take things from strangers, and I don't think that that's right," and we'd just paid four thousand dollars for the commercial, and spent a day and a half with the kids and animals. You know, it takes a long time to get a thirty-second commercial shot; and I thought, "Man, I'm not gonna do that again." And we kept thinkin' and thinkin', and finally they come up with the idea that they'd call me Uncle Mose, and by doin' that I'm not a stranger to them, and they're not a stranger to me.
>
> We had a dog that could ride a skateboard, and could climb a sliding board and slide down there, and he always had a Conn's bag around his neck. Every kid remembers that, the parents knew it. . . . We just thought it did us a lot of good; it still does. I know I'll be in a gas station in a different town, and they'd say, "You're ready on pump number thirteen, Uncle Mose." And if they recognize you, you know, other people [join in].
>
> I was in a store on the north end of town helping the salesman. A woman came by with her son, and said, "Now you can pick one thing — what do you want?" and he said, "I want the Uncle Mose potato chips." He didn't say Conn's; he said Uncle Mose.

Company mascots were a big part of promotion for many. Wise had its owl; Chesty had the boy with the protruding pectoral muscles; Lay's, for a time, had its smiling spud. At least three companies used clowns, a perennial favorite for attracting kiddies: Guy's in Kansas City, Golden Flake of Alabama, and Red Dot of Wisconsin.

Red Dot's clown, Ta-To, was used mostly on packaging but occasionally was trotted out for public appearances — likely, a production-line employee was drafted into wearing a clown costume. But in 1946 Ta-To broke into radio when Red Dot hired Two Ton Baker, the Music Maker, to be Ta-To's voice. A "singing favorite with Chicago audiences,"

Two Ton, it was said, "sits on a piano stool like an iceberg on a highball glass":

> Ho-ho-ho
> The folks all laugh when I'm around
> 'Cause I'm the Red Dot potato chip clown.
> It's potato chip time . . . the folks all tease,
> Give us Red Dot . . . RED DOT potato chips, please.
> They're crisp . . . dry . . . tasty, and on sale EVERY WHERE!
> Ho-ho-ho . . .

In the South, Golden Flake's clown, Goldie, similarly made appearances on packaging and in person but also made the transition to TV. Julie Strauss, now director of marketing at Golden Flake Foods, got her first job with the company when Goldie was the Golden Flake television auction mascot. Strauss's task was to count empty bags of chips turned in by customers for auction items. Golden Flake bags were comparable to box tops or Green Stamps—a one dollar bag was worth one hundred points, a twenty-five-cent bag worth twenty-five points—and went toward items like bicycles or snapshot cameras. Auctions were broadcast in five TV markets as segments during shows, moving to radio when television became too expensive, according to Strauss. "It's a stinky, smelly job counting those bags," she adds, explaining that it was up to her to verify that a customer had actually turned in five hundred thousand points to win something like a wagon. "We'll still get letters from people saying they rediscovered a bicycle in the basement that they won on a Golden Flake auction," says Strauss

Golden Flake went on to use other mascots as Goldie started to look old-fashioned. The Golden Flake Gobbler, whom Strauss describes as a "Shaggy Cookie Monster-type character," replaced Goldie for a while in the 1970s; Sir Snack-a-lot came later and didn't last long—according to Strauss, he was supposed to be a knight, but they "couldn't get the guys to wear tights" when it came time to dress up for the promotion. Today, Golden Flake has gone full circle, with Goldie returned to active duty as a public service mascot, waving "Buckle up" on the back of Golden Flake truck, or saying "Do not litter" on the back of a bag of chips.

The potato chip auction format was not uncommon. In Kansas City, where the Kitty Clover brand was king, a televised kiddie auction was

Golden Flake Junior Auction. (courtesy of Golden Flake Snack Foods, Inc., with thanks to Tim Hollis)

Golden Flake delivery truck. (courtesy of Golden Flake Snack Foods, Inc.)

hosted by a man named Fred Broski. Broski recalls the time a kid named Jack Krump, whose uncle worked for Kitty Clover, was on the auction:

> *Fred Broski:* Every time you bought a bag of Kitty Clover potato chips there'd be a little coupon on the back. You'd get twenty-five points maybe for a small bag and fifty points for a larger bag, and for a bigger bag you'd get a hundred points, and maybe for the great big jumbo bag, at that time might sell for eighty-nine cents, maybe five hundred points.
>
> Well, the kids would all bring their points, all their coupons, to the TV show, and they'd bid for prizes. The TV station would buy all these prizes. They would buy games and toys and baseballs and basketballs, and then they always had a grand prize like a bicycle.

> *Jack Krump:* I had an uncle who worked for Kitty Clover, and they were the sponsor of the Junior Auction. And his kids couldn't be on it, so he provided me with boxes of the bags with coupons on the back. And I just filled up a paper sack, a grocery sack, with these coupons. We'd go down the day I was supposed to be on the auction, and they had a table full of toys, and I was just gonna buy everything that was on there.
>
> I got on there, and the first item that came up that I wanted was some Tonka toys and boats. The bidding started, and the kids were bidding a hundred, a hundred fifty, and I looked in my bag, and I just said, "Ten thousand."

> *Fred Broski:* He had ten thousand in one bag and ten thousand in another bag and ten thousand in another bag. It was like printing up counterfeit money.

After that, said Broski, they changed the rules about how many prizes a given kid could win. Over time, kids became more sophisticated about bidding generally, working it out in advance so that there was no more suspense to the process. "Needless to say," said Broski, "the show didn't last, but it was a lot of fun."

Celebrity was another angle for appealing to a general audience. Even regional chippers sometimes enlisted movie and television stars to enhance advertising. In California, Nancy Kulp (Miss Hathaway from *The Beverly Hillbillies*) played a chip inspector for Bell Brand; in the Philadelphia, Pittsburgh, Baltimore, and New York City markets, Jonathan Winters made a commercial for Herr's. Winters played a suite of characters called the Fussler Brothers—a construction worker, a scholarly nerd, and a goofball wearing a beanie with a propeller. Herr's vice president of marketing Dick White recalls that they filmed each brother separately—plus their white-haired mother, also played by Winters—splicing and combining the parts for the final commercial. "Commercials take a long time to make—ten or twelve hours," says White. "I'll tell you, the whole day—the whole time—he was in character." White recalls that Winters played a cat, a Martian, and a baseball pitcher, among other characters, losing no opportunity to goof off with the Herr's staff and film crew. "He entertained us the whole day. Over the last twenty-five years it's been the most memorable commercial we ever made," says White.

Other celebrities looked on chip commercials as more of a day job. Frito-Lay's "Betcha can't eat just one," circa 1963, was a good campaign to begin with, but it really took off two years later when Bert Lahr, most famous as the Cowardly Lion in MGM's 1939 *Wizard of Oz,* was recruited for the series. Although many of us grew up within television reach of a Kitty Clover or a Golden Flake or a Conn's, Frito-Lay's national capability was an added overlay on these efforts—and any American old enough to have seen TV in the '60s remembers the Lahr commercials.

In each rendition, it was the same story. Lahr, often costumed as a historical figure such as Christopher Columbus, would try to eat only one chip from the Lay's bag but always failed, after which he proceeded to sheepishly nibble away at the entire bag. Magazine advertisements showed him as George Washington or Caesar; in one, he is naked above the waist in a blonde wig and makeup as Eve in the Garden of Eden, while a cartoon snake curls around a Lay's chip bag overhead. In a biography of his father, *Notes on a Cowardly Lion,* John Lahr says that Lahr eyed his work for Lay's warily, even as he welcomed the income. "His laughter was meant for people, not merchandise," writes the younger Lahr. Bert Lahr confided to John: "I wonder if these ads have been good for my career? Here's the strange thing—after all these years on stage, the biggest success I've ever had is in these trite commercials. It's stupid." John Lahr writes: "Cab drivers stop their cars to yell, 'Bet you can't eat one!'; grandmothers accost him like one of their own to ask if he really eats potato chips"—to which he reportedly replied, "Don't eat 'em, they'll kill ya." The commercials provided Lahr with $75,000 a year, no small amount of money in the 1960s, and far more than he made in his Broadway stints during the era. John Lahr credits him with inventing the catchphrase "de-Lay-cious."

Boomers also fondly recall ads for Lay's Ruffles, which, like the Lahr ads, met with great success. "RRRRuffles have RRRR-ridges!" a voice exclaimed in alveolar trill, as the rolling *R* shook the background, making the TV screen shudder and the camera bounce in the course of causing earthquakes or worse.

But by the end of the sixties, one product's TV promotion was to outdo them all, and no person old enough to watch television or walk into a supermarket in the United States by the early 1970s was unaware of it. It was more than an advertisement: it was a phenomenon. It was unlike anything seen in potato chips since the invention of waxed bags or the Ferry cooker, and for several years, it rattled everyone—even Frito-Lay.

Procter's (and General Mills') Gamble

The 1960s were a time when household technological improvements were viewed almost universally as a good thing, and ease of food preparation was prominent in the minds of food companies and the housewives they served. There was increasing use of additives to improve shelf life, of dehydration, and of reconstitution of foods to alter texture and to enhance attractiveness. Until the early 1970s, the idea that food additives might be undesirable or detrimental was mostly not a consideration in North America. Given the new developments in food processing, it should have been no surprise that someone would come up with a prefabricated potato chip; yet, when prefab chips appeared in the late 1960s, they succeeded in wrenching the old-time potato chip world into complete upheaval. "The arrival of Pringles would seem to present the industry with the most serious challenge in its history," announced SFA's *Potato Chipper* in June 1972.

The idea of a prefabricated chip was not original with Pringles. According to the 1976 *Snack Food Blue Book*, "At least 40 prefabricated chips and snacks [were] introduced into the U.S. market during the years from 1964 to 1974," although it seems most of these were nonpotato chips, such as General Mills' Bugles. In 1966 Sealtest tested Chipnics in the Roanoke, Virginia, market but failed. General Mills succeeded with Chipos in 1967. Made of dehydrated potato flakes, the Chipos product was reconstituted, flash-fried, and enhanced for shelf life with BHA and BHT.

The Weaver Potato Chip Company of Lincoln, Nebraska, was the first to sound the call to arms. With the support of Noss's Snack Food Association (at that time called PCII for Potato Chip Institute International and by then headed by a succession of chip executives after Noss), Weaver took General Mills to court for using the term *potato chip* to describe a product that, by 1969, had been developed with the sweat of many small companies for over one hundred years. The main factor contributing to this last straw? According to the *Snack Food Blue Book,* "Chippers were especially dismayed by the insistence of these corporate giants in using the unqualified designation of potato chips in the advertising and labeling of these prefabricated products. The feeling was this was unfair coattail riding on the popularity of real chips." Harvey Noss, the undying advocate for all things potato chip, captured the prevailing sentiment: "A potato chip is a thin raw slice of potato fried in deep fat. Period. The industry has spent millions establishing this." PCII's attorney said, "Our contention was that these were not slices of potatoes fried crisp and, therefore, it was deceptive to call them potato chips. General Mills was trying to take a free ride on the millions of dollars spent on advertising real potato chips."

In the 1971 trial, PCII and Weaver contended that the term *chip* was described, even by the Library of Congress, as "slices of raw potato fried until crisp," whereas General Mills contended that *chip* was a generic term. A compromise, although not perceived as such by traditional chippers, was reached in 1971 when the judge ruled that the term *potato chip* could be retained if the package carried a prominent declaration that Chipos were made from "dried or dehydrated potatoes."

If it was General Mills that first successfully marketed a dehydrated, reconstituted, prefabricated potato flake product, Procter & Gamble outperformed it in tactics. Where General Mills sold Chipos in a box, P&G devised a tennis ball canister, where the perfectly formed half-moon Pringles could be stacked unbroken. PCII pleaded with the government, this time via Congress, to force removal of the potato chip appellation. Charles Seyfert, heading up a "Stay in Business" committee to look into the issue, proclaimed: "The dairy, citrus fruit, and wool industries have protected themselves against misleading labels and advertising. We, the makers of real potato chips, are asking the same kind of protection." Joseph Seyfert, who followed his father, Charles, into the business, today recalls that the senior Seyfert "took the Pringles comparison to heart," believing that Procter & Gamble was slandering the good name of potato chips. According to the son, Charles even started a boycott of P&G brands by sending PCII members a letter and list of P&G items that they and their family and friends should avoid. The tactic, the younger Seyfert says, "was successful enough to have gotten their [Procter & Gamble's] attention."

Comedian Mark Russell, appearing on the PBS *MacNeil/Lehrer Report* in 1975, put a slant on the event that spoke to the political sensibility of the times:

> My fellow Americans, I believe that the quality of life in America today is deteriorating because of the presence in our homes of canned potato chips. May I say that the Pringles controversy is an ever-growing menace. When we were children, were potato chips packed in an air-tight can? No, potato chips were meant to be free—BORN FREE—bouncing around in a little bag.
>
> All Pringles are exactly the same. You can buy one in Washington, D.C., then go out to San Francisco and buy another that's exactly the same. Now, if that isn't Communism, I don't know what is.

Once again, it was ruled that the fake product could be called a potato chip if its label stated that the product was "made from dried potatoes." Terrified, some traditional chippers rushed to make their own reconstituted chip, most of them using the same cylindrical can: Laura Scudder came out with Dittos; Frito-Lay came out with Munchos, Crunch Bunch, and Crunch Barrel; General Mills added Mrs. Bumby's Potato Chips; and Planters came out with . . . Planters Potato Chips. The tennis ball canister seemed to be key, but this "novelty" was hardly anything new, since snacks like British biscuits had appeared in such canisters since the 1930s.

On some deep level, it seemed the success of the newfangled chips did more than simply make chippers fear a loss of sales. It was almost as if the reconstituted chips hit a sore spot—made the chippers feel as if they had disappointed the public, somehow failing with the product they had lovingly served to eager Americans for decades. PCII president Verl A. Walker grudgingly admitted: "All of a sudden traditional chippers are competing with a product that is very close to what our customers have been telling us they have been wanting for twenty years—fresh, crisp, perfectly shaped unbroken chips, appetizing in color, no grease and no defects, and in a moisture-proof container that's easy to store and re-seal." But Walker was not so grudging as to deny the primary drawback of the new product, adding "the only thing that's missing is the natural potato flavor!"

Chippers like Wise and Jays stressed that this was exactly the point: the new chips weren't "natural" or "real." By the 1970s, for a public becoming increasingly aware of food additives, it was a timely approach. Meeting the controversy head on, the text of one television ad ran:

> These newfangled potato chips are made from dehydrated potatoes, vegetable shortening, mono- and diglycerides, salt, with ascorbic acid and BHA added to preserve freshness.
> Wise Potato Chips are made from potatoes, vegetable oil, salt.
> The newfangled potato chip?
> Or Wise oldfangled potato chips?
> . . . you decide.
> Wise Potato Chips . . . naturally delicious.

In the end, it didn't seem to matter. After the initial flare-up, sales of Pringles appeared to boost the overall market, helping sales of real potato chips—which many consumers still preferred anyway. Lest their shelf space be taken over by "tennis ball tubes," it also prodded some companies to pay greater attention to the quality of their traditional chips, forcing them to improve their own products.

Setting the Stage

Prior to television, the "fun" elements inherent in potato chip marketing—flashy foil bags, gaudily colored cartoon logos, mascots such as clowns, bees, owls, bluebirds, kids, cowboys, humanized smiling spuds—were mostly associated with packaging and other two-dimensional extensions of packaging, like print and billboard advertising. With the advent of television, the inborn fun of potato chips came right into the American home. The advertisements even took on the fourth dimension of continuity: viewers could look forward to the next installment of Bert Lahr's effort to eat only one Lay's potato chip.

But behind the scenes, all was not fun. A shakeout was in the making, and even the U.S. government was beginning to take notice. In 1963, after Lay had bought four more chip companies and shortly after the Frito-Lay merger, the Federal Trade Commission began to focus on its activities. Judging by FTC documents, the matter appears to have drawn out through a complexity of settlement offers and collateral suits, initially involving only divestiture of certain of Frito-Lay's acquired chip plants. But in 1965 Frito-Lay merged with Pepsi-Cola to become PepsiCo, providing even more potential market muscle. It seemed to be a natural combination—"Potato chips make you thirsty; Pepsi satisfies thirst"—but the FTC didn't approve of such language, ruling in 1968 that PepsiCo could not create advertising "tie-ins" between Pepsi and salty snacks. PepsiCo was also "barred from acquiring any snack or soft drink maker for a period of ten years." In 1968 the FTC ordered Frito-Lay to sell ten of its twenty-eight plants to Nefco, Inc., of Little Rock, Arkansas, for $9.6 million. The sale included the old Num Num plant in Cleveland and a Frito Company plant in Columbus, Ohio. Also sold were plants owned by Nicolay-Dancey—makers of New Era potato chips—in Detroit and Chicago; Red Dot's plants in Ottumwa, Iowa, Grand Forks, North Dakota, and Madison and Rhinelander, Wisconsin; and the Brooks plant of Springfield, Missouri. A tenth plant in Portland, Oregon, was sold to a former Frito-Lay employee. One estimate had it that chips from the plants would have amounted to 31 percent of Frito-Lay's chip sales.

Further, Frito-Lay was to buy a significant portion of the output from the sold plants: during the first eight months after divestiture, it would buy "at least 90 percent of the potato products manufactured at the plant the last full preceding year of the divestiture"; over the next two years, the amount of product it purchased would decline to 75, 50, and 25 percent—after which the new plant owners were presumably on their own to produce a product under their own label. Several retired former chip executives recall the 1968 FTC case. Victor Sabatino, a former vice president at Wise and CEO of Guy's, remembers that this strategy was not as beneficial for the new owners as it may have seemed at first glance; in the first year, says Sabatino, the regional was "glad to take Frito's money" and make almost all of their product for Frito-Lay; but in the meantime, the chipper was so busy making Lay's chips that it had little time to devote to its own product. "Most of the plants didn't have the time to develop their own name," says Sabatino, "and by year three, they're going 'Oh crap!' By year four, it was too late, and most of them went out of business."

Herman Lay did not address the 1968 FTC case in a 1969 interview but, while his company may have benefited from acquisitions, on some level he seemed uncomfortable with the idea of monopoly: "I must say that I can't, from the standpoint of my basic philosophy, disagree with the premise that monopolies are not good for business. . . . On the other hand, I have not seen a true monopoly in the country, and basically I do not feel that business mergers necessarily develop monopolies, but more often create additional competition."

Monopoly or not, Frito-Lay's predilection for growth provided it with built-in mechanisms to incorporate its expansion into day-to-day planning, even as its increasing size and nationwide distribution capabilities made such goals easier. In addition to persistent marketing research, Frito-Lay's "store-door" distribution—bypassing warehouses by sending the route men right into the store—became the envy of the industry. A study by Frito-Lay determined that in addition to standard snack aisle displays, secondary end-of-aisle displays—endcaps—could add 17 percent to total sales. Where most companies were content just to get snacks to the retailers' warehouses to be distributed by store employees, Frito-Lay route men physically entered each store and checked shelves regularly, making sure stocks were orderly, fresh, and full. Frito-Lay replaced smaller stepvans with tractor-trailer semis, cutting down on the number of drivers and further enabling efficient distribution.

Others rushed to emulate Frito-Lay's strategies. Even before the Pringles years, a succession of attempts by others to try its consolidation approach had occurred, although some gave up early on. In 1960 Sunshine Biscuits acquired Blue Bell and Humpty Dumpty of Maine; a few years after Laura Scudder's death, Pet Foods bought Scudder, in 1962.

It got serious in 1977 when a company called Acton Corporation bought Mrs. Ihrie's in Baltimore and Old Vienna of St. Louis. Acton also acquired Gordon's of Louisville, a company with a penchant for using imagery of an antique red delivery van in its advertising. Acton was not a snack food company—it was a cable television and telephone firm—but by default immediately become the nation's second-largest potato chip and corn chip maker. "We're only four plants away from having national distribution," bragged Acton's chief in late 1977. Meanwhile, a company called Culbro, formerly the General Cigar Company, acquired Bachman's, which then acquired Chesty, KAS, and Kitty Clover—all of the Midwest—and capped it with Cain's Marcelle Potato Chip Company, a venerated old chipper ensconced in the rippled chip tradition of north central Ohio.

The buying action didn't last long on the part of Acton and Culbro. By the end of the 1970s they were having second thoughts, as Culbro sold its Bachman's unit, and Acton sold its southwestern food division to Borden. Borden had been in chips since 1964, when it acquired the then forty-three-year-old Wise company from the original family, giving it a major chip presence in the Northeast. By the late 1970s, Borden added Morton Foods, Sta-Krisp, Dentler-Facs of Texas, and Dickey's of New Orleans—the same Dickey's where a young John Kelley got his first field job as an engineer in the late 1940s (chapter 3). In 1979 Borden acquired Guy's of Missouri and Buckeye of Ohio.

With Acton and Culbro waning, Borden now had a respectable midwestern presence to couple with Wise in the Northeast. Borden too had thoughts about going up against Frito-Lay, or at least thoughts about going "national." And, unlike some of the others, Borden had the will and resources to pull it off. Or at least to come close.

5

Full Combat

The snack aisle is littered with bodies and blood. There's over
40 points market share up for grabs.

David Poldoian, president of Eagle Snacks in 1995

In 1982 Borden made only one purchase, but it was one that solidified an already important direction; it bought Seyfert, a dominant Indiana chipper, in a move that augmented Borden's already formidable Midwest presence.

It didn't stop there. Borden next acquired Geiser's of Milwaukee and Clover Club of Utah, solidifying markets in the mountain states and upper Midwest. Jays—the big Chicago chipper started by alleged Capone torpedo Leonard Japp Sr.—was added to the Borden stable in 1986. In 1987 Culbro sold its Snacktime unit to Borden, which included regional chippers Chesty, Cain's, Kitty Clover, and a kettle chip called Krunchers. Where Frito-Lay's way had been to infiltrate every new market with its nationwide Lay's brand, using national TV ads with stars like Bert Lahr, Borden's way was to maintain regional brandsmanship. John Geuss, a vice president and general manager at Guy's Snacks in 1989, observed: "Guy Caldwell spent 50 years growing that brand [Guy's Snacks of Missouri] and educating the consumer to know that it stood for quality. Attempting to switch would be both risky and expensive. The same is true of Jays in Chicago [and] the Wise name on the East coast."

Famous as the company of Elsie the cow, by the mid-1980s Borden was in the process of becoming everything to everybody. In addition to salty snacks and Elmer's glue, Borden was turning out Cracker Jack, Campfire marshmallows, Meadow Gold milk, Classico spaghetti sauce, Wyler's soups, Cremora coffee creamer, and ReaLemon lemon juice — and those were just the consumer foods. Borden was also in chemicals — its CEO in the mid-1980s, Romeo Ventres, was a former engineer who had spent most of his life in the chemicals business. Its Chemicals and Plastics Ltd. Partnership produced things like PVC resins, methanol, and nitrogen products. Borden's expansion was accomplished through some ninety buys from 1986 to 1991 alone.

Ventres had seen how chemical companies lived or died by the size and efficiency of their operations; successful companies either had one large factory making one thing, or one large factory making a lot of small things. He set about to reconfigure Borden's acquired plants into "hyperplants" to run large volumes of single products or multiproducts.

The hyperplant doctrine maximized capacity with a "complete product line to eliminate reshipping" at single locations with "centralized access to markets served." It could take advantage of low-cost labor and economical ingredients using one properly placed location, and allow for hiring of specialized experts who could optimize production.

"If you have small individual plants, you can't really afford the specialized highly technical disciplines that you can have with a big plant," said Geuss. "You need people in quality assurance functions who have degrees in food science. You need people who have technical disciplines, and can understand the computers that make the equipment operate."

It was a good idea for Frito-Lay, who marketed the same chip nationwide, but it didn't necessarily make sense for Borden's chips, where the approach was to maintain regional brand appeal. Borden snack division president George Waydo advised against the hyperplant idea for Borden's chips, at least where combining brands was concerned.

"At that time I compared our sizes," said Waydo. "In virtually every case, our plants were as big or bigger than Frito-Lay's. Every chip was made different to be unique to its marketplace. It made no sense to put it all under one roof. I convinced Ventres that there was no use in consolidation. The concept didn't fit in with the Borden snack line." Waydo argued that producing several regional chip brands at one location would necessitate frequent changes of fryer oil — one chip brand might use cottonseed oil where another used corn oil—and complicate packaging and distribution.

Even so, the hyperplant concept was embraced within each regional company's snack line, and some Borden plants were enlarged to produce diverse arrays of snacks under each regional's name; other regional Borden-owned plants were closed. The redesigned Guy's potato chip plant in Liberty, Missouri, now produced potato chips, tortilla chips, corn chips, fried pork rinds, fried and baked puffed cheese curls, popcorn, snacking and baking nuts, and canister snacks. When it finally closed in 2000, long after Borden's tenure, Guy's employed a thousand workers.

By 1989 Borden had salty snacks available in forty-six states and was number two in the United States after Frito-Lay. Borden had, among others, Wise, Buckeye, Snacktime, Laura Scudder, Clover Club, Guy's, Jays, Seyfert's, and Southwest Snacks, plus salty snack units in Puerto Rico, Ecuador, Spain, and Malaysia.

The Eagle Rises

While Borden was consolidating regional chippers, another contestant tried to go national in 1979.

Flush with cash from its successful battles with Miller, Anheuser-Busch saw beer and salty snacks as a better fit than cable television and cigars had been for Acton and Culbro; Anheuser-Busch already had built-in distribution possibilities via its beer routes. Although many states prohibited advertising alcohol and foods together, it was a fitting combination under one roof, especially with a place to sell them like Busch Stadium, home of the St. Louis Cardinals baseball team, also owned by Anheuser-Busch since 1953.

Initially, Eagle snacks—Anheuser-Busch's new snack line—gave away snacks, especially honey-roasted peanuts, on airlines. Bars, taverns, and airports were other venues where it was easy to introduce new snacks through beer vendors; in supermarkets, they were sold in liquor departments next to Budweiser beer displays. Distribution was built in; for most of these outlets, Anheuser-Busch's own beer distributors did the work. Like Frito-Lay and Borden, Eagle had it all—peanuts, potato chips, pretzels, puffed cheese products, tortilla chips. At first, Eagle contracted production out to others — for example, Vitner's of Chicago produced Eagle potato chips and continued to do so for Eagle's entire existence. But as volumes grew, Eagle also phased in its own plants — eventually buying one from Vitner, which it never opened.

Eagle not only gave away chips on airlines; it also paid money — big money — to put them in stores. Payment for shelf space — slotting fees — allegedly started by Coke and Pepsi during the cola wars, was becoming common in many food genres in supermarkets by the 1980s. Often appropriately called pay-to-stay or pay-to-play, slotting was a good, if expensive, way for Eagle to get in the door. Slotting payments guaranteed not just placement but prime placement — an endcap at the head of an aisle, a free-standing display near the door. Customers in the deliberate act of getting a weekly chip fix knew the way to the snack aisle, but not so impulse buyers, a type thought to account for much of snack foods' profits. They would be more likely to buy a product with prime positioning. New products, like Eagle's, were doomed to invisibility if buried among sixty feet of competing chip bags, but placed near the door they had a chance to make an impact.

The slotting trend grew gradually to include not only soda pop, cereal, and snacks but fresh produce as well. Up to now, Frito-Lay had not engaged much in slotting, not because it couldn't afford to but because it didn't have to. But now that Eagle was doing it, everyone was obliged to play along or risk losing shelf space. A Department of Justice document from a later investigation credits Eagle with starting the trend: "When Eagle entered the market, it was an unknown and unrecognized product. Unless they had adequate shelving space they were not going to succeed. Anheuser-Busch decided to purchase space to increase visibility. The result of this action was that it forced everyone else into purchasing shelf space."

It is hard to imagine Eagle and Frito-Lay ignoring the fact that not everyone could afford slotting fees. The net effect was to cut out small players, such as many regional chippers. It was particularly difficult for a new chipper to enter the field if first it had to come up with money just to get into the store. Chippers complained that the chip industry was becoming less and less a food business — where shelf space was based on quality — and more and more a real estate business, where shelf space was based on pocketbook size. A typical four-foot-wide grocery rack having multiple shelves was counted as four feet. Prices ranged from $150 per foot to $500 per foot in the 1980s and 1990s to $1,000 a foot annually in 2005. To do business in a single large metropolitan chain could amount to a million dollars a year. Slotting fees were—and continue to be, for the most part—word-of-mouth transactions between retailer and supplier; they were not even reported in retailers' financial statements. "It seems that these fees are the 'dirty little secret' in retailing," said Senator Christopher S. Bond, at Senate committee hearings on the topic in 2000. "Often nothing is in writing between the manufacturer and the retailer, and the amount of money paid in slotting fees is usually known only to supermarkets, their brokers and distributors."

While Eagle was busy trying to get shelf space for its snacks through beer distributors and slotting fees when necessary, it also took a page from Borden by buying out another regional chipper and leaving the original name and product intact. Eagle bought Cape Cod, a tiny company based in Hyannis, Massachusetts, that had been in business only five years. Cape Cod had a handmade kettle chip, similar to the early chips that every chipper made before 1929. By 1980, when Steve Bernard started Cape Cod, some fifty years had passed since the invention of Ferry's continuous cooker. Except for small pockets of markets, mostly in Pennsylvania and Ohio, the kettle chip was outmoded.

But now it was getting a revamp. Kettle cooking produced a harder, thicker chip, one totally different from the average picnic-style chip then ubiquitous throughout the United States. Snacktime's Krunchers was also a kettle-style chip, now part of the Borden line since the acquisition. But Cape Cod's elegant presentation helped it compete with Krunchers; Cape Cod's packaging and product embodied a high-end "gourmet" aspect compared with Krunchers' cartoon sensibility. Cape Cod was a special-edition chip, like an exclusive gold-leafed imprint of a book publisher. Because the Cape Cod chip was unlike Eagle's regular potato chip, Eagle could distribute it alongside its continuously cooked chips everywhere, not just in Cape Cod's natal Massachusetts locale.

While Borden was adding companies like Scudder to build its California base and had snacks available in forty-six states under differing regional names, by 1988 Eagle chips were available in all fifty states under the Eagle name. Eagle promoted its chips in a series of successful advertising campaigns featuring television's Odd Couple, Tony Randall and Jack Klugman. By 1994 Eagle's sales were up an estimated 7 percent for that year alone.

Except that a 7 percent increase isn't that much when you only have 6 percent market share in salty snacks to begin with. Despite Anheuser-Busch's clout and use of slotting fees, Eagle had trouble getting noticed by consumers, a fact that was reflected in market share that never rose above 5 to 6.5 percent any given year for Eagle's entire sixteen-year history. Even in the small but crucial drug and convenience stores where slotting was not prevalent, and Frito-Lay not so dominant, small regional brands—including Borden's regionals—competed with Eagle. Eagle seemed caught between the two, where it flailed despite Anheuser-Busch's deep pockets. Don Carr, former owner of Kay and Ray's of Pennsylvania, worked for Gibble's but also worked in equipment during Eagle's era. His company served two Eagle plants. "It was astonishing the money they spent," says Carr about Eagle, "not only on production, but the money they spent trying to get into stores."

Some said that distribution was a key issue. Local Anheuser-Busch distributors saw chip distribution as "more diversion than delight." While a few bags of chips or peanuts could be sold in the beer aisle, the majority would have to go to the snack aisle, requiring trips to two different parts of the store. To add to the confusion, Eagle used its Campbell Taggart bread distributors for chips too, as well as independent distributors—nonpayroll jobbers who contracted with Eagle to distribute its product and the snacks of other companies. And Eagle switched back and forth between central operations. Starting in St. Louis, it moved to Dallas, then back again.

"They kept changing what they would do," says an anonymous individual in the flexible packaging industry. "They would move to St. Louis, then move to Dallas, then move back to St. Louis again. Eagle tried to have the beer guys sell it—that's never gonna work. Then the bakery guys. By the time they got the snack guys to sell the snack foods, they'd become a quagmire of red ink."

Kevin Bowler, the former president of Eagle who left to buy an Anheuser-Busch wholesalership in Daytona Beach in April of 1995, believes it was not so simple. "I think the answer you have is bar talk versus factual talk," says Bowler about the accusation that Eagle's distribution was disorganized. "We had beer guys who did great—we had some who did not—that is normal distribution based on statistical models. Same for independents we used and for bakeries." Bowler says that problems for Eagle were less about distribution at local and regional levels and more about finding the right combination at the national level—a difficult accomplishment to initiate from scratch. It was a catch-22 when it came to catching Frito-Lay, whose shelf space was already guaranteed because of existing volume. "The biggest challenges were scale," says Bowler. "Our relative cost differential at the manufacturing side was not onerous. Our cost to national market—remember, not regional market—was a challenge for a 'ramp up' company. Cost from plant to distributor was significantly higher (distance and how we shipped versus [Frito-Lay] model) . . . scale on delivery trucks (dollars per stop and number of) . . . mix of stops (supermarkets—c-stores— mass merchandisers) . . . absolute dollars associated with volume-based [Frito-Lay] programs vs. our size dollar sales."

One asset Eagle did have was a great potato chip. On the surface that would seem to be a good thing. But despite Eagle's difficulties, the combination of Eagle's good product and Anheuser-Busch's bulging wallets forced Frito-Lay to take notice. "I think that what happened when Anheuser-Busch came into the picture," says the anonymous individual in the flexible packaging industry, "was that Frito-Lay saw them as a worthy opponent, and didn't want them to get off the beachhead."

Part of Frito-Lay's (by now often referred to as "Frito" in the industry) concern had to do with circumstances at Frito-Lay itself. In 1991, while Eagle chip sales were growing, Frito-Lay's snack products were taking a beating in every category. Focus groups using taste tests conducted by Frito-Lay showed that consumers preferred Eagle potato chips to the Lay's chip, which was "viewed as too greasy, too bland, and too boring." Meanwhile, Keebler and Nabisco were making rumblings with their own chip and snack lines. Keebler was marketing several chip brands nationwide—O'Boises, Tato Skins, Ripplins—and both Keebler and Nabisco garnered a place in the top ten salty snack makers nationally. Procter & Gamble's ever-present Pringles lingered steadfast in the background, staying in the top five—usually second or third in chip brand sales only after Lay's. Frito watched its market share erode from a high of 42 to 38 percent by 1991.

Enrico Entering

When Coca-Cola's 1985 "New Coke" debacle resulted in the recall of the new product scant months later, PepsiCo CEO Roger Enrico boasted in a full-page newspaper ad that "the other guy blinked" in the face of competition. The implication was that Coke had tried to become more like Pepsi and failed.

Described as having a shy demeanor that masked an intensely competitive personality, Enrico was credited with keeping Pepsi-Cola close on Coke's heels in the "cola wars." As PepsiCo's Frito-Lay division continued to struggle into the late 1980s, a decision was made to call in Enrico to take charge in January 1991. Enrico allegedly vowed: "We're going to make a major change in the way we manage this company."

Characterizing Frito-Lay as having a "bulging payroll" and a "bloated lineup," *Business Week* printed speculations in July 1991 that Enrico might eliminate as many as four hundred to six hundred positions. The next year, after laying off eighteen hundred employees—mostly in administration and management—Enrico moved to hire younger, hipper staffers. He changed packaging, dropping outmoded flavor and size combinations. New television advertisements trotted out celebrities like George Foreman, Larry Bird, and Kareem Abdul-Jabbar. Four more plants were sold. To keep up with the others, prices were slashed.

Thanks to Eagle parent Anheuser-Busch's deep pockets, price slashing was the new rule for staying in the game, and Frito was obliged to play along. Eagle priced its products as much as 20 percent lower than Frito's, and it wasn't the only one to keep up with; Keebler was cutting prices too. Sustained by profits on corn products like Fritos, Doritos, and Tostitos, Frito could afford to slash potato chips and stay solvent overall. In 1991 it introduced a low-margined twenty-five-cent potato chip package to be placed handily near cash registers and reduced allowable snack profit margins from 21 to 17 percent.

Behind the facade of marketing, Frito went to the drawing board and back to the lab. In addition to devising a low-fat baked potato chip (Baked! Lay's), Frito went about improving its conventional Lay's and Ruffles chips, changing from soy to cottonseed oil—the first time the formulas had ever been tinkered with.

It seemed to work. Months after many of Enrico's changes, Frito's profits grew by 15 percent in the first half of 1992 alone, while Borden's share slipped dramatically. In 1996 *U.S. News and World Report* proclaimed that the chances were 94 percent that every American household had at least one Frito-Lay product.

Borden Fades to Corn

Despite Borden's having double Eagle's market share in salty snacks during some of the 1980s, attempts by Eagle, Keebler, Nabisco, and Frito-Lay to grow nationally labeled potato chip brands seem to have perennially tempted Borden to do the same. Snack division president Waydo fought a constant battle against it: "It is not unusual for one of our bright marketing people to say, 'Think of the economies of scale if we could convert our U.S. snack food business to one common brand!' and present a series of twelve beautifully colored boards showing how Guy's potato chips over twelve gradual changes could become Wise potato chips. We saw people fail by making regional acquisitions and then destroying fine regional companies by making them common brands. We said, 'We are not going to do that.'"

In addition to coordinating a huge stable of disparate regionals, Borden had the difficulty of integrating new corn products into the mix. Most of the companies Borden acquired were potato chippers, but corn was the part of the snack industry with the most growth, and Frito was beating everyone with it. While the water content of potatoes makes them an inefficient raw material, with 100 pounds of potatoes yielding about 25 to 30 pounds of chips, corn is the other way around. Because the kernels are dried, water, and later oil, are added during processing to yield pulp for making corn chips — so that 100 pounds of corn meal results in 100 to 108 pounds of product. The inherently efficient corn chip was also a wide-open marketing opportunity; by the 1980s potato chips had been tweaked and modified for over 125 years, but corn chip niches were still relatively unexplored. Frito-Lay had come up with Doritos — a lighter, larger toasted tortilla than Fritos — only about fifteen years earlier and was still breaking out new corn products like Tostitos and Santitas. With a majority of its product in corn already,

Frito could afford to take losses in potato chips. The majority of Frito-Lay's product was in high-profit corn snacks, but Borden's was the other way around, with 80 percent in potato chips and 20 percent in corn. Former Guy's executive Vic Sabatino indicates that it took awhile for Borden to come around: "Borden's production was almost as efficient as Frito's. It was just that we had the wrong product mix. They would ask me, 'Why are our costs so out of whack?' I told them it was because we were selling the wrong product. It took years and years to convince them."

When Borden headquarters finally realized that corn was the way to go "nose-to-nose" against Frito, it encountered difficulty from its regional components. "Borden got the right strategy: grow the corn-based products and force Frito to spend against their corn," Sabatino says. "But because they were built out of regional companies, there was resistance on those companies' parts—who wanted their own brand names—like 'Cain's Corn Chips'—and they could never get continuity."

Whereas Waydo believed there was a lot to lose by nationalizing Borden's old regional potato chip stable, there seemed nothing to lose by trying to nationalize a new corn chip brand in new regional markets. Borden based the new national corn and cheese product line on its oldest member: Wise. Joseph Seyfert says that the idea was to "generate a series of national products" using the distribution system already built in from the regional components; according to Sabatino, regionals were allowed to keep their local potato chip brand but would gradually phase in Wise-branded corn and cheese products. But Borden's regional chippers didn't like it and wanted to retain their identities on the corn and cheese bags as well. A compromise was reached whereby Borden allowed each regional to put its "bug," or logo, on the bottom of the Wise package. Now, a bag of Wise corn chips sold in Indiana or Ohio carried the Wise logo on top and a small banner logo for Seyfert, Cain, or Buckeye on the bottom corner. Sabatino says it was a "minivictory" for the regional sales forces, who had wanted to keep their own brand names all along—but it didn't sell. Borden's third try at making a common look was to let each regional make its own corn and cheese product on the Wise-branded bag, but keep the original company's name at top.

Vic Sabatino: It was supposed to look the same for each bag, except with a different name. It was the "smile" design from the Wise bag, with an arch under which appeared the brand name. The idea was to sell it that way for a couple of years, remove the regional's name, and then call it Wise. But the regionals didn't agree; they didn't go along. It was a disaster.

Julie Strauss, Golden Flake Foods, Alabama: Part of Borden's problem was that they had no economy of scale. They had to print images of five different companies on all their bags; they had to print the trucks all different.

Anonymous individual, flexible packaging industry: Borden could never make a decision. They would go back and forth between having one brand and using niche brands. They were successful on Cheez Doodles, but that's all.

George Waydo says that profit margins went down as production costs stayed the same, and it was not possible to continually produce chips, drop prices, and give away product while keeping books in the black. It was the BOGO era—"buy one get one" free; if Borden was already spending 8 to 10 percent of the price of the product on promotion and advertising, and then had to give away a second bag on top of that, profits would have to drop.

"Remember, this was the era of hostile takeovers," says Waydo. "People were waiting in the wings to take over your company. We had pressure to keep our income up; to generate income to discourage suitors.

"If Borden had stuck around another year or two—because Anheuser-Busch and Keebler both left—it could have held on. I argued vigorously at meetings that Anheuser-Busch and Keebler were losing their shirts. Our volume was not growing, but our spending accelerated, and profits dropped dramatically."

"The problems at Borden were masked by inflation and acquisitions," echoes Sabatino. "Apparent sales were up, but units were down. It was all smoke and mirrors."

Joseph Seyfert believes that Borden's collage approach could have been successful, but in the heightened atmosphere of the Potato Chip

Wars—with Borden now preoccupied by BOGO offers, price cuts, and throwing out undersized chips for better-looking product—"it became a matter of 'who's king of the mountain.'" Such distractions led to an unraveling of Waydo's initially fitting approach.

Borden watched its salty snack market share slip from a high of 12 percent to 5 percent by 1996, three years after Waydo left as president to become its consultant. A 1994 *Forbes* magazine broadcast "Poor Elsie! How Inept Management Milks Borden Dry" on its cover, and inside gave details of ballooning debt and an "inefficient patchwork of declining brands and loosely related products" throughout all of Borden's product lines—not just snack foods. Plants closed down.

> *Vic Sabatino:* I remember one night pounding on the chairman's car in the parking lot, telling him that I couldn't shut down plants as fast as we were losing business.

> *George Waydo:* I fought vigorously to stay in the wars. We would never be Frito-Lay, but could be a profitable second national brand. It wasn't that they didn't listen to me, it was just that they couldn't do what I wanted to do. I could understand. I didn't agree, but I could understand. The realities were that snacks were just one piece of the pie.

Borden announced in January of 1994 that it would sell its salty snack concerns "under the divestment portion of its restructuring program to focus its resources on fewer businesses." It sold Clover Club and Guy's in the fall of that year and continued to sell off every regional chipper it owned, except Moore's and Wise—the original Borden flagchip brand.

Caught in the Crossfire

By the late 1980s predatory price slashing and purchasing of shelf space were the new rules for staying in business; at least, that was how the big boys were doing it.

But throughout most of the twentieth century, chippers had not only partied together, but sometimes shared recipes, new technologies, or even employees, in a pinch. Battles among potato chippers were limited to occasional incursions into each other's territories, or disputes over routes along borders. "They fought tooth and nail on the streets," is the way Alan Klein, owner of Mister Bee Potato Chips in Parkersburg, West Virginia, puts it, recalling the old-school ethic of an era when people like Harvey Noss were in charge. "But it was clean; you didn't price cut. You sold on quality, not price. But when the big companies came in, they worried about returns to stockholders. It became a different industry. It took all the fun out of it."

While Borden, Eagle, Keebler, and Frito-Lay were battling it out in the Potato Chip Wars, the regionals were caught in the middle. It was a completely new paradigm, to which some could not adapt fast enough. A source quoted in a later investigation said that "before the chip wars, Frito would take a price increase once a year and the regionals would follow suit." But "once Eagle came in, Eagle would act and Frito would respond more frequently than once a year. This activity caught all the regionals in the crossfire."

Some of the regionals who shut their doors were the very ones who tried hardest to imitate Frito-Lay's, Borden's, and Eagle's strategies—either by acquiring other chippers or by taking on complete snack lines of corn, cheese, pretzels, popcorn, nuts—instead of staying small, and staying with potato chips.

"A lot of regionals were hurt by trying to be like Frito-Lay—trying to match them item-for-item," observes the anonymous individual in the chip packaging industry about such a tack. "You can't do that, or you're gonna die."

It wasn't just a matter of adding products. Some tried to do what Herman Lay had done earlier—buy out smaller chippers to acquire their plant capacity. But that strategy could backfire, too, according to the packager, who comments that "if you do that, you're buying someone else's problems."

The stories of several companies during this time suggest that there may be something to such arguments. Out west, G.F. Industries, Inc., bought out veteran regionals Blue Bell, Bell Brand, and Granny Goose—who already had Scudder. Once considered the West's dominant snack company, Scudder by now had changed hands several times since Laura Scudder's death in 1959. Together the G.F. companies produced and sold potato chips, tortilla chips, cheese puffs, kettle chips, popcorn, and corn chips, and employed 1,250 people. But in April 1995, press releases from each of the subsidiary companies announced their likely closures, which involved 250 to 600 employees depending on the company. Also out west, Clover Club Foods of Utah filed for Chapter 11 bankruptcy in 1995. In the South, Lance cut five hundred jobs, shut two plants, and took a $21.9 million loss for the fourth quarter of 1995 alone. *Business North Carolina* attributed Lance's problems to competition with, among others, Eagle and Frito-Lay. "You're talking about 'slotting allowances' and charging for shelf space," said a Lance board member. "You used to go into a store, and it was just us, or maybe Tom's had a rack there. When I was a kid, you'd go into a filling station and, while the young man was servicing your car, you'd get a Coke and pack of crackers. Maybe we haven't been paying enough attention to that in recent years." Amidst the accelerated atmosphere of price cutting, said the Lance CEO, "now, any time since 1990 that we put in a price increase, we have not been able to make it stick."

In Pennsylvania, the heart of traditional potato chip country, three big regionals were down for the count. Gibble's and Charles Chips both filed for Chapter 11 in 1993, with Charles's debt at $18 million in 1992. In December 1996, Bon Ton Foods—a veteran turn-of-the-century chipper, whose packaging still used circa-1890s imagery of a woman in a bonnet and a big red bow—announced plans to cut seventy jobs.

"That's a story in and of itself," says Herb Hoover, formerly of the E. K. Bare potato brokerage in Lancaster County, Pennsylvania. "El-Ge, which was close to Bon Ton, bought out Bon Ton. Then the combined company bought out Mrs. Ihrie's; then they bought Bickle's. Now the single company [Hanover Foods] uses as many potatoes as would be made by one small plant—about one semi-load a day. When they were separate the combined companies used enough for twelve to fifteen semi-loads a day."

Hoover's account provides a glimpse into the way slipping sales resulted in the shattering of family-owned companies, with remnant coalitions of survivors picking crumbs from the wake. In New York City, Bon Ton lost its distributor in favor of Utz, a sister chipper also based in Hanover, Pennsylvania. Years earlier, Utz employees had come to Bon Ton's aid, working alongside Bon Ton employees after floods had trapped the night shift on the factory roof. Over twenty years later, the miniwar between Bon Ton and Utz was played out two states away, as the Bon Ton billboard at Yankee Stadium was replaced by one for Utz in 1996.

Although costs were up and profit margins were down for everyone, it is not always clear to what extent the loss of regionals during the Great Potato Chip Wars was a direct consequence, or indirect effect, of the new paradigm of slotting fees and price slashing. In the early years, everyone was making money; now it was a different story: Bob Jones, of Jones Potato Chip Company, Mansfield, Ohio, maintains that it was different in the old days.

"Going back to the '30s and '40s, chips were a weekend treat, and a lot of people didn't even eat them," says Jones. "If all you did was make good chips, you could grow. And it was more profitable in the '40s and '50s. In the '70s, there were more pressures related to doing business. The people that got really rich in this industry did so earlier."

Florida potato shortages didn't help. When prices were driven up, large companies could pay whatever it cost to secure Floridas for spring chip production. But not so smaller companies. During a shortage in 1987, Gibble's, a midsized Pennsylvania chipper that once served eleven states, could not get enough potatoes to stay on the shelves. Don Carr, former owner of Kay and Ray's and a Gibble's plant manager, says that the supermarkets didn't have much sympathy, with the grocers taking the stance: "If you can't stay on the shelves, you lose the space. Along with that," Carr adds, "you had players like Eagle and the slotting fees. Between slotting and the high price of potatoes, Gibble actually lost stores—lost sales volume—and never really recovered."

After going into Chapter 11 bankruptcy in 1993, Gibble's was bought by Consolidated Biscuit of Ohio, but continued to do poorly. The 1996 Snack Food Association's membership directory showed "Nibble with Gibble's" having 200 employees and 60 route trucks, down from 430 employees and 175 route trucks in 1987-88. Consolidated Biscuit transformed the Gibble's continuously cooked lard chip— a near-novelty in the industry—into a standard vegetable oil chip. Although there was an attempt to come up with a baked chip, Gibble's mostly became just another producer of a vegetable oil potato chip sold as a "private label" product under a supermarket's name. It was a higher volume but lower profit-margined chip business than the previous Gibble's niche.

"The Gibble's plant wasn't necessarily geared toward doing private label," says Carr. "For the private label product, they needed to run a machine that did three thousand pounds per hour. But Gibble's would have to run two machines for that kind of production. Gibble's was more geared to making a quality product than a low cost product."

Consolidated Biscuit and Gibble's were soon to feel the full force of difficulties associated with private labeling. Consolidated also made cookies for Nabisco, who, it turned out, had more capacity for cookies than needed, so canceled its private label contracts with Consolidated. According to Carr, Consolidated was then forced to choose between selling Gibble's or shutting it down. In late 1996 Gibble's was sold to Martin's Famous Pastry Shoppes Inc. Under Martin's ownership, Gibble's today continues to make a thin, crispy chip that regularly wins taste tests, likely due in part to the tastiness of lard, although the lard aspect is rarely mentioned in product reviews.

In the Midwest, Hiland, a former powerhouse that sold chips in eight Midwest and Great Plains states, was not as lucky as Gibble's. Hiland too was struggling when purchased by Curtice-Burns, who in 1988 outbid Borden for the company. Even more hands-off than Borden, Curtice-Burns encouraged its regional stable — Snyder of Berlin, Husman's of Cincinnati, Nalley's and Tim's Cascade Style Potato Chips of Washington State — to cater to local chip styles and marketing preferences. Hiland needed work, but the thinking was that sufficient brand interest existed to "stage a comeback." Marketers developed Midwest-sourced ingredients, added corn oil to suit "midwestern tastes," and introduced the slogan "The flavor of America's Heartland" on Hiland packages. Production enhancements included seven form-fill-seal machines with computerized scales for packaging; a wastewater disposal system, an additional warehouse, and — notoriously — an innovative chip package.

Hiland's package concept — the "Bowl Bag" — was the most novel approach to chip packaging since the Pringles tennis ball can. Chip eaters no longer needed to transport a bowl to a tailgate party — the bag could be unzipped and made into its own bowl. Hiland turned the bag sideways so that the zipper ran the full length of what would normally be the side, about nineteen inches — "an unusual orientation for a flexible film-packaged product," said *Packaging Digest*. "We're optimistic that this development is going to be a big winner for us," said a Hiland vice president at the time.

Unfortunately, the sideways labeling was also the product's downfall. Displayed horizontally, it needed twice the necessary space on the snack shelves, halving its own sales potential. The "re-sealable" strip closure didn't work reliably, and the product was marketed for the Fourth of July rather than tailgating season. It languished on the shelves, where no one bought it. John Blough, now director of operations at Snyder of Berlin, mentions that the package even won a "packaging blunder of the year" award in one of the trade magazines.

Or, maybe it was ahead of its time. Thirteen years later, in 2005, Frito-Lay reintroduced the concept, using the same name—Bowl Bag—perfecting the seal, orienting it vertically, and this time coordinating its release with the football bowl games.

But a packaging flop, although potentially serious, by itself would not be enough to take down a company unless other fundamentals were also amiss. According to Blough, bigger problems at Hiland were the erosion of the brand name, a process in place long before Curtice-Burns acquired it. Despite Curtice-Burns's policy of not buying "turnaround-positioned" companies—and despite efforts to enhance product, marketing, production, and distribution—Curtice-Burns couldn't make a go of it and sold Hiland to Weaver of Nebraska in 1993.

"I think we overestimated the strength of the brand," says Blough. "The weaknesses at Hiland were in the marketing area. [By the time Curtice-Burns became involved,] Frito-Lay already had their shelf space."

Some believe that it was mainly the poorly managed regionals—those who had gotten by with negligent management when profit margins were better—who were paying the price for excess in an increasingly constricted retail environment. True, profit margins were decreasing, and slotting fees were a barrier to new outlets—but the regionals who eventually disappeared had only themselves to blame.

Rob Hess of the E. K. Bare potato brokerage of Lancaster County observes that some of the plants that went belly-up endured not only mismanagement but divorce settlements, as the nature of the American marriage changed. Wives in many cases had been as instrumental as their husbands in starting chip businesses, working side-by-side and around the clock; they justifiably felt entitled to part of the family business after a divorce. In some cases, the wife might inherit the entire company. In the late 1920s, Helen Friedman, an early employee of Magic City Foods in Birmingham, Alabama (today the makers of Golden Flake potato chips), and later part owner, married Frank Mosher, another owner. When they divorced she received the entire company—today one of the South's largest chip companies.

Some of the attrition in the chip industry was just due to the nature of family businesses—according to some, it's rare that any family business survives more than two or three generations, period. A passage in the 1976 *Snack Food Blue Book,* written in the midst of the 1970s pre-Eagle part of the shakeout, suggests that death and taxes ruined some family chippers: "There was, it should be noted, nothing sinister in the erosion of numbers. It's just that it was difficult for the persons who founded chip companies during the early growth years of the industry to get out their equity as they became older and neared retirement age. Even when there were family members to inherit the business, the burden of inheritance taxes could be devastating. The result was a natural tendency to sell out to large corporations."

In New England, Frank Dodd, who became a general manager at John E. Cain Company in 1968, recalls that by the late 1970s the Cain family no longer wanted to "invest in what was necessary to stay in the industry. Quite honestly," Dodd says, "potato chip people were seat-of-the-pants people."

These seat-of-the-pants types were increasingly finding that the do-it-yourself technologies that might have worked in the 1930s no longer sufficed. Along with constant (and expensive) advances in machinery, more and more necessary was the use of marketing research for targeting product; with competition for shelf space, distribution methods had to be constantly evaluated and updated. It no longer sufficed for someone's aunt or mom to do the bookkeeping; employees with business degrees were required to manage accounts, and a corporate structure was needed to maintain it all. Some, like Herman Lay, embraced the new necessities, inventing and tweaking them as they went along; others, perhaps like New England's Cain family, seemed to want no part of it. Acquiring tools like continuous cookers and packaging machines during the 1930s and 1950s was one thing. By the 1970s, chips had come so far from grandma's kitchen-stove methodology that some family chippers must have wondered what business they'd been born into.

The overall effect was pronounced. The SFA's chipper membership in the continental United States, although representing only a sample of the chippers who chose to join, declined from 114 to 95, to 63, to 48 from 1943, 1977, 1988, and 1996, respectively. Formerly broken into six membership regions having their own summer and winter meetings, the 1976–77 SFA membership directory indicated four regions. By 1988 the directory's "regional map" specified only "Eastern" and "Western" regions, and the 1996 membership directory made no mention of regions at all.

The Eagle Fries

By the mid-1990s, as a heightened state of competition wreaked havoc on the weary regionals, Eagle—the one often credited with starting the Wars to begin with—had yet to post a profit after sixteen years in business. In 1995 *Brandweek* focused on Eagle's problems, but ended on a positive note: "To be sure, Eagle appears focused on building for long term, and, barriers be damned, isn't planning to shrink from the fight anytime soon." Eagle president David Poldoian added, "A simple effort to pound us out of existence isn't going to work. We are here to stay."

Only a month later, it was a different story. As Borden's regional stable was fading with little notice from the media, newspapers around the country carried lead stories about a "surprise announcement" from Anheuser-Busch:

> *Wall Street Journal:* Anheuser-Busch Cos., accelerating its back-to-beer strategy, said it will sell its unprofitable Eagle Snacks business and the St. Louis Cardinals major league baseball team, along with the club's Busch Memorial Stadium home.

> *New York Times:* The announcement marks the end of a more than sixteen-year effort by Anheuser-Busch, the world's largest brewer, to expand into the snack food business. Although beer and salty foods have a natural affinity, it was not enough for Anheuser-Busch to find the same profits in Eagle brand potato chips and pretzels as in Budweiser and Bud Light.

The division was said to have lost $25 million in 1995 alone. Because Eagle would have required an "infusion of capital" to reach full potential, said company officials, they decided instead to use the money to refocus on brewing. Former president Kevin Bowler had left Eagle a scant six months earlier. As with Borden, Bowler suggests that Eagle was close—very close—to eking out a permanent place as a national snack company, but the interests of the larger company—Anheuser-Busch—prompted a return to "fundamentals." Bowler says that Eagle had a reasonable plan to implement the necessary changes; however, "in '95 the clarion call in boardrooms was to recommit to core competencies; you could argue Eagle and bread were not." To the boardroom, stock repurchases, rather than chips and snacks, became a better use of dollars to grow earnings per share. Eagle would carry existing business to the end of 1995, when it expected to sell to a prospective buyer who was already in place.

On October 26, 1995, Frito president and CEO Steve Reinemund sent a congratulatory letter to Frito-Lay associates. The letter was complimentary, but urged against complacency in the new world order: "As you may have already learned, Anheuser-Busch surrendered yesterday after fifteen years in the salty snacks business and another year of losses at its Eagle Snacks division. . . . Eagle succeeded in building a stable of national brands that could now be acquired by an even tougher competitor."

Several tried. It was reported that Nabisco had looked into buying Eagle, as reportedly did seven "financial groups" of investors with no history in snack foods—a type of owner becoming more and more commonplace in the potato chip industry—but no buyer ever materialized. *BusinessWeek* quoted a prospective buyer who soured on the idea after learning more: "Here was a company with poor market position, poor execution, fragmented distribution, and no cost or quality advantage." On February 7, 1996, Anheuser-Busch Companies, Inc. announced that it was finally closing business at the Eagle plants. Four Eagle plants—in Robersonville, North Carolina, Fayetteville, Tennessee, Visalia, California, and the old El-Ge plant in York, Pennsylvania—would be sold to Frito-Lay. Eagle held onto the Cape Cod plant in Hyannis, Massachusetts, for the time being. Overall Eagle reportedly took a $206 million write-off.

Borden still had Wise and, for a time, Moore's, but for all practical purposes it was out of the fight. Keebler had announced plans to quit, too, and Nabisco seemed to have lost its appetite for salty snacks. Close to the time of Eagle's announcement about its impending sale, Frito-Lay's portion of the salty snack market had risen to over 50 percent from a low of 38 percent in 1991; Eagle was third at 5 percent. In potato chips, Lay's and Ruffles alone accounted for 34.5 percent of the category nationwide; Eagle was behind Pringles and combined generic "private label" potato chips at 5.3 percent.

Eagle was finally gone, and the smoke was clearing from the field. With Frito-Lay getting Eagle's old plants, the only thing standing between it and market domination was a motley handful of regionals who had fallen under Frito's and Eagle's radar. All that was needed for the Eagle plant sale to go forward was approval from the U.S. Department of Justice. A mere formality.

6

Trust and Antitrust

There is a paradox at the center of antitrust. If you have companies competing tooth and nail to produce a better product at a lower price, eventually somebody will start to win. If one wins and gets high market share, they will then start to acquire a monopoly. They can then start to raise their prices.

James W. Lovett,
antitrust attorney

When Frito agreed to buy four of Eagle's five chip plants—subject to Department of Justice (DOJ) approval—the lives of former Eagle employees, to the tune of 300 to 450 people per plant, suddenly went on hold. Some former Eagle workers reportedly cried when they got word of the closings.

In 2001 I made a Freedom of Information Act (FOIA) inquiry to the DOJ about the Eagle plant sale. Among the items I received were a two-inch stack of what I counted to be 432 pages of handwritten letters, all addressed to Anne K. Bingaman, then an assistant attorney general in the Antitrust Division under President Clinton. Names of the authors were redacted—blacked out.

From York County, at the former El-Ge plant, which had over three hundred employees:

Our jobs are important to us all in Eagle Snacks of York, Pa. I hope the sale to Frito Lay is approved. I have over 20 years of dedicated service.

Bills must be paid when due. We do not need any more plant closings in our county as there is enough unemployed people now.

Sincerely,

[Redacted]

From Robersonville, North Carolina:

To whom it may concern:

I work at Eagle Snacks Inc. in Robersonville, NC. Frito-Lay is in the process of buying our plant & we would really appreciate your department approving this sale as soon as possible. We have 420 people in our plant alone. We all need jobs. The Frito-Lay company wants to open us back up, but we need your approval.

Please consider this for the economic welfare of our employees as well as our county.

Thank you,

[Redacted]

From Fayetteville, Tennessee:

Frito-Lay has bought the building and I understand they intend to open back up in the near future. I'm writing this letter to ask if any way possible, that yall could speed up the opening process. The job market is extremely low in Lincoln Co. and none of us want to leave our hometown to work, but we may be forced to if we have no other choice. Please hurry—we need the jobs.

Sincerely,

A very hard worker,

[Redacted]

The former Eagle workers need not have worried. Department of Justice approval went ahead in May 1996. In the next few months Frito announced plans to reopen the plants.

But not all former workers for Eagle were technically Eagle employees. Even before the plant transaction was approved, some former Eagle comrades were beginning to feel as if they had been left outdoors in the cold.

The California Clan

Frito's "store-door" delivery system was built on a program of company-owned routes using proven methods: competitive shelf-stocking programs based on employee loyalty. Frito-Lay had decades to perfect the system. By comparison, Eagle's eager reach for shelf space seemed almost opportunistic—a grope for distribution openings through almost any gap by any method, using beer staff, bread staff, snack staff, independents, and slotting fees—whatever worked.

Independent distributors usually have an established clientele and can be a good way for chippers to "break" new markets. As independent "jobbers," they pay their own benefits, buy their own trucks and warehouses, withhold their own taxes, and pay their own employees, if any. Frito-Lay announced its intent to rehire Eagle employees—but rehiring Eagle employees would have no effect on independent distributors, who formerly worked on behalf of Eagle. Either way, the Eagle independents—specifically, a group of them in California—would be out of a job.

On April 18, 1996, twenty-one former Eagle independent distributors in California filed suit over Anheuser-Busch's sale of Eagle to Frito-Lay, asking the court to enter a temporary restraining order to enjoin the sale: "If Frito Lay acquires the Eagle Snacks plants, plaintiffs will be irreparably harmed. Plaintiffs all rely on the distribution of Eagle Snacks pursuant to their distributor agreements for their livelihood and support as well as support for their families."

It wasn't just their own livelihoods the independents were reputedly concerned about. They claimed the proposed transaction to be an antitrust violation of section 7 of the Clayton Act—the mergers were likely to lessen competition, or to create monopoly. The accompanying complaint for damages specified that Eagle had entered into a "conspiracy" with its "number one competitor" rather than sell the plants to new competitors. The sale would destroy the "good will" of Eagle Snacks, and was done with the intent to lessen competition, monopolize the market, and fix prices.

In a response dated April 25, 1996, an executive from Frito said that the acquisition involved only four plants, did not include acquisition of Eagle's inventory or market research, and would rehire former Eagle employees (but made no mention of rehiring the Eagle distributors): "This is a purely bricks-and-mortar transaction, undertaken by Frito-Lay as the least costly, most efficient way to remedy its capacity needs . . . Frito-Lay currently intends to hire between 100-150

supervisory and between 1000–1400 non-supervisory employees to operate the plants. Personnel who were employed at the four plants at the
time of their closure will be given first consideration by Frito-Lay for
job openings."

If it wasn't so before, Frito-Lay's newly anointed role as the only
national player left in the Great Potato Chip Wars now provided it a
unique standing. Frito's response attributed its new position to its own
creativity, justifying its newfound stature as further reason for the plant
acquisition to go forward: "As a result of its commitment to continuous
product innovation, new product introductions, and high quality standards, Frito-Lay is now in the midst of a period of dramatic growth for
its salty snack products. Acquisition of the plants will relieve Frito-
Lay's present and anticipated capacity problems."

David Poldoian, the Eagle president who toward the end had fought
against Frito in the Wars, now sided against his former Eagle distributors, stating that the lawsuit against the Frito-Lay purchase was "totally without merit."

The presiding judge concurred. In a paper dated April 25, 1996,
U.S. District Court Judge Edward J. Garcia denied the former Eagle
distributors' motion for reasons that seemed to have more to do with
weaknesses in the plaintiffs' case than Eagle's or Frito's potential culpa-
bility. Judge Garcia acknowledged that "while it is true that a lessening
of competition is recognized as irreparable injury," the court could not
determine if competition would in fact be affected, "since plaintiffs have
presented no evidence of the same." The former Eagle independents
had not provided "a single shred of evidence" that the acquisition would
deter competition. With no further obstacles to the sale, there seemed
to be clear sailing ahead for Frito-Lay. In late April the DOJ closed the
investigation of the Eagle plant sale.

But sometime—before or during—their review of materials about
the plant sale, the Justice staff must have seen something, somewhere,
that aroused their interest.

The Department of Justice Launches

Memorial Day weekend is the second biggest weekend for potato chip
sales in the country, after the Fourth of July. On the Friday before the

1996 Memorial Day weekend, viewers heard two commentators on *NBC Nightly News:*

> *Tom Brokaw:* And as you prepare to tear into one more giant, economy bag of snacks this Memorial Day weekend, you may be wondering if you're getting the best price. Well, the Justice Department is wondering the same thing and it is investigating the giant Frito-Lay.

> *Pete Williams:* Justice Department investigators want to know if snack food giant Frito-Lay is taking up so much room on supermarket shelves that its competitors can't reach consumers. Frito-Lay is the blue chip of the salty snack food business with more than half the $15 billion market. Smaller companies complain that Frito-Lay is unfairly muscling them out of business by paying supermarkets to give its products prime store shelf space.

The new Justice investigation was separate and apart from the investigation of the Eagle plant sale. Executives at Borden and Country Club said that DOJ officials had called over the past three weeks. But no one had yet notified Frito that it was under investigation. Frito-Lay spokesperson Lynn Markley said, "We would certainly take [any inquiries] seriously, but we have not been accused of anything and we have not been contacted by the Justice Department."

Two weeks later, a lead *Time* magazine story, "Frito-Lay under Snack Attack," detailed the Justice investigation as it explained the Wars and slotting fees to the American public. Bemused food industry experts, who had seen slotting go unchallenged for over a decade, wondered why an investigation of Frito was taking place now, or even at all. They pointed to other food makers—Campbell's, Kellogg's, Gerber—who were even more dominant in their markets than Frito, had been using similar tactics longer, and had never been investigated in this manner. Anyway, it was the retail supermarkets, not Frito-Lay or Eagle, who were the true culprits in slotting. An editorial in *Food Processing* admonished, "Don't blame Frito-Lay. Or Con-Agra. Or Kellogg's. Or any other company involved in this scam. It's the retailers that government ought to be focusing on. . . . I don't recall Frito-Lay, or any other company, walking up to the supermarket big shots begging to pay for the opportunity just to be on the shelf."

Although word of the investigation was announced in May 1996, it turned out the DOJ had been receiving—or soliciting—complaints about Frito-Lay and the snack food industry for some time. Some complaints had arrived just after Anheuser-Busch's October 1995 announcement about Eagle, but some came even before then, as much as a year before the current investigation, when Eagle was supposedly still very much in the running. A letter dated June 22, 1995—four months before Anheuser-Busch's announcement about closing Eagle—hints at an impending shake-up, but redacted text makes it impossible to know if it addressed rumors about Eagle's closing, or something else; the letter (its source redacted) to Justice legal assistant Wendy Saltzman, said that "we also learned today that what is reported as rumor on [redacted] will become a fact today or in the very near future."

A seventeen-page "confidential memorandum," also dated June 22, 1995, outlined for the DOJ the entirety of the snack food market—products, customer purchasing habits, distribution, merchandising, shelving. It was a serious attempt to summarize available information for government officials. The memo's conclusion indicated that this was not the first time the source (redacted) had been in contact with Justice officials: "We once again appreciate the opportunity to present these concerns about an important and large consumer market to the Department."

Now that an investigation was officially underway, more letters—some unsolicited and some in response to DOJ requests—arrived at the department. It was the release of a dam held back for years.

The Complaints

My FOIA request in 2001 yielded 1,937 pages of information (including the 432 pages of letters from former Eagle employees). Except for a handful of instances where a clerk apparently erred, all of the information—letters, transcripts of interviews, transcripts of meetings—had sources and other portions redacted, with blacked-out names, sentences, paragraphs, and pages. Withheld from my request entirely were 115 documents—724 pages.

Of the documents I did receive, forty-one were letters written to the DOJ about the snack food industry; a few of these were copies of letters received and then forwarded by members of Congress. Fifty documents were transcripts of phone or in-person interviews with individuals in the snack food or grocery industries. With redaction of almost all names, there is, of course, no way to know how many unique individuals were involved. Of the ninety-one total documents, at least twenty expressed concerns about slotting and fee payments in exchange for shelf space; eight letters mentioned monopolistic behavior or concerns about anticompetitive activity; at least fourteen letters or interviews mentioned "exclusivity" or "exclusion"; at least eight alleged payment to grocers in exchange for excluding competitors from shelves. Some letters were simply follow-ups asking if the Justice staff had received an earlier letter; others only made vague complaints about the situation in the snack food industry and enclosed the latest *Wall Street Journal* article.

On the basis of such complaints, on August 19, 1996, the U.S. Department of Justice issued a Civil Investigative Demand to Frito-Lay, Inc., to determine whether there had been a violation of section 2 of the Sherman Antitrust Act, specifying "explicit or de facto exclusive dealing arrangements and other exclusionary practices." The demand required that responses and documents be presented within about a month, on September 21, 1996.

The Demands

The Department of Justice demanded a surfeit of information. Frito had to not only provide basic data about plant locations, distribution, and marketing but identify everyone in Frito-Lay responsible for retail promotion, marketing, sales, and their dates of service—especially those responsible for approving policies related to retail pricing, rebates, shelf-space payments, and "exclusive promotions." For each of its twenty-two sales areas, Frito had to identify retail channels, specify total sales by product, and name persons responsible for pricing. It also had to itemize production details for its forty-two plants, including number of routes and total sales within 100 miles, 150 miles, and 200 miles. The demand specifically asked for information about outlets, sales volumes, and shelf space in Northern California, Southern California, San Antonio, Dallas, Houston, and Chicago.

Frito had to supply its own data about those markets, including expenditures for shelf space and identities of each person approving price changes; it had to identify retail outlets for which it was the sole supplier (excluding generic "private label" brands), outlets where it lost shelf space, and the competitors to whom it lost the space.

In addition to data, Frito-Lay was required to supply all documents — since 1991 — related to business, operating, budgets, marketing, forecasts, studies, surveys. It had to supply internal documents related to complaints — "allegations that your company is not behaving in a competitive manner, including, but not limited to, retail outlet and competitor complaints, threatened, pending, or completed lawsuits, and federal and state investigations."

Not only did Frito-Lay have to specify data about itself; it had to do so about others. Frito had to identify each company that had "entered, attempted to enter, or exited" from manufacture of similar products, the competitor's products, the competitor's market area, and the dates the competitor entered and exited.

The demand should not have been too much of a surprise to Frito-Lay by this time. Slightly earlier, before it issued the Civil Investigative Demand, the DOJ had met with Frito officials. On a Friday afternoon in late July 1996, Justice attorneys talked with Frito-Lay counsels Mark Fritz and others about the investigation. When questioning got around to shelf fees, the Frito reps explained that they would

> prefer not to pay for shelf space because they want their payment programs to promote performance improvement. Similarly, they do not pay for exclusivity or condition the payments that are made. They believe that exclusivity does not necessarily promote growth in sales. They typically try to make an objective case using IRI [Information Resources, Inc.] data and discussing how a store can improve their own sales by further promoting Frito-Lay. . . . Fritz states that some supermarkets may demand payment for shelf space. In these circumstances they will pay, however, they may try to reduce their programming funds or they may attach additional performance criteria.

Although it is hard to know what data are missing, copies of Frito-Lay data I received from the Department of Justice Civil Investigative Demand do not contradict this view. Among the materials the DOJ obtained from Frito was a workbook titled "Customer Focused Selling." It appears to have accompanied a slide or overhead presentation and includes sections where users could calculate "penny profit" and profit margin, homework exercises, and solutions. One section advised on sales calls, with examples of sales pitches to the grocer client: "I've got a great idea to increase your sales. I can show you a way to maximize sales and profits per square foot, without taking additional space. Would you like to hear more?" Or "How would you like to increase your sales by 10 percent? A theme display by the dairy section would take advantage of the high traffic in that area. What do you think about my idea?"

Topic 7 in the workbook listed common objections that dealt directly with acquiring space from competitors. There was no mention about offering money or contracts to exclude competitors, but it suggested ways to meet the store owner's needs. For example, if a store owner complained "I'm getting a better deal from your competitor" or "I don't have enough space in the gondola [shelf], at the end of the aisle, etc.," the Frito-Lay salesperson should not "be shy about showing how space currently used by our competitors (or by other categories) could give your customer a better return. Point out how Frito-Lay products would satisfy the customer's needs better." Another common objection from a store owner might be: "Other snack food companies have offered me one free fill (or one free case with the purchase of 10). Why should I give the space to you if you can't offer the same kind of arrangement?" The workbook outlined this response:

> Emphasize the business results. "Instead of a one-time offer, you'll be able to enjoy the benefits we provide for as long as you can do business with us. We can offer you:
>> The most popular snacks on the market
>> National advertising
>> The highest rate of return on any snacks
>> A wide variety of brands to appeal to a variety of customer tastes."
> Explain the benefits Frito-Lay can offer: "As far as a grand opening special for you, what I can do is set up a special event, with window banners and special displays."
> If the objection is about the initial cost: "I can set up a charge for you right now. In reality, you won't have to pay for the products until they've already sold."

Nowhere were the words "exclusive" or "exclusion" mentioned; nowhere was there talk about offering payments of cash or merchandise to remove a competitor, or conditions to be imposed on a competitor in exchange for rebates; nowhere did it mention moving a competitor's rack or what to do with the competitor's rack when the space was taken.

Other data the DOJ apparently received from Frito included the demographics data it requested for western markets where Frito-Lay had few competitors. Both Nielsen Scantrack and IRI InfoScan data listed demographics for western cities such as San Francisco and Sacramento, showing population, number of households, and percentage of chains versus independents. Printouts listed names of supermarkets, their numbers of units, and percentage of market share. One presentation contained Frito-Lay data about the Atlanta market, a part of the country where Frito's regional competitors were supposedly the strongest. It showed Frito with $67.4 million market share in salty snacks total, over Golden Flake—one of the southeast's biggest regionals—at only $5.3 million. But, with that exception, nowhere did I find listings of competing chip brands or companies, their market shares, or unit prices; no expenditures for shelf space, identities of persons approving price changes, retail outlets for which Frito was the sole supplier, or identifications of outlets where they lost shelf space.

Results from an observational study included in the FOIA request and apparently contracted for by Frito-Lay showed that salty snacks were among "the highest impulse categories in the supermarket." Impulse (as opposed to planned) purchases were 70 percent overall among all supermarket purchases, whereas salty snacks alone—presumably also a component of the former category—were even higher, at 82 percent. The finding didn't speak well for the alleged benefits of potato chip quality, customer brand loyalty, or consumer interest in company histories printed on the backs of chip bags. According to one document, "Despite their use of salty snacks, consumers are very *uninvolved* with the category and spend less than 1 minute shopping for salty snacks."

Although the DOJ demanded a variety of internal Frito-Lay correspondence, the only such correspondence included in my FOIA request concerned a Kroger Customer-Management Agreement. Dated February 10, 1997—months after DOJ's compliance date, September 1996, for initial handover of materials—it talked about crediting $3,000 to Kroger stores if they moved an endcap and placed one "incremental perimeter rack" for Frito-Lay. But "if they do not follow the recommendations of the category study and take the rack and move the endcap they will not get the $3000 credit."

Buried among the nearly two thousand pages of documents I received was a memo written by DOJ staff about the final decision and deliberative process of the Antitrust Division. On DOJ stationery, dated April 23, 1998 — two years since the official opening of the investigation into Frito-Lay — and headed "Recommendation to Close Investigation: Frito-Lay, Inc.," it began, "We opened this investigation in April 1996, on the strength of complaints from competitors that Frito-Lay, Inc. ('Frito') has exclusive contracts with retailers." The rest of the paragraph was redacted. Next paragraph: "Nevertheless, competitors insisted that Frito was able to obtain sole supplier status in certain types of stores, such as convenience stores. As for other larger retail outlets, competitors complained that Frito was currently dominating the shelf space, and engaging in constant efforts to obtain additional space, invariably at the expense of, and to the detriment of, its rivals. Competitors claimed that Frito's efforts were driving them out of business because reduced space meant reduced sales and increased costs." Most of pages 2 and 3 was redacted, but DOJ authors went on to detail why the investigation was to be closed: "The most promising of our theories are set forth below. Much credit should be given to Jill Ptacek and Dick Doidge [DOJ attorneys], whose earlier memoranda contain somewhat deeper analysis and cover every possible theory we could come up with, however promising." Pages 4 to 14 — presumably the content of DOJ's analysis and reasons for closing the investigation — were entirely redacted.

An Ending, of Sorts

On December 22, 1998, the *Wall Street Journal* reported that "the Justice Department has closed its investigation into alleged anticompetitive practices by PepsiCo Inc.'s Frito-Lay division without taking any action. The investigation, started in 1996 as a look at the entire salty-snack industry, focused on complaints by smaller companies that Frito-Lay, which controls more than half the market, was improperly locking out rivals by using a common practice of buying shelf space in retail stores and securing exclusive promotions." The next day, the *New York Times* ran a similar story and quoted Frito-Lay spokeswoman Lynn Markley: "We are very pleased with their decision."

Industry analysts did not seem especially surprised at the result, pointing out that Frito was too savvy to have done anything explicitly illegal; besides, the areas in which Frito and others traded—slotting in particular—were "gray areas" of antitrust activity. "Some industry analysts said the lack of action suggests Frito-Lay's retail practices, while aggressive, apparently weren't illegal," explained the *Wall Street Journal* piece. "Payment of fees to retailers and exclusive promotions are becoming increasingly common in a number of industries."

James W. Lovett, an attorney for a small snack company in the DOJ investigation believes that Frito-Lay's financing and acumen allowed it to operate

> right on the line. In fairness to them—and I'm sure that some route manager somewhere probably did something illegal—as a general corporate rule, they probably didn't do anything that violated antitrust laws. They were too smart. It's all about shades of gray. Frito-Lay was very aggressive about pursuing the lines where the shades of gray were. In every investigation I have been involved in, when they drop the investigation, it's because they don't think they can win the case. Either they concluded that Frito-Lay hadn't done anything wrong, or that Frito-Lay had done things wrong in the margins, but it wasn't enough to warrant a case.

George Thompson, an analyst at Prudential Securities, agreed with the basic premise: "The problem is Frito-Lay is kind of damned for being so big, but big doesn't necessarily mean bad. I'm sure they are very aggressive, but my experience has been that they are also very aware of what their position is relative to everyone else and they have to be very, very careful."

Frito-Lay indicated to me that the investigation was a vindication of sorts, not only for whatever alleged role it may have played in the Great Potato Chip Wars but for its approach—an approach increasingly followed, in part or whole, by nearly everyone else in the industry: "The conclusion of the Justice Department review speaks well for our business practices and we're very pleased with their decision. There are no mysteries about how Frito-Lay succeeds. Our marketplace advantages come from quality, value, innovation, and our route system delivery."

Antitrust scholar Gregory Gundlach talks about two ways to view slotting. On the one hand, favorable displays can improve market efficiency and thus benefit consumers with improved screening of new products, better use of shelving, and more efficient signage. On the other hand, slotting may carry conditions that exclude or disadvantage a competitor. According to Gundlach, three conditions can be put on payment: access, position, and promotion. If a dominant player can restrict something like access, slotting can wreak havoc with competition. Gundlach speculates that the DOJ may have dropped the case because the former view prevailed: perhaps they believed slotting practices are actually beneficial. "By this standard of thinking," says Gundlach, "even if the case is pursued, at the end of the day, they [the DOJ] believed nothing was wrong."

In any event, if the field wasn't cleared after the sell offs of Borden and Eagle, it was clear now.

7

The Heartland
Ohio and Pennsylvania

Stable climates with muted seasons allow more kinds of organisms to specialize on narrower pieces of the environment, to outcompete the generalists around them, and so to persist for longer periods of time. Species are packed more tightly. No niche, it seems, goes unfilled.

E. O. Wilson, *The Diversity of Life*

You've never seen anything like it. This area's like no other in the world.

Ken Potter, retired owner,
Martin's Potato Chips, Inc., Thomasville, Pennsylvania

Things were rather quiet in the years after the Great Potato Chip Wars.

In 1999 Cape Cod, independent once again after Eagle's demise, was bought by Lance, a large southern snack manufacturer. Guy's Foods, the former midwestern chunk of Borden's regional chip puzzle, sought bankruptcy protection in February 2000, closing up its gigantic plant a month later. In 2000 Borden sold Wise to a New York equity firm. Seyfert's, also formerly of the Borden stable, ended up with Troyer Farms of northwest Pennsylvania—the latter a true independent family-owned chip company rather than an investment group.

Flash forward to 2004. That summer I made a week-long journey to the center of America's potato chip heartland—Lancaster and York counties, Pennsylvania. Between visits to chip plants, I stop for lunch at the Shady Maple, a supermarket in East Earl, Pennsylvania.

It is lunchtime, and things are hopping. Kids fidget in chrome double-decker shopping carts that bring to mind extended-cab pickup trucks: two-seaters, with two child seats, one behind the other, perhaps six feet long. In front of the store, behind banks of picture windows, a glass display case is next to a lunch counter. The case contains maybe one hundred toy trucks, made by companies like Ertl, with logos of Pennsylvania products, including potato chips—toy trucks for Utz, Martin's, Good's, Gibble's. People line up at a counter twenty deep to buy lunch—a BBQ chicken special for three dollars. Lunch comes with a bag of plain chips that people accept without a second glance—Utz chips, in the white bag, made in the next county in Hanover.

Although there are probably larger, the Shady Maple in East Earl is the largest supermarket I've ever seen. Staffed most visibly by Mennonite counter girls, it employs 350 people in 110,000 square feet of space. An independent, unaffiliated with any chain, the Shady Maple sells fourteen brands of potato chips—that is, fourteen different chip companies having independent corporate lineages—not counting different flavors and styles. Potato chips alone occupy some seventy-six feet of horizontal shelf space. Herr's, headquartered some thirty miles away in Nottingham, leads the way at the Shady Maple with eighteen feet of space; Utz is second with twelve feet; Martin's, also from next-door Hanover, and Lay's/Ruffles are tied at eight feet each. Also represented are Bickle, Original Good's, King's, Gibble's, Ralph Good's, Dieffenbach, Kay & Ray's, Zerbe's, Wise, and Cape Cod.

Dan Holinger, grocery manager, East Earl: Lancaster County is the chip capital of the country. Most of the chip companies we have here—King's, Dieffenbach, Good's—people come here looking for those particular chips.

Herb Hoover, former Lancaster County chipping potato broker: This is the potato chip Mecca of the world. One time, we went into a local grocery store here, and found eleven companies with 124 choices—between the different combinations of oils, sizes, flavorings, and everything.

Greg Hake, owner, Hake's Grocery, York County, Pennsylvania: We're in the potato chip area; we love our chips around here. We eat Martin's . . . and

Utz. We have Frito-Lay; Frito-Lay has their Doritos—there, they sort of dominate. But when you get beyond that, when you get to the Lay's chips, we just don't eat them as much. We like Martin's . . . and Utz.

Terry Groff, grocery manager, Weaver Market, Adamstown: People in the rest of the U.S.—they have the Wise and the Lay's—but they've never had a good chip.

On my visit to the heart of what guidebooks call the Potato Chip Belt in York and Lancaster counties in southeast central Pennsylvania, I visited nine supermarkets—both independent and chain—making visual estimates of chip shelf space by company. In Lancaster County, not one supermarket represented fewer than ten potato chip companies, and Frito-Lay led in shelf space at only one of them.

If Frito-Lay was going to quash the vulnerable regional chippers after the "failure" of the Department of Justice investigation, nobody told people about it in Lancaster County, Pennsylvania.

The Bigger Boys

Today, Pennsylvania has sixteen independent chip companies (not including Wise and Frito-Lay, who have plants in Pennsylvania but are headquartered elsewhere), the most of any state of the Union. Ten of these sixteen are in York and Lancaster counties alone. The smaller companies are exceedingly local, servicing only the immediate counties proximate to their home base; few of the smaller companies pay slotting fees. The small chippers I have talked with mostly feel that they don't need to—people will find and buy their chips, regardless. The larger of the Pennsylvania chippers are akin to regional versions of Frito-Lay and Eagle, with complete snack portfolios of pretzels, tortillas, popcorn products, and multiple lines of potato chips. They may use the same Nielsen and Information Resources, Inc. data that Frito-Lay has, and they may pay slotting for extensive free-standing displays and endcaps.

Utz is in York County, Pennsylvania—also the home of Snyder's of Hanover, Martin's, Bickel's, and Hanover Foods. Utz owns the Baltimore/Washington chip market and now has distribution in New York City, New England, and down into the Atlantic seaboard. In 2005, market surveys rated Utz fourth in potato chips in the country, with over $88 million in unit sales compared with Frito-Lay's $1.5 billion.

South of the "Lard Belt" in Lancaster is Chester County, the home of Herr's. Herr's nearly owns the Philadelphia chip market and now has distribution in New Jersey, West Virginia, Ohio, New England, and increasingly into the South. In 2005, market surveys rated Herr's seventh in potato chips in the country, with over $48 million in unit sales.

Utz's and Herr's unit sales are almost two orders of magnitude less than Frito-Lay's, but are respectably large for regionals. Like Herr's, Utz has only two potato chip plants compared with Frito-Lay's thirty-three, but the main plant in Hanover looks as if it could take up two city blocks—over 500,000 square feet, the size of ten NCAA football fields. Why have Utz and Herr's remained and prospered, while other regionals with big aspirations did not?

As mentioned previously, attrition—presumably enhanced in the environment created by the Potato Chip Wars—is likely part of it. Some suggest that there's no reason other Pennsylvania chippers—El-Ge, Mrs. Ihrie's, Groff's, Bon Ton—couldn't be where Utz and Herr's find themselves today. For whatever reason—family decisions, inherent deficiencies, or attributes on the parts of Utz and Herr's—the others largely disappeared, leaving companies like Utz, Herr's, and Wise with the remaining market share. Bob Jones, president of Jones Potato Chip Company in Mansfield, Ohio, believes that "there's probably a hundred different reasons why they [family-owned chip companies] went out of business."

But if you remain, the next goal is to know your niches and to remain strong within them. Expanding can be risky—new flavors, for instance, cost thousands in lab fees, packaging design, and especially display space, for which supermarkets are more likely to charge slotting.

"Unless you've got a really, really super winner," says Bob Shearer of Shearer's Foods, in Brewster, Ohio, "packaging is expensive; there are plates to make the film, and if it doesn't sell, you're stuck. And we don't ever have enough room or shelf space."

"There's more to printing a bag than you might think," says Don Noss. "Most are three or five color. The dyes alone for a job can cost $300,000. It takes three or four hours just to set it up."

"When I was young, there were three flavors—vanilla, chocolate, and strawberry," comments Daryl Thomas of Herr's. "Now there's forty-some flavors. The challenge is to find a niche with staying power, and not just some flash-in-the-pan."

One Ohio chipper, who wished to remain anonymous for the comment, believes that the trick to survival is one of balance—of being aggressive on one hand, but staying within boundaries on the other, so as not to attract the unwelcome attention of large competitors. "The trick is to know your market," he said. "If you don't know your market, you're going to die, but expanding—that's a big challenge. What you have to do is be strong, but stay within your niche."

In 2004, six years after the DOJ cleared Frito-Lay of wrongdoing, Frito conducted a series of taste tests between its Lay's potato chip and those of some big regionals—Utz, Herr's, Jays in Chicago, Cape Cod in Massachusetts, and Old Dutch in Minnesota. In each case, Lay's won the taste tests. Philadelphia billboards proclaimed: "Philadelphia prefers the taste of LAY's over HERR'S." The same thing happened to Utz. The ad campaign ran on billboards, radio, and television.

"They're doing some 'taste testing' out there on the street," John Davis, sales manager at Utz, told me in 2004, "and they're trying to claim that they're number one and they're better than we are. But we just had a pep rally, as it were—a sales meeting—and we told everybody the thing we put on the back of our hats is 'Who are they kidding?' because we know where we stand."

"Even the big guys need an enemy—somebody to rally the troops," observed Daryl Thomas. "We focus on companies that we bump into strategically more so than those that are just on the radar; Frito-Lay does the same thing. In that respect it's flattering. The fact that they take so much notice speaks well for us."

In Chicago, Jays took Lay's to court over the taste tests and won. Even without the Frito campaign, it had been a rough few years at Jays; one by one, the family members who ran the company passed away. CEO Leonard Japp Jr. died in 1999, followed by grandson Leonard Japp III in 2000, the same year founder Leonard Japp Sr.—the one who started the company by allegedly running chips to Al Capone's speakeasies—died at age ninety-six. In early 2004 the struggling family-owned company filed for bankruptcy and was bought out, but was then targeted by the Frito campaign. In Chicago, Frito's survey of three hundred people labeled Jays chips as "unflavored" in the tests, while Lay's were called "classic"—a distinction the judge didn't care for. In addition, the surveys were conducted in suburban malls rather than in the city itself. After a court ruling in favor of Jays, Frito-Lay agreed not to run the ads for two years, and to pay Jays' legal fees for the court battle.

A Frito-Lay spokesman took issue with the ruling, pointing out that it, too, was part of Chicago's snack food culture: "People often forget, Frito-Lay is local too. We've been doing business in Chicago for decades with more than five hundred employees servicing the area. We respectfully disagree with the judge's ruling regarding our advertising claim."

In any event, after the Jays ruling, the other chippers did not take Frito to court. Nationwide, Frito took down the billboards and ended the campaign.

No Lard? No Thanks

As larger chippers like Jays, Herr's, and Utz use advanced marketing techniques to maintain and spread out from regional footholds, other traditional companies in Pennsylvania and Ohio seem blissfully unaware of marketing, retaining the mom-and-pop marketing techniques of tradition, word-of-mouth, and products of distinction.

Like lard. Although local guidebooks call Lancaster and York counties in Pennsylvania the Potato Chip Belt, an equally apt description might be the Lard Belt.

Until its recent acquisition, Original Good's of New Holland was the oldest continuously operating chip company in the United States. Original Good's was, and is, known for its lard kettle chip. Good's is not alone in the region—Zerbe's, in Denver, Pennsylvania, ten miles north of the former Original Good's factory, makes a similar lard chip; fifteen miles northeast, in Mohnton, King's makes a somewhat lighter lard chip; twenty miles northwest in Womelsdorf, Dieffenbach makes a massive, slatelike lard kettle chip. Grocery manager Terry Groff of Weaver Markets says that, when it comes to potato chips, Lancaster County's motto is: "No lard? No thanks."

But lard has disadvantages; it can be expensive, it has a shorter shelf life, it can be harder to ship, and it is avoided by a sector of the public who since the 1970s have become increasingly health conscious.

Mose Mesre, Conn's Potato Chips, Ohio: Over in Pennsylvania, they fry their chips in lard over there. They love those hard crunchy chips. You can't tell them that lard's no good; it's what they want.

Glenn Weber, King's Potato Chips, Lancaster County: The lard taste is pretty particular to the Pennsylvania Dutch—Berks and Lancaster counties. Outside this area, you get those people who really rave about it, but the market isn't that strong that you could go out there and build a business on it.

Herb Hoover: In this part of Pennsylvania, lard is still the old standby, although recently it's fallen out of favor with the younger chippers.

William Backer, Backer's Potato Chips, Missouri: It's like pies—there's no better pie dough than lard. It makes it flaky and crispy. But lard chips don't last long on the shelf—maybe six weeks—and those animal fats are hard on a person.

Among locals, Original Good's is called Blue Goods to distinguish its blue logo from Red Goods, another Lancaster lard chipper. Started in a kitchen in 1886, a mere thirty-three years after Katie Wick's invention, Original Good's stayed in farmers' markets on and off into modern times—into the mid-1980s—which may be why the brand is sometimes overlooked by scholars of snack food trivia. By the early 1980s, Original Good's was sold at a single farmers' market—a living fossil in the chip world. Lewis Good, owner of the company before its recent sale, says that his father "would sell everything he could make, and he could have sold a lot more. They were just hauling them out. They would line up at that farmers' market." His wife, Lynn, adds that "Christmases were something else."

When Lewis Good—fifth-generation descendant of founder Anna Good—took over from his father in 1984, he increased distribution, moving into local and chain supermarkets. He found his traditional kettle chip, cooked in lard, was ready for expansion.

"That was the challenge," elaborates Good. "We needed to take on more stores to serve our customers, because they just didn't have time to

Inspecting potatoes at Original Good's plant, summer 2004. (courtesy of Lewis Good)

drive to the Giant where they buy groceries, and then drive down here to Yoder's, just for the potato chips."

Which is why he sold out to nearby Ralph Good, a distant relative, in 2005. When I visited the Original Good's plant prior to the sale in 2004, local Mennonite girls in prayer caps and calico dresses worked the packaging equipment and two kettle fryers. Now, those two kettles are twelve miles away in Adamstown, at the Ralph Good's plant. Ralph Good's products have larger regional distribution—seven counties to Original Good's two. According to Lewis Good, the move was a positive one. They needed to take their chip to the next level, and the common Good's name made the merger a natural fit.

Like Original Good's, cousin Ralph Good's also makes a lard chip. Unlike Original Good's, the Ralph Good's chip is a continuously cooked picnic-style chip. The Ralph Good's chip combines the old and new. As thin a chip as any in the industry, it gets a twang from the traditional lard medium that no vegetable oil can provide. Like the earliest chips, the lard in which both Good's chips are fried provides an extra dose of the savory, much the way that bacon or ham livens up split pea soup. Similar to the Gibble chip, Ralph Good's has a thinness—as thin as or thinner than a Lay's—that results in an ultrawhite chip with a combination of crispness and flavor that is stunning. Now that Original Good's are made side-by-side with the Ralph Good's chip, owner Greg Good says they have their hands full.

Although the Lancaster County lard chippers I talked with are aware of Frito-Lay, competition, and slotting fees, the concerns seem vague and distant—mostly it's something they hear about but don't seem to have experienced themselves. When I asked Greg Good how they keep their niche in a world dominated by Frito-Lay and the regional giants, it was almost as if he didn't know what I was talking about: "We just keep it the same. . . . People still like that product. . . . They've grown up on the chip, and they still like that lard chip around here."

One aspect that may set Lancaster County and its lard chippers apart is its Mennonite heritage. The Amish population of Lancaster County is estimated at 25,000, and the broader Mennonite community comprises another 30,000 people in a county with a total population of 470,000. This total of 55,000 people of Anabaptist faith is only 11 percent of the county but, combined with nonmember Mennonite descendants, amounts to a healthy chunk of the population that could be loyal to traditional chip styles and brand names. Two Lancaster County supermarket managers I talked with acknowledged that local Mennonite product loyalty could explain Lancaster County's chip diversity. But the grocery manager at the Shady Maple says his clientele are often from outside the county and are just looking for something different.

"A lot of our customers come from a distance—from suburbs of Philadelphia," says Dan Holinger. "A lot of them come here to get products they can't get at home. They might not shop here weekly, but once every two weeks. They might drive forty-five miles."

Others similarly suggest that proximity of markets, a diverse customer base, and ease of transportation have made for a diversity of chippers in places like Ohio and Pennsylvania. The anonymous individual in the flexible packaging industry believes these factors play a role. "Further west," he said, "there's fewer companies. There's less money per call, because they're spread out. The higher population densities east of the Alleghenies gives a better chance to make a profit."

Until recent times, lard also remained the medium of choice for some small traditional Ohio chippers, although today, only one Ohio lard cooker—Gold'n Krisp—remains, compared with seven in Pennsylvania.

Amazingly, it seems almost as if every small Ohio city once had its own chip company or, in some cases, several. One need only look at the city of Massillon, thirty miles south of Akron, which today has a population around thirty thousand. The Rider family (chapter 1) once supplied potatoes for three chippers in Massillon alone: Gold'n Krisp, Kitch'n Cook'd, and Gee-Gee's. It also supplied four more in Cleveland, only forty-five miles away: Dan Dee, Num Num, Restemeier, and Johnnie's. Another four clients—Salem, O.K., Flaherty, and Tyler's—were in Akron. Today, the Riders serve only Gold'n Krisp and Wagner's, a company recently reborn to the southwest in Miamisburg. Now, Ira Rider, the retired family patriarch, observes, "There's no chip plant in Cleveland, and there's no chip plant in Akron." At one time, the Riders had ten employees. With Ira retired, now it's just his son Ed and Ed's wife, Betty, running the business. Ed and Betty's son wanted to take over, but they talked him out if it.

But Ohio, while having fewer family chippers today than Pennsylvania, still has its own venerated potato chip heritage. One of these old respected Ohio companies—Jones of Mansfield—exemplifies the challenges faced by traditional family-owned chippers in the modern snack food world. Through its persistence, Jones also provides insights into why others have failed.

Jones Town

Parts of Mansfield, Ohio, have seen better days.

When I visited there in 2004, I saw dilapidated multistory houses that were literally falling apart. The roof of one yellow clapboard house, occupied as far as I could tell, had caved onto the porch, bent and rounded around the vertical beams like a chocolate bar in the sun, melted into place via decades of gravity. A few miles north, the rusty brown roof and linked buildings of the Mansfield Steel Works, the largest building I have ever seen, seemed to extend for miles—but is actually "only" a mile long. Formerly employing thousands, it was another

Founder Fred Jones with the old bag, late 1960s.
(courtesy of Jones Potato Chip Company)

casualty in America's transformation from an industrial economy to a service economy . . . like the appliance factories, tire companies, and a remaining GM plant that once kept Mansfield busy.

But all is not lost. On the outskirts of town, as in most of America, there are well-attended malls, as well as a beautiful nature reserve with nature trails and a public estate and horticultural garden open to visitors. Even parts of the inner city have been restored, with shiny retro-refurbished neon signs for the City News and Coney Island Diner. There is a classic art deco dry cleaner and a lovely little '30s-era white brick Texaco station, recently converted to a law office.

It is not far from here, close to the railroad tracks, that the Jones Potato Chip Company has its home.

Bob Jones is a big man; he looks like a former linebacker. His face resembles George Wendt from television's *Cheers,* but he is more physically imposing, like Hoss Cartwright from *Bonanza.* Along one wall in Jones's office is a pile of potato chip bags—he likes to keep up with what the competition is doing; leaning against another wall is a framed version of the older Jones bag, not yet hung when I was there.

The Jones bag was redesigned recently, and the old one is history. With a drawing of a boy and girl on it, the old one looked antiquated. It was also a dead ringer for the old Ballreich potato chip bag, with only slight differences in the kids' hairstyles and clothing. Ballreich, based about fifty miles northwest in Tiffin, is another old Ohio chip company;

Bob Jones's father once worked for the Ballreichs, and they helped Jones get his start. But by the 1990s, Bob Jones felt that the bag with the pictures of kids eating potato chips was holding them back; it was a good packaging vehicle in the 1950s and 1960s, but not so the late 1990s.

"It got to a point where buyers would say, 'Your chips are pretty good, but your bag looks terrible,'" says Jones about the old bag. A distributor Jones was negotiating with in Pennsylvania even told him: "We can't sell a product that looks like that." The packaging change was an emotional issue for customers who had grown up with the old Jones bag.

"I had an e-mail exchange with one woman who said, 'My little boy will never have the Jones bag that I had.' In polite terms, I said, 'He probably doesn't care.' I mean, he isn't going to like her music; he isn't going to like her . . . anything, you know?"

Jones lifted the frame to better show me the old bag. This version of the old bag was bright yellow—barbeque chips—where the bag for regular Jones chips was blue. He set the frame back down to lean against the wall.

"I finally told her: 'This can be his. The old bag was your bag. Let this be his.' In the end, after two or three e-mail exchanges, her husband was starting to take my side. After five or six e-mails they just said: 'I can see your point. Keep making good chips.'"

The new Jones bag is surprisingly breezy, contemporary, and competitive for a company so tiny. Although it is not like Frito-Lay's logo or packaging, it is nonetheless modern, sassy, and efficient. It no longer has the drawings of the kids, but retains the old Jones logo, with the oval that surrounded it, modifying it with a swirling, dynamic "brushstroke." Old customers might be saddened by the loss of the old bag but would at least recognize the product. Customers new to Jones—exactly the customers Bob Jones would like to attract—wouldn't know anything about the old bag anyway.

It's those new customers that could make the difference to Jones's staying in business. "Our volume is down . . ." Jones hesitated as he talked with me. "It's been shrinking for a few years, and we've been trying to find ways to reinvigorate our potato chip volume.

"What used to keep us busy locally—and I mean in six or eight counties . . . That used to keep us plenty busy, and we never worried very much about other towns or locations. But now—and I think it's pretty typical of other parts of the country—the same amount of people don't support the amount we used to be able to sell. So we have to work harder, drive farther . . ."

Jones company dominates Mansfield, but it's a small market. The trick for Jones to acquire new territory is to get that foot in the door, to make his brand known elsewhere, to expand.

"When we go into other territories," he said, "we really struggle for small amounts of space. We're not known. Here, we've been around since the 1940s, and really, I think it's the only reason we've survived. Because we're one of the smallest companies you're going to find out there."

Jones's production equipment costs just as much to purchase and maintain as for a Frito-Lay or a Wise. Potatoes and oil cost him the same, the price and supply of which are both subject to a capricious market. Even where Jones gets someone else to produce items like pretzels and popcorn, he still has to pay a designer for the graphics, and pay for the printing and laminated film for the package. Each added chip flavor—and there are scores nowadays—adds yet another permutation, requiring more colors and images. Each bag size—2.5 ounces, 6 ounces, 8 ounces, 12 ounces—adds another modification. Frito-Lay or Wise can divide those expenses over millions of bags. But for Jones, the numbers might be in the thousands.

Simply put, for a company of Jones's size, there is no economy of scale.

"Every year you're seeing new and upgraded versions of everything [from the large companies] . . . you see cartoons, the latest movie tie-ins . . . those types of changes at our volume are impossible. So you try to keep it fresh, but there's limits," said Jones.

It's not just the flavors and the packaging. Since its inception, Jones has made a specific chip style, indigenous to central Ohio. It's a wavy chip, *marcelled* in this part of the country, cooked in partially hydrogenated soybean oil—what chippers call a "dry chip" with a "soft crunch." But now Jones has also been forced to explore different frying oils and chip styles. If he wants to branch out to Cincinnati and Cleveland and Detroit, he needs to adopt a profile that consumers in those markets will like.

"If you've spent the last twenty or thirty years eating a product made in cottonseed or corn oil," says Jones, "you're going to like that. We don't make that style of chip. People don't know what kind of oil goes into it, they just like that taste. As I move into some of those markets, my chips don't taste like that . . . so to a degree we have to be similar, just to get people to say, 'Oh, I like these.' We're trying to have as many taste profiles as we can."

Satisfying "taste profiles" means resetting the cooker for every chip batch that comes down the line. It means changing out the oils and the flavors. It might mean adjusting the quantity or duration of rinsing water for potato slices before frying, or changing the cooking temperature or slice thickness. Jones has only one cooker at one plant.

Today, his business is 60 percent chips, which are produced in-house, and about 40 percent products made for him by others—corn snacks, pork skins, jerkies, sunflower seeds, and cakes. Jones believes that maintaining this diversity, which is challenging enough for a large company like a Frito, Herr's, or Utz, is necessary for him to compete at all. Those companies serve multiple states—but Jones serves only a handful of counties in central and northern Ohio.

"If we just did potato chips, we probably couldn't survive, because there's just too many other needs. Some people don't even eat potato chips."

For a time Jones tried distributing products with other companies' names as a way to get into new stores; for the most part, it didn't work out. Jones made some money as the distributor, but the profit margins in selling someone else's product were so small that he decided he'd rather make the pennies on Jones-branded items, so he no longer distributes others' products.

With one glaring exception.

Raps and Chumpies

In 1994 African American businessman James Lindsay saw inner city youth as an untapped potential for potato chips. He started Rap Snacks, a potato chip geared specifically toward urban minority kids, replete with celebrity endorsements from rap stars. At about the same time that Lindsay was getting Rap Snacks going, chips called Chumpies and Homegirls were being marketed to distributors in Philadelphia, Baltimore, and New Jersey. Lindsay's Rap Snacks packages carry images of young black men and women in hoodies and backward ball caps posed against brick wall motifs—not exactly the imagery evoked by Amish kettles in Lancaster County.

"Rap Snacks was a way to create a market that didn't exist before," says Lindsay. "It's a new extension of the marketplace. I saw snack foods as being hungry for something different—something besides Frito-Lay and Wise in the world."

As of 2007, the outlets for Lindsay's product are convenience stores and mom-and-pop stores, but he is looking to change that. In late 2006 he launched Sylvia's chips, in a marketing agreement with the famous Harlem soul food restaurant of the same name. He believes an un-tapped adult minority audience is eager for his product—and that it's time such a product was marketed to adult African Americans with positive role models.

"Look at how many African Americans are on product placements," Lindsay observes. "Look at Aunt Jemima and Uncle Ben. There's forty million African Americans in the country, but you don't see their pic-tures on product placements." At the time of this writing, Sylvia's chips are being test-marketed in Detroit and Kansas City; Lindsay says the chips are doing "very well."

Lindsay believes that his spicy flavor profile—Louisiana Hot, Honey Barbeque, Lemon Pepper—is a major aspect of his appeal. Re-cently, Lindsay moved headquarters from Philadelphia to Greensboro, North Carolina. He likes the friendlier people in the South and looks forward to expanding his product in that more dispersed market.

How is he expanding? Rap Snacks—among the most nontraditional of chippers—has made a distribution agreement with Jones—one of the most traditional of family-owned chippers. It's worked out well for both; Rap now has a good distributor, and Jones can get a foot in the door of markets he could never have reached on his own. "It allows me to get into stores that otherwise wouldn't take my product," observes Bob Jones.

In today's postmodern world of potato chips, there are no strange bedfellows.

Making Waves

Bob Jones believes that, compared to larger cities, his small-town base and the outlying area he serve provides a market relatively free from competition.

"Most of our business is in an area where the influence of larger cities is not over-burdensome," says Jones. "The community's kind of like an island, in a way. Many of the companies that went out of business—their products maybe weren't all that distinctive. One of the things my dad did when he first started—there were no wavy potato chips in this area, so that's what he started with."

While lard is a venerated chip tradition entrenched in parts of Pennsylvania, the small swath of north-central-west Ohio that includes Jones has other traditions. There, two related companies retain a potato chip custom with a name unique to Ohio: the marcelled potato chip.

> *Bob Jones, president, Jones Potato Chip Company:* I think our brand name in a relatively small area is synonymous with marcelled chips—but we still put *wavy* on the bag in case customers don't know what it means. . . . We actually tried to make regular-style chips, and it didn't work out that well. And the people who buy competitive brands . . . when they hear the name "Jones" they don't think of anything other than a wavy chip, and if that's not what they want, they don't give us a second thought.
>
> *Sue Ballreich, Ballreich Potato Chips, Tiffin, Ohio:* A lot of people hear *marcelled* and think it's a flavor.

The story of the marcelled appellation in Ohio—as opposed to names like *wavy, rippled,* or *ruffled*—dates to the early twentieth century, long before the 1950s and '60s craze for rippled dipping chips. As the story goes, after World War I, Fred Ballreich, who served as a baker in the war, returned to the states and started making potato chips. Ballreich soon adopted the marcelled name, from the French hairstyle he had seen, to describe his wavy chips. Or so the legend goes. The name spread in central and northwest Ohio, with one company—Cain's Marcelle Potato Chip Company of Bowling Green, later added to the Borden stable—incorporating the term in its name. The territory of another extinct Ohio company, Mar-cel, still favors wavy chips today, as evidenced by Conn's sales in that area. Mose Mesre, of Conn's in Zanesville, says that "whereas in most places we sell two to three times as many regulars, up there it's two to three times as many wavies."

It turns out that the Jones and Ballreich companies share more than a tradition of marcelled chips. The two companies' chips do not taste

Jones trucks, early 1950s. (courtesy of Jones Potato Chip Company)

exactly the same, but they have another family resemblance that is mostly unique to Ohio: the "soft crunch"—a textural aspect that often goes with what chippers call a "dry chip" profile. Ballreich and Jones are not the only Ohioans to have this style; so do Conn's, which is about seventy-five miles southeast of Jones, and Mister Bee, a West Virginia company started by a veteran Ohio chipper and about sixty more miles southeast.

"Soft" in the context of crunch does not mean wilted or limp. Rather, the muted crispness integral to this chip style is a silky smoothness that yields gradually to the teeth. Unlike a Lay's or a Wise with the grittier bite, Ballreich, Conn's, Mister Bee, and Jones employ a consistency almost like a Triscuit wafer. They tend to be white and light, like a cumulus cloud turned into a potato chip; they are homogeneous and delicate, like potato-derived cotton candy; yet there is enough edge to distinguish a slightly papery crispiness. More important, whereas many conventional potato chips are little more than vehicles for oil and salt, the central Ohio soft crunchers impart a uniquely "potato-y" taste. The consumer takes from the chip the smell and taste of raw potatoes—white, sliced, and firm—and a mild suggestion of "vegetarian" below-ground roots and tubers, an aspect mostly absent from the Lay's-Utz-Wise conventional chip. The taste profile of these Ohio brands can be surprising to the uninitiated, and is not for everyone. But the fact that regular working Americans living in this geographically distinct pocket prefer such a gustatorily subtle chip for daily picnic and lunchbox use is startling, especially in a nation dominated by the Lay's-Wise-Herr's-Utz full-crunch model.

As I tried to unravel the mystery of the soft crunch, it seemed to me at first that water was key, because Jones, Conn's, Ballreich, and Mister Bee all rinse their chips extensively before frying. Potatoes being processed for chipping typically follow a discrete series of steps: a destoner removes rocks, a peeler (a series of rollers with bristle brushes that sands the skin off) washes them, and a slicer (bladed rings that spin inside a drum) slices them. In the slicer, they may be rinsed with water. The uncooked chips—surprisingly thick, limp, and moist—emerge below the slicer, where they may be rinsed again in a tumbler that shakes off more starchy water. Depending upon the company, they may be rinsed once and then sprayed once again, as they are moved toward the cooker, where they will be dropped into hot oil.

I tried to pin down some chippers about the soft crunch, but didn't get any firm answers. It seemed there were many variables involved. Bob Jones acknowledged that Jones may wash off more starch, "but it could be the thickness and the oil type and temperature." Sue Ballreich admitted to washing potato slices, but the Ballreich frying temperature varied with the potato variety and moisture content. "When a potato gets to our factory," said Ballreich, "it is washed, peeled, inspected, sliced, tumbled, rinsed, and shaken before being cooked. Our unique taste comes from our marcelled cut, which is a thin crisp wavy chip bursting with potato taste! At least that's how we describe our product that our customers can't get enough of."

One extinct Ohio company, not far from Jones and Conn's, took water processing to an extreme. Ira Rider, the retired potato buyer from Wooster, recalls that Akron-based O.K. potato chip company had potatoes sliced into long troughs, "like cattle troughs" and stirred by an employee whose job was to "get that starch out. Now," adds Rider, "there are some places I know of that sliced them the night before in water and let them soak—and that would give them a lighter chip." According to

Rider's son, Ed, O.K.'s idea was to soak the slices to keep them from sticking together; stirring kept the "bubbles" out of the chip, making them flatter and whiter. "That was the greatest thing about O.K. potato chips," says Rider; "the length of time he took to do the slices."

But water by itself does not seem to be the answer to the soft crunch, because it turns out that today almost all continuously cooked brands rinse their slices to wash off surface starch. Except for kettle chips, whose consumers usually demand the "hard bite," sliced potatoes are almost always rinsed before going into the fryer. Therefore, the secret to the soft crunch must not be water alone.

But there's the oil. The common denominator of a certain cooking oil is the other reason that water is probably not the only agent of the soft-crunch taste profile. All of the Ohio chippers who make soft-crunchers—Jones, Ballreich, Conn's, and Mister Bee—use partially hydrogenated soybean oil, whereas other chippers increasingly use liquid cottonseed, sunflower, peanut, or corn oils.

Comparison of two kettle chippers hundreds of miles from Ohio, who also use partially hydrogenated soybean oil, provides further insight.

Sterzing's, a tiny batch-kettle chipper in Burlington, Iowa, makes a thick, robust kettle chip. Like the Ohioans, Sterzing's cooks in partially hydrogenated soybean oil—it tastes like a Ballreich or a Conn's on steroids—and it also has the soft crunch. Like Jones, Ballreich, Conn's, and Mister Bee, Sterzing's rinses its chips—twice. Yet Sterzing's batch-kettle process is usually thought responsible for the hard-bite profile associated with kettle chips.

Martin's in York County, Pennsylvania, also produces a kettle chip cooked in partially hydrogenated soybean oil. Unlike Sterzing's, Martin's drops freshly sliced potatoes directly into oil, bypassing the rinse. Martin's has tactile hardness but retains the potato-y taste of the soft-crunch style, resulting in a truly "vegetarian" chip, replete with essences of parsnip, turnips, celery, and potatoes. Butch Potter, CEO of Martin's, believes that hydrogenated soybean oil gives the chip its potato-y quality; it's a combination of taste and the fact that soybean oil is solid at room temperature.

"When you eat a typical chip, you taste the oil first. Soybean oil is bland. Because hydrogenated oil is more of a solid, it has a high melting point," and so does not melt upon mouth contact. But with chips cooked in hydrogenated soybean oil, says Potter, "the oil doesn't get in the way of the potato."

Thus, it appears that both water *and* partially hydrogenated cooking oil are the key to the soft crunch.

Heat could be yet another key variable. Don Noss believes that Ballreich's unique chip has to do with frying at lower temperature, although the Ballreich executives I asked would not confirm that. But Conn's, an Ohio soft cruncher very similar in taste and texture to Ballreich, emphasizes low temperature. Thomas George, vice president of Conn's, says, "We fry lower than anyone else—at 325 degrees." George maintains that "a lot of them fry at 400 or 450 degrees." George also believes that Conn's cooks their chips just a bit longer at that lower temperature.

The aggregate of these fussy contributions to chip taste—thickness, oil, water, temperature, time—indicates that maintaining chip profile is more art than science. For Conn's, tradition, or at least a healthy respect for the complexity of the unquantifiable, influences chip preparation in a way that almost suggests superstition. When Conn's left its 1950s–1960s era factory a couple of years ago, it had the opportunity to update its old continuous cookers but ultimately decided not to. Conn's didn't know exactly what the old cookers did for its special profile, but it wasn't taking any chances. "If we changed to a newer fryer," says Thomas George, "we think there's a possibility—we don't know—that we would change the chip."

Altering the oil offers further insight into the mystery—as one chipper found to his chagrin.

Partially hydrogenated soybean oil happens to be high in trans fats—the subject of much controversy since their negative role on heart health became widely publicized in the early 2000s. Nevertheless, Mister Bee Potato Chip Company owner Alan Klein can attest to its merits. In 2006 Klein tried to switch Mister Bee from its time-tested but unhealthy fifty-five-year-old trans-fat recipe to something healthier—unsaturated cottonseed oil. Like a politician who waffled under public pressure, Klein learned by bitter example what can happen when you flip-flop.

"I knew it would be a dramatic change," says Klein, "but everyone was saying 'no trans fats, no trans fats.' But we had such a negative reaction with the new stuff. People just did not like it. I had a woman call me from fifty miles away who called me every foul word in the English language. She told me that if she wanted to eat healthy, she'd eat carrot sticks. Our sales dropped 11 percent in four months. So we switched back to the old recipe, and sales took off. We're doing better now than before, probably due to all the publicity."

One assumes that such a drastic public reaction could only have been provoked by a distinctive and radical change in taste profile—likely a loss of the soft crunch—that resulted simply from changing the cooking oil.

Chip manufacturing elements like these—water, temperature, cookers, oils—embody a complexity of tradeoffs that are reflected in the sensibilities of the chip companies themselves. Some smaller, older companies, like Conn's, will not change their chip recipes, feeling that to do so would risk losing the customer base that got them where they are today. Others, like Mister Bee, might experiment to find out how far they can go to attract new customers without alienating their base. Still others, usually bigger boys like Frito-Lay or Utz, can afford to do both. If they want to test something new, they can add completely novel product lines on top of their conventional ones—like the five separate lines of kettle chips, each cooked in a different oil, that Utz sells in addition to their continuously cooked chips.

If it was just a matter of taste, such complexities might not even arise; as Bob Jones knows, these kinds of changes involve investment and expense. But as with Mister Bee's exploratory adventure into cottonseed oil, what increasingly brings such complexities to light is an American public concerned about something other than taste; something they may, or may not, be willing to sacrifice for flavor.

That thing is health.

8

A Few
of Our Favorite Things
Fats, Carbs, and Calories

Now let me tell you something. Fat-free potato chips are just
about like picking up a piece of cardboard—that brown craft
paper—and trying to eat that. We tried it, and the public did
not accept it.

Mose Mesre,

Conn's Potato Chip Company, Zanesville, Ohio

The craze on carbohydrates is worse now than ever. Having
said that, there are people who need a bag of potato chips now
and then. For those people, we exist.

Glenn Weber,

King's Potato Chips, Lancaster County, Pennsylvania

If you look at the nutrition labeling on the backs of most of today's potato chip bags—it doesn't matter if the chips are kettle cooked, cooked
in lard, or whatever—you will not find much variation in the total calories provided by different types of chips. They tend to have 150 to 160
total calories per one-ounce serving, and "calories from fat" are usually
rated at 80 or 90.

Sifting through the fifty-some bags in my contemporary chip bag collection, I found that Snyder's of Hanover had the lowest calorie count, 140, with 60 calories from fat. The highest were Ballreich, which uses partially hydrogenated soybean oil, and Zerbe's, a tiny Lancaster County lard chipper, tied at 170 total calories, 110 from fat. Surprisingly, most other lard chippers were in the middle or even the low end of the total calorie range.

But it's not so much the total fat that counts. What seems to matter in dietary health is the *type* of fat.

Phats of the Land

The names and types of fats — saturated fats, unsaturated fats, polyunsaturated fats, hydrogenation, trans fats — pose an endless continuum of confusion for the consumer. An example is the relative health rankings of butter versus margarine, which seem to trade places every ten years, depending on recent research.

One thing is almost certain: although fats and oils are necessary for good nutrition, they are too abundant in the modern American diet. The technical name alone for this category of biological macromolecules — fatty acids — does not evoke a flattering or appetizing image.

Saturated fats are usually — but not always — animal fats, such as lard, and tend to be solid at room temperature. These are cited as having bad effects on health because they elevate bad cholesterol (low-density lipoprotein — LDL). Unsaturated fats, more often "plant fats" from nuts and seeds, are those with one or more double bonds, thus rendering some of the individual carbon atoms in the molecule "*un*-saturated" — without hydrogen atoms. Unsaturated fats can be either monounsaturated (one double bond) or polyunsaturated (two or more double bonds). Fats with double bonds tend to have lower melting points; that is, vegetable oils are "melted" (liquid) at room temperature.

Although more healthful for the most part, plant oils historically used in cooking were not without a downside. Through the end of the nineteenth century vegetable cooking oils were susceptible to rancidity. In chemical terms, the prevalence of double bonds made them easily oxidized, resulting in spoiling and loss of stability. "Hardening" of oils into something more solid — partial hydrogenation — was an invaluable aid to food manufacturers when introduced in 1903. Physically, the process of partial hydrogenation made vegetable oils more like animal fats, and gave them longer shelf life.

In the process of partial hydrogenation, some double bonds in a fat might be removed, while one or more "cis" double bonds are formed into "trans" double bonds. Where cis fats have hydrogens on the same side of the double bond, trans fats have the hydrogens on the opposite sides, enabling them to pack together solidly—making them firmer, like lard. Although naturally present in animals that "chew the cud" and evident in butter, beef, and mutton, trans fats are otherwise rare in nature. Trans fats have the same molecular formula as the original unsaturated fat they came from, with the same numbers of atoms, but by the process of hydrogenation acquired beneficial properties not present in their unmodified progenitors. In addition to diminishing rancidity, hydrogenation allowed food producers to manipulate the fats' melting point—the textures of shortenings could be optimized for blending with flours for pastries. Vegetable-based fats could thus replace lard and butter, the general thinking being that any vegetable-based spread must be more healthful than an animal fat. Melting points could be customized. For chippers, oils had better stability during frying, cooking temperatures could be modified, stored oils were more resistant to rancidity, and, best of all, chips could stay on shelves longer.

But health studies in the 1990s revealed that trans fats might be even worse than saturated animal fats. Not only did trans fats raise "bad" cholesterol—LDL—they lowered the "good" cholesterol—HDL—an effect that had not been observed before, in any type of fat. There were even indications that total negative effects of trans fats on heart health were more than the sum of their LDL and HDL detriments and possibly caused inflammation. A cardiologist and public health expert said recently that trans fats are "the most dangerous ingredient in our diet."

For many chippers, it was a nonissue. Except for Ohio chippers in the soft crunch tradition, many or most didn't use hydrogenated oils to begin with, or if they did, it was in combination with other oils and could be eliminated without much effect.

One such chipper was Golden Flake, a major southeast regional based in Birmingham, Alabama. Before 2006 ingredients on Golden

Flake bags listed potatoes "cooked in a blend of one or more of the following oils: liquid and/or partially hydrogenated corn, cottonseed, or soybean, salt." Golden Flake director of marketing Julie Strauss indicates that Golden Flake's decision in 2006 to eliminate hydrogenated oils involved no small amount of work.

"Who knew before that there was bad stuff in it?" she says. "We tested for eight, ten, twelve months. It's a big deal; you don't just change it overnight."

Strauss says they tested different blends and combinations, using regular taste tests and blind taste tests, all the while trying to retain the Golden Flake taste and feel. Today, all of Golden Flake's products are 100 percent trans-fat free. Strauss explains that the "mouth feel" of chips cooked in liquid oils is different—as mentioned in chapter 7, they're what chippers call a wet chip, whereas chips cooked in lard or hydrogenated oils are dry chips.

"We've had some die-hards complain," she adds. "They've said, 'Why are they greasy all of a sudden?'" But for the most part, Strauss says, the transition has gone smoothly.

But for other chippers, like the Ohio chippers, it would be unthinkable to leave their hydrogenated oil niche behind. It provides the crucial local base upon which, they believe, their narrowly defined livelihood depends, and negative publicity be damned. As we have seen, Jones, like its marcelled cousin Ballreich and its nonmarcelled cousins Conn's and Mister Bee, gets its unique taste from partially hydrogenated oils. Don Markov, director of sales at Jones Potato Chip Company, agrees that chips from hydrogenated oil render the fingers less oily when you're eating them. "With hydrogenated oil," says Markov, "we can adjust it to make it melt in your mouth. Oils like peanut oil build up in your mouth." Markov says that people eating a wet chip cooked in peanut or cottonseed oil will actually eat fewer chips at a sitting, because the oil that accumulates in the mouth inhibits the appetite. Chips cooked in lard or hydrogenated oils solidify at room temperature, but the heat of human body temperature breaks them down. They literally melt in your mouth on contact, exactly like chocolate or butter.

Up against pressure from reformers advocating for more healthful food, chippers using partially hydrogenated oils remain philosophical, yet persistent.

"We did not and will not change our oil," says Thomas George, vice president of Conn's. "Here's my feeling: if you eat chips—I don't care if they're mine, or Mike-sell's, or whatever—you're eating a snack. Potato chips are a snack. We know that potato chips are not good in excess. If people are overly concerned about trans fats, they would not be eating chips at all."

Butch Potter, of Martin's in Pennsylvania, agrees. In his opinion, it isn't "anywhere close to a proven issue. There's all these things now where today it's true, but tomorrow it's a different story. I don't want to say that we're not concerned with health, but I think that time will be on our side. Many consumers who are more likely to follow advice from their television set are less likely to eat potato chips anyway."

When Mister Bee, one of the smallest traditional chip companies in the country, switched from partially hydrogenated soybean oil to cottonseed oil and back again, newspapers all over the nation, including *USA Today,* carried the story. After returning to the old recipe, Alan Klein suggested to his advertising agent that they run a new billboard promo with a photo of him bending over while being kicked in the behind by a woman. The agent declined—opting for a more demure billboard that simply said, "We're back"—but wasn't too humble to add that she had warned him against making the switch to begin with.

Other than the taste profile, the biggest benefit of hydrogenated soybean oil is shelf life. "A long time ago, you sold what you made every day—there weren't any Wal-Marts," says Klein. "When you went in, you left enough product so that next time there would be one or two bags left on the shelf. Now, marketing people want gigantic displays— they want it full all the time. The way you used to sell was to keep the product as fresh as you could. I had always been told that a chip is at its peak when it leaves the cooker, and every hour after that, it deteriorates."

Almost a decade before the dangers of trans fats became known, chippers had tried to mitigate the effects of fats in general. In 1993 Louise's of Kentucky came out with a no-fat microwaved chip. Although Louise's didn't last long, Frito-Lay could read the change in the winds. Deciding to get with the trend, Frito's scientists tried everything from heated dryers to microwaves to giant toasters to create a baked chip with little or no fattening oils. Immediately it was clear that a sliced potato would not work; it had to be potato flakes, not altogether dissimilar from the material that went into Pringles. The first attempt flopped, and the Frito-Lay board chairman allegedly told lab scientists eagerly awaiting his response: "Do you really think this product deserves the Lay's name?" But in October 1994, the right combination of added sugars, fats, and pressure treatments was discovered, and Baked Lay's chips "flew off the shelves." Where regular fried potato chips have total fat levels in the aforementioned 10-gram range, today Baked Lay's total fat scores are only 1.6 grams per ounce—an impressive reduction.

A tasty baked chip that people actually liked was certainly an asset, but because it was not made from sliced potatoes, it was no more a true potato chip than a Pringles. Plus, the mouth-feel of a potato chip, whether dry or wet, is inseparable from the fact that it is fried in fat. The essential challenge thus remained: to create a potato chip that tasted and felt like a potato chip but contained no adverse dietary detriments from fats.

Days of Olestra

Procter & Gamble, the same people who had roused traditional chippers over Pringles in the 1970s, had been developing "sucrose polyesters"—combinations of table sugar and fat—since the late 1960s, obtaining a first patent in 1971. Naming the generic compound *olestra*, P&G insisted on calling its commercial version *Olean*—the same difference as *aspirin* and *Bayer*. It went to the FDA for testing in 1987. By the time olestra was ready for prime time in 1996, P&G scientists had spent twenty-five years in research, nine years in FDA involvement, and reputedly several hundred million dollars in development. A nonbiological molecule synthesized from otherwise metabolizable biological macromolecules, the olestra molecule was large and indigestible—a key attribute both to its desirable nonfat qualities and to certain less desirable properties.

It didn't take long for information to leak that olestra caused diarrhea and intestinal cramps in some consumers. But at the beginning of 1996, during the same period that Eagle's plants were being acquired by Frito-Lay and the Department of Justice was preparing to investigate the snack industry, Frito-Lay became the first to test-market chips fried in the new compound. Frito-Lay sold the chips, first called MAX, for six months in Cedar Rapids, Iowa, Eau Claire, Wisconsin, and Grand Junction, Colorado.

As far as other chippers were concerned, Frito's deal with P&G had the makings of the same old story. Once again, Frito-Lay was disadvantaging competitors, this time with an exclusive twelve-month contract, supposedly costing "in the eight figures," with P&G for exclusive supply of olestra (except for small amounts that others could release in test markets only). Frito insisted that the exclusivity was justified; it was taking a major risk, since success with Olean was not guaranteed. To boot, it had signed the contract for olestra back in 1992 and had been waiting a long time. Other chippers were jumping on the bandwagon, taking advantage of Frito's foresight and investment. As it turned out, Frito was right about the risk. Like the New Coke debacle of the 1980s, olestra drew unwelcome publicity. The reason it didn't add fat calories to the body was precisely because it passed through the body—too rapidly for some.

"It travels through the body unchanged, just like fiber," announced the P&G Web site. Its structure "prevents digestive enzymes from breaking it down. That means neither the fat nor the sugar are absorbed by the body." But much attention in the media was devoted to the fact that this lack of absorption resulted in diarrhea or intestinal cramps from chips cooked in the nonoil. Only a year after the test, olestra, with its attendant problems of diarrhea and vitamin depletions, "hasn't exactly set the world on fire," said one news story. Another story skirted such problems and quoted a truck driver: "I smoke cigarettes, I drink beer, I'm eating brats. This brat I'm holding in my hand will do three times what the chips will do." A Frito dietitian on hand in the test-market stores advised customers to limit their intake to a one-ounce serving—about half the size of your average small bag of chips—to which a Cedar Rapids columnist quipped: "The problem is that if you are the kind of person who can eat just one serving, you don't need low-fat chips in the first place."

Many customers couldn't tell the difference anyway. Defenders of the chip said that only one in three thousand (0.033 percent) bags sold caused patrons to suffer diarrhea or cramps, although consumer groups claimed the actual percentage was higher. Less well known was the fact that choosing olestra over fat reduced the body's uptake of vitamins, because fat helps the body absorb vitamins, whereas vitamins reacted neutrally to olestra. Olestra was thus accused of depleting the body of carotenes and vitamins, which was not quite true; it was more that dietary vitamins and carotenes that would normally have been absorbed in part due to dietary fat would not respond to olestra. P&G attempted to make up for this by adding vitamins and carotenes to the olestra, but they were still required to announce the bad news about diarrhea, cramps, and vitamin depletions on the label.

Dietitians weren't the only ones to highlight the questionable values of olestra. The Center for Science in the Public Interest ran ads in the Columbus, Ohio, market asking watchers if they would feed their dog a can of food that could cause cramping and loose stools, after which the dog food can on the advertisement morphed into a can of Pringles cooked in olestra. Pringles countered with its own ads, as the whole exchange started to take on the character of a negative political campaign.

Late that year P&G announced that twelve other "marketers" had signed up to buy Olean in addition to Frito. By 1997 new tests with Frito's version of the chip in Indiana markets used the name WOW! instead of MAX. Products with olestra were required to carry a diarrhea warning label—up until recently, that is.

Today, there are no such federal labeling requirements for olestra. Where regular fried potato chips have total fat levels in the range of ten grams per serving, and Baked Lay's total fat scores are only three grams, a bag of Lay's Light Original Potato Chips—the latest name for olestra chips—contain exactly zero grams of fat per serving.

At the same time, concerns about fats have led to dramatic changes across other lines of Lay's chips. In 2006 Frito embarked on a major move to convert all its other potato chips from cottonseed oil to sunflower oil—reducing saturated fat content by 50 percent. According to Jared Dougherty, public relations manager for Frito-Lay, "This move alone removes 60 million pounds of saturated fat from the American diet," a figure that sheds considerable light on just how much Lay's potato chips dominate the American potato chip market. The change to sunflower oil—by most accounts, an expensive oil—is "part of Frito-Lay's commitment to healthier foods," the expense of which Dougherty says has not been passed on to consumers.

Potatoes Really ARE Nutritious?

By now, concerns about nutrients like fats should have been old hat for chippers, who had lived through intermittent and often faddish concerns about their product of choice for decades. Since at least the late 1960s, it seemed that if a sentence began with the term *junk food*, the next two words were likely to be *potato chips*.

Detractors became pervasive by the early 1970s, when even President Nixon's advisor on food and nutrition "publicly questioned the food value of potato chips." Ever poised for battle on behalf of the chippers, Noss's potato chip association once again went on the counterattack, issuing press releases about the nutritional benefits of chips and emphasizing that they were usually cooked in vegetable oils, rather than animal fats. The USDA even approved a promotional photo of a teacher eating an apple next to a child eating a bag of chips, captioned: "Let the teachers have their apples, and the kids have their chips." After a storm of protest from the apple industry and cafeteria administrators—according to the Snack Food Association, even Senator George McGovern sided with the apple producers—the ad was canceled.

Today the FDA's required "Nutrition Facts" label on the back of potato chip bags carries information about calories, fat, vitamins, and protein content. It appears functional and boring at first glance, but reveals a lot about chips. Most one-ounce potato chip servings contain something like 5 percent of daily recommended carbohydrates, 12 percent of recommended daily fiber, and 4 percent of sodium (from salt added after cooking). Research by some food scientists finds much to praise about the nutritional benefits of potatoes. Researchers report that "the nutritional or biological value of protein in potatoes is rather high" and "the nutritional value of potato protein is as good or better than whole egg, and better than beef, tuna, whole milk, wheat flour, corn, rice, soybean, and kidney bean protein."

Potato chips actually do contain protein. In my collection of contemporary chip bags, nutritional information always rates protein per one-ounce serving (twenty-eight grams) at one or two grams. It also indicates mostly minimal vitamin content; vitamin A and calcium are almost always 0 percent of the average daily requirement and iron 2 percent. The exception is vitamin C, which ranges from 8 to 30 percent of the minimum daily requirement, most often 15 percent. "On a national basis," say researchers, "potatoes contribute more Vitamin C to the U.S. food supply than any other one major food."

Other negative aspects of potato chip nutrition include starch, which causes cramps in large amounts; pesticide residues, usually not much of a factor because they affect only the tops of potato plants; and glycoalkaloids. Solanine, one of these glycoalkaloids—note the common word-root with the potato's genus, *Solanum*—is considered a poison. It is related to nicotine, which is found, of course, in tobacco, another nightshade. Like many such plant compounds, solanine is toxic to insects and likely functions as a "natural pesticide," but also produces negative effects in mammals. "About 100 mg of solanine," say researchers, "will produce nausea, headache, and gastrointestinal pains in a man." There have been cases of poisoning where solanine growth resulted from "green potatoes" improperly stored in lighted conditions. Except for such incidents—and cases of poisoning from nightshade berries, which have been documented since antiquity—most of us today accept that potatoes are safe to eat.

But one scientist believes that glycoalkaloids such as solanine are only part of a larger health issue inherent in all members of the potato plant family.

The Arthritis Connection

In 1950 Dr. Norman Childers, a professor of horticulture with graduate degrees in plant physiology, nutrition, agriculture, and horticulture, had a three-phase colostomy. His surgeon believed that diverticulitis leading to his intestinal problems was aggravated by Childers's heavy consumption of spiced V-8 vegetable juice.

After the operation, Childers experimented with his diet. He noticed that tomatoes and potatoes, both from the nightshade family, seemed to cause soreness in his joints and muscles within an hour of eating. Childers spread word of his findings to acquaintances with arthritic problems, many of whom had similar relief when they strictly eliminated from their diets tomatoes, potatoes, eggplant, peppers, and nightshade-based seasonings like chili powder and paprika. The network of arthritis sufferers trying Childers's diet grew by word-of-mouth.

Childers collected testimonials from individuals such as these:

I have been on the No-Nightshades diet for now over 13 years. After about 8 or 9 months on the Diet my hands were free of pains. I also got rid of the pains and swelling in my ankles, the right knee and stiffness in my neck. I had to have custom-made inner soles for my shoes. All that now is a thing of the past.—G. K.

I am 50 years, have had the same problem very badly for 20 years in feet, back, hands, hips, elbows, shoulders and neck with lighter problems in ankles, knees, and chest; have taken indocin and butazolidin pills, ate nightshades regularly and in quantity sometimes. I have been on your Diet for 6 months. Ninety percent of the pain has left, was retired 6 years ago with rheumatoid arthritis and degenerative spinal disease. I have several other people in this area on the Diet which has worked well for them too.—G. B. S.

As word of the "no nightshades" approach spread—Childers and colleagues now try to avoid the word *diet* because of its association with weight loss—he assembled survey data from more than seven hundred people over several decades. Of those who followed the regimen, 556, almost 73 percent, obtained some kind of positive benefit; of the people who "rigidly followed" the approach, almost 92 percent gained relief from arthritic symptoms. On survey forms, some of the latter marked "unbelievable" improvements, such as "discarding wheelchairs, walkers, canes." The response he saw in himself was enough for Childers to devote the rest of his free time to promoting his regimen, about which he has published at least one scientific paper and a self-published a book, *Arthritis: Childers' Diet That Stops It!* "Livestock people have known about nightshades for over one hundred years," says Childers. "They hire their kids to pull out nightshade plants in the fields, because they know what it does to the livestock. But what holds for livestock holds for people."

Scientists could only speculate about the reasons nightshades were so bad for cattle. A study by George K. Davis of the University of Florida documents "a calcification (hardening) of certain tissues of cattle" when fed the leaves of *Solanum malacoxylon,* a nightshade in the same genus as potato. The effects seemed similar to effects of excessive vitamin D_3 administered experimentally. Photos that accompany Davis's article show skinny cattle with curved spines and enlarged joints, or feeding cattle bent down on front knees due to tendon damage from nightshades; other photos document calcified cartilage, or phosphate deposits pushing into animals' blood vessels. Every once in a while, explicit instances of nightshade poisoning in humans come to light, such as the case of three schoolchildren who died allegedly from eating the fruits of a potato plant. The difficulty is that much of the information about nightshades is anecdotal in nature; other than Childers's diet surveys, little or no research has been conducted with humans.

Meanwhile, Childers continues to send out his book to followers. A color photo shows him in his mid-nineties with smooth, clear skin, his red hair only partly edged in white. At the time of this writing, Childers is ninety-six years old, and his yearly newsletter goes to an estimated nine thousand people; he believes he has sold fifty thousand copies of his book. When I asked Childers if the link between nightshades and arthritis had more to do with vitamin D_3 than with glycoalkaloids like solanine, he was the first to say that no one seems to know for sure.

"We need research on it," he admits. "The problem needs basic research, of which we don't have much." And some research and opinions cast doubt on the alleged link between nightshades and arthritis. Apparently, epidemiological studies comparing populations consuming many potatoes with those who eat few have not shown differences in incidence of arthritis.

Potatoes and tomatoes are integral to the modern North American diet—it's hard for most to imagine summer without tomatoes or burgers without fries. It's not only potato chips that are nightshades but also pizza toppings, chili ingredients, and french fries. Nightshades are in nondescript processed food components like "potato starch" or pepper-based seasonings—in things like baby foods, breads, crackers, fish cakes, muffins, soups, meat pies, and dressings. It's a lot to give up.

"People accept it very slowly," says Childers about giving up nightshades. "And it's only after they're in great pain that they come around to it."

If the arthritic problems ascribed to the nightshade family are in fact due to glycoalkaloids such as solanine, there may be good news for potato chip diehards. A 2006 study found that the potato processing that is standard to any potato chip operation—peeling, slicing, washing, and frying—leads to significant reduction of nitrates and the toxin solanine in potato chips. Of all the potato products in the study, chips scored lowest, with original levels of solanine reduced to 14-18 percent of the original amount by the end of the chip processing line.

Were he alive today, Harvey Noss would be wearing the news on his T-shirt.

Simple Carbs, Complex Carbs

Fats, meanwhile, are only part of what goes into a potato chip. They are an added part at that—fats are added in oils during frying. In contrast, because potato chips for the most part are carbohydrates, it is hard to imagine a time when chip makers could ever produce a "low-carb" or "carb-free" potato chip. Carbohydrate content of a one-ounce serving of potato chips may average only 5 percent of the minimum daily requirement, but at fifteen grams per serving it averages 54 percent of the content of a potato chip compared with fats' roughly 36 percent.

Potato growers like Don Ramseyer (chapter 1) work hard to make sure that sugars—simple carbohydrates—do not accumulate in stored potatoes, because sugars can turn chips brown and lend them an "off" flavor and texture. But certain potato varieties, high in sugar to begin with, can lend chips a unique taste, something desirable for the "gourmet taste profile," today a major growth niche in the industry. It's a double-edged sword; a little sugar lends the chip something special; too much renders it a piece of burnt umber.

Kettle brand chips, one of several potato chips marketed in natural food stores, use only Russet Burbank potatoes—a high-sugar potato that Kettle brand representative Jim Green calls "tough to work with. . . . The good news is that Russets have all these sugars in them, and the bad news is that Russets have all these sugars in them. . . . So the sugars make them tough to work with, but also, we feel when properly cooked, they make the best tasting potato chips. The trick is to cook potatoes that have just the right amount of sugars in them. Sugars, when cooked, caramelize. Too high of a sugar content and they caramelize too much, the chips turn out too dark, and it affects the taste. A little dark is good; too much in our opinion is not."

On the other hand, certain customers want "too much dark." At Jones in Mansfield, Ohio, which uses a conventional chipping potato like Snowden or Atlantic, rejected dark brown chips are picked off the line and hand-packaged in clear plastic for sale at the outlet store. Kay & Ray's, a lard chipper in central Pennsylvania, has gone a step further; it started production of high-sugar brown chips after then owner Don Carr realized that some customers actually prefer them. Carr says:

> Potatoes get a higher sugar content, especially in winter time, if the potatoes get chilled. Originally we would pick out the brown chips, and sell them at reduced price. I got to asking customers if they bought brown chips because they were cheap, or because they liked the dark chips. Most everyone said they liked the dark chip.
>
> Around 1993 there was a small potato shortage, and the price went up. I purchased a load of potatoes out of New York at a cheap price—the load was totally dark—and was not sure how to deal with it. I sold part for tablestock; for the rest I decided that if that many people liked it, make a chip. We went to the print shop, got a clear bag and put a label on it for the dark chips—got it authorized for retail. Even if it didn't sell, it would occupy regular shelf space. As it turned out, the darks began to sell, and we've been doing it ever since

Carr estimates that the Kay & Ray dark chips, which look like crunchy caramelized sugar maple leaves in the clear fourteen-ounce bag, are 10 to 12 percent of the total Kay & Ray chip volume; they've even had to add a smaller six-ounce bag for customers who prefer the regular chips but like a small bag of dark chips on the side.

But the main carbohydrate component of potato is starch, which, as we have seen, is easily converted to sugar in raw potatoes under the wrong storage conditions. In potato chip form, there seems to be nothing wrong with starch; although a research study from the 1930s documented "violent stomach cramps" in medical students fed raw potato starch mixed in ice cream, enough so that the experiment had to stop. But apparently the moderate amount of starch bound up in the potato matter of chips has no such effect; as with most starch, it is easily converted into glucose by the body.

But while facsimiles of potato chips can be made without fats, it appears that a potato chip can't be a potato chip without carbohydrates. So it was with some trepidation, in a country where over two-thirds of adults are overweight and almost a third clinically obese, that chippers considered low-carb diets in the early 2000s.

The Carb Bubble Builds

The idea of a low-carb diet did not originate in the 1990s or even the 1970s. In the early nineteenth century, a French lawyer and lay physician named Jean-Anthelme Brillat-Savarin (1755–1826) observed that obese people had cravings for carbohydrates like breads and pastries. He also observed that carnivorous animals did not get fat unless they too were fed carbohydrates like breads and pastries. He advised avoiding starch, sugar, and flours and recommended "light meats" and vegetables.

In the 1960s Robert C. Atkins was a medical doctor in New York City, specializing in cardiology. The story goes that when his ID photo was taken for a part-time consulting job at AT&T, he was "horrified" at his image, thinking, "My god, I have three chins."

In researching ways to lose weight, Atkins noted that literature on fasting said that subjects experienced a sharp decrease in hunger after the first few days. The loss of appetite was attributed to excessive ketones in the body, which supposedly caused appetite suppression. Atkins seemed to have stumbled onto a dietary golden chalice: a weight-loss diet without hunger. As Atkins tried eliminating carbohydrates, he monitored ketone presence in his urine as a further confirmation of success. He found that adding small amounts of carbohydrate had no effect on ketone levels and that weight loss continued even with small amounts of sweet fruits like strawberries—with whipped cream! In the first six weeks of his new diet, he lost twenty-five pounds and found that he could eat whenever he wished, as long as he kept the carbohydrates low. "It was so exciting," he is reported to have said. "It was almost as if the more you ate, the more you lost."

The theory seemed biologically sound, if perhaps not nutritionally prudent. When carbohydrate intake is low, the body is forced to break down dietary proteins to produce glucose, the fundamental sugar used throughout the body. The act of breaking proteins' amino acids to glucose requires energy, supplied from—you guessed it—body fat. But the body fats in the process are broken down incompletely, leaving "ketone bodies" as a waste product (acetone is a type of ketone). Apparently, there's nothing inherently wrong with ketosis—which is not to be confused with ketoacidosis, a potentially life-threatening condition associated with type 1 diabetes in which ketone accumulation is severe.

In the early 1970s Atkins promoted his low-carb diet, promising weight loss in only fourteen days. The first two weeks of the diet, the "induction phase," were the roughest. While eating high-protein meats, dieters had to restrict carb intake to as little as twenty grams per day. If potato chips were allowed, the equivalent would be twenty-five to thirty potato chips per day, based on the nutrition labeling on modern chip bags—although vegetables like asparagus were preferred. As the diet progressed into later stages, carbs could be added back in five- and ten-gram increments until a "target" weight was achieved, at which time the patient would have determined a personal daily carbohydrate intake to keep him at equilibrium—"between 45 and 100 grams of net carbs a day."

Two other low-carb diets, the South Beach Diet and the Zone, were variations on the theme, differing in details—the South Beach Diet was lower in saturated fat—but all emphasized that any carbohydrates taken in should be *good* carbohydrates, like broccoli and cauliflower. Potatoes (and presumably potato chips) were specifically discouraged, or permitted reluctantly.

The results for new dieters were startling. Patients reported losing as much as fifty pounds in five months; one person lost sixty pounds in two and a half months. As the low carb trend peaked in 2004, *Time* magazine ran an article whose title, "The Low-Carb Frenzy," captured the bandwagon atmosphere. It estimated that twenty-six million Americans were on serious low-carb diets, with another seventy million limiting carb intake. Heinz, General Mills, Subway, Kraft, Breyer's, and beer companies such as Coor's added low-carb lines; T.G.I. Friday's menu added Atkins-approved menu items. Surveys estimated that more than 9 percent of American adults were on some kind of low-carb diet; elsewhere, traditional diet programs like Weight Watchers and Jenny Craig were losing members. In response, Frito-Lay released low-carb versions of Tostitos and Doritos in the Edge product line, which used soy protein in their respective corn chip recipes.

But the potato chippers were stuck. The crucial distinction between a corn chip mash, in which protein can be substituted for corn, versus a chip made of sliced potatoes, rendered them helpless. By 2005 overall U.S. potato consumption had dropped an estimated 5 percent since 2002.

Nutritional scientists, caught unawares by the dietary onslaught, acknowledged the paucity of research, adding that small sample sizes, lack of dieters' stick-to-itiveness, and suspect self-reporting by patients made reliable research difficult. And at first, the few studies seemed to find only good things about the low-carb diets. One literature review indicated that the Atkins diet might actually be better in terms of colorectal cancer risk, although it was difficult separating out confounding factors, such as high dietary fat, high caloric intake, and obesity. Another study found that subjects "loved the diet" and that carbohydrates were "clearly stimulating their excessive appetites." Another noted that low-carb dieters replaced "bad carb" consumption in a good way—they increased salad greens by 54 percent and "green vegetables" by 34 percent. A study that randomly assigned twenty adults to a high-protein low-fat diet or a high-carbohydrate low-fat diet group found that both diets were equally effective at reducing body weight, but that the "high-protein" subjects felt better, "more satiated," in the first four weeks; however, they were careful to distinguish their high-protein low-fat diet from "high-protein, high-fat, low-carbohydrate Atkins-like diet plans," which they believed were harmful because of the potential to raise bad cholesterol.

Nutritionists, long skeptical of the low-carb diets, in some cases had to grudgingly admit they seemed to work, but nonetheless implored dieters not to forget their veggies; often, they noted with alarm how the low-carb diets ignored the U.S. Dietary Guidelines. A University of Colorado nutritionist, expressing concern that dieters would avoid the range of nutritionally valuable fruits, vegetables, and whole grains, observed that "the Atkins diet is anything but healthy"; others noted that low-carb diets were associated with increased protein loads to the kidneys, alterations in acid balance, and loss of bone minerals. A sports nutritionist complained, "Thanks to the Atkins diet, an extraordinary number of today's athletes are experiencing needless fatigue."

As the mass of data accumulated, the preponderance of evidence began to tilt in the direction of equivocation, or at least to come out on the side of the second law of thermodynamics, or, there is no such thing as a free lunch. A six-month study found that patients on low-carb diets lost the most weight—about three times as much as the low-fat dieters—but a longer study, showing similar results at first, revealed that after a year the two groups became even. Another found that in the end, the key to a successful diet was keeping calories low—whether from fats or carbs didn't matter—and just plain sticking to the diet. One group of researchers, comparing low-carb versus traditional low-fat diets, found that the diet did not determine who lost weight initially, but the people who were successful in the long term were the traditional low-fat dieters.

At about the same time, average citizens seemed to grow tired of it. The carb bubble burst in 2005, with the estimated percent of Americans on the diet down from 9 percent to 2 percent. Companies peddling low-carb products found themselves in the midst of a shakeout, as even Atkins Nutritionals was forced to file for Chapter 11 bankruptcy in summer 2005. Heartened by the trend reversal, the American Institute for Cancer Research urged dieters to "come back to common sense. Eat a balanced diet weighted toward vegetables and fruits, reduce portion sizes and increase physical activity." The president of the Idaho Potato Commission reported that potato growers were "jumping up and down in their fields" in response to word of the turnaround.

The potato chippers, having repeatedly endured such fads since the '60s, mostly watched with a weary "I told you so" stoicism, despite having taken a minor beating.

"Five or six months ago," said Bob Shearer in summer 2004, then president of Shearer's Foods, Inc., "we were concerned about the low-carb thing and how it was affecting business, and now I'm not as concerned about it as I was then. I don't see that as a major factor."

"Every time they come up with something different, people jump on it," said Thomas George, of Conn's, "and then it settles down. Pork rinds were big during the low-carb trend. We used to sell a ton, but it's cut back, and people are back to chips."

"It's a different journey for different people," says Frito-Lay's Jared Dougherty about health and low-carb diets. "For some people, its low fat; for others, it's low carb; for others it's about protein. There's a core group of individuals that continue on low-carb diets. Our meat snacks appeal to them." Although low-carb interest has diminished in recent years, Dougherty says Frito-Lay's Oberto line of meat snacks has continued to grow.

By the mid-2000s chippers had successfully dealt with a questionable low-carb controversy by waiting it out. They had met a seemingly valid trans fat concern either by altering recipes slightly, like Golden Flake, or by sticking to their enjoy-snacks-in-moderation guns, like Conn's and Mister Bee. Unfortunately, before the end of the decade, one more health concern would hit them; as of this writing, the jury is still out on this one.

The Acrylamide Scare

In early 2002 researchers in Sweden announced that they had discovered acrylamide in everyday starchy fried foods.

Acrylamide is a compound formed when asparagine, an amino acid found in protein, reacts with glucose at high temperatures. It is a precursor to a polymer used in certain cosmetics, plastics, and packaging materials. Acrylamide had previously been found to "cause genetic, neurological and reproductive damage in animals" and, after experiments with laboratory rats, was classified as a "probable human carcinogen." Evidence of the potential toxicity of the chemical surfaced only in 1997, when cows that drank from an acrylamide-laced stream in Sweden began to "stagger, collapse, and die." While newspaper and TV news reports in 2002 covered the story widely as one more thing to be frightened about, it quickly faded from the front pages, perhaps yielding to other concerns in America at the time.

Although popular press reports invariably mentioned potato chips and french fries when addressing acrylamides in food, it turned out that breads (especially crusts), cereals, coffee, biscuits, and many more foods were also sources. Even home-cooked foods were not immune; it was thought that half the acrylamide ingested came from foods cooked at home, such as baked potatoes. But the data were highly variable; a USDA database of foods tested showed that the acrylamide level of one processed food product sample could be two or three times greater than that of another sample of exactly the same thing. For example, the acrylamide level of "Popeyes french fries, location 3" on the USDA database was 1,030 parts per billion, and the level of "Popeyes french fries, location

1" was 301 ppb. The story was similar for potato chips. Acrylamide levels of twenty-five bags of Lay's Classic from different code dates and bags varied from 249 to 549 ppb. Amazingly, the second highest chip on the USDA chart was Baked! Lay's Original Naturally Baked Potato Crisps (only 1.6 grams of fat per ounce) at 1,096 ppb. The lowest was Utz's Home Style Kettle-Cooked Potato Chips, at 117 ppb, cooked in— guess what?—trans-fat gorged, partially hydrogenated soybean oil.

If it's not one thing, it's something else. Meanwhile, other products— from Cheerios, to Hershey's Cocoa, to Lipton Onion Soup and Dip Mix, to Maxwell House French Roast, to "chopped ripe olives"—had appreciable acrylamide levels as well. Chips made from sweet potatoes were among the highest of all, with Blue Mesa Grill Sweet Potato Chips topping out at 4,080 parts per billion.

The verdict remains out on whether acrylamide is harmful to humans. Tests with lab animals were done at "very high doses"—1,000 to 100,000 times that to which humans are exposed. Studies so far are conflicting, negative, or vague; for example, data from a long-term sample of nurses as subjects indicated a positive relationship between acrylamide and breast cancer, but a study of Swedish women found no association, as did another using Swiss and Italian subjects.

Meanwhile, for potatoes, it appears that sugar—the scourge of chippers and growers anyway, because of its habit of turning chips brown— may be exactly the agent of acrylamide creation. Research to date suggests that lowering sugars may be the best way to reduce acrylamides, something that chippers would be happy to accomplish in and of itself anyway. In addition to maintaining proper potato storage temperatures, lab-documented ways to reduce acrylamide include frequent change of frying oils; lower frying temperature; dipping potato slices in citric acid; and soaking, blanching, or predrying potato chips before frying—the soaking a reason for resurrecting the recipe of the extinct O.K. Potato Chip Company (chapter 7), which soaked sliced potatoes in water troughs before frying.

The average American who knows about trans fats and low-carb diets likely has not yet heard, or at least not yet retained information, about acrylamides—at least outside of California. In 2005 California's attorney general filed suit against Frito-Lay, McDonald's, and Burger King, among others, to show acrylamide levels on product labels. Under voter-approved Proposition 65, California required food manufacturers to label products known to cause harm to consumers. One draft of the warning would have read: "Warning: Baking, roasting, frying, and toasting starchy foods forms acrylamide, a chemical known to the state of California to cause cancer." Food manufacturers, horrified by an explicit cancer warning on their packages, countered that acrylamide was different because it was not a food additive but was created by cooking; in addition, it has likely been present in the food supply since humans discovered cooking. The FDA also questioned the wisdom of the listing, saying that the labeling could cause "unnecessary public alarm," further adding that California's attempt to regulate acrylamide could conflict with federal law.

The Snack Food Association, again poised for battle, backed a proposed "national uniformity law," which would trump state laws such as California's Prop 65. Indeed, it was said, the same across-the-board approach was used "when Congress established uniform requirements for nutrition labeling, allergen labeling, meat and poultry standards, over-the-counter medicines, medical devices and pesticide tolerances." In March 2006 SFA announced partial victory when the U.S. House of Representatives voted 283 to 139 to approve the National Uniformity for Food Act. In April, California withdrew rules that would have required the acrylamide labeling, citing "voluminous" public comments, but, undeterred, added that it would submit new proposals for regulation soon.

Emeritus chemistry professor Robert L. Wolke singled out potato chips when he expressed his concerns about acrylamide in the *Washington Post:*

> I love potato chips. Doesn't everyone? But I have just thrown away half a bag of them, and I intend to buy no more. Why? Because the chemical acrylamide, a probable carcinogen, has been found in fried starchy foods, especially potato chips and French fries.
>
> . . . But why did I swear off potato chips, when the jury has barely begun to consider the hazards of acrylamide at potato-chip consumption levels? When no safe maximum level of acrylamide in human foods has been determined? Well, it's a lot easier to quit potato chips than to quit smoking, and there are many alternative salty crunchy-munchies that can accompany my cocktail without endangering my

health—at least not so far as has been discovered. So I switched to peanuts. Will their time come?

The Snack Food Association's health policy advisor, Lisa Katic, responded to the letter in an important industry newsletter:

> Katic said that if he is going to stop eating potato chips because of acrylamide, then what about breakfast cereals, brewed coffee, soft bread, bagels and soup mixes where levels of acrylamide also are present?
>
> "It is inappropriate to single out one food and suggest the elimination of our product without regard to those, which may be more frequently consumed," Katic said.
>
> She pointed out that the 2006 Exposure Assessment of Acrylamide conducted by the Food & Drug Administration indicated that 100 percent of the population consumes acrylamide as part of its diet. She added that the World Health Organization advises consumers not to change their dietary choices, but to follow established guidelines and eat a well-balanced diet consisting of a wide variety of foods.

Katic's concerns about diet added to another doubt voiced by the federal government and other food experts: consumers who worried about acrylamide might fail to cook foods thoroughly and end up with food poisoning instead, a malady far more immediate and severe than a component whose toxicity in foods was yet to be confirmed. In August 2006 an industry consultant stated that the national uniformity regulations had bipartisan support, but that "election-year politics has made this not necessarily be the case, especially in the Senate."

Although the U.S. House of Representatives approved the act in 2006 and lobbying by the food industry remains in progress, complete passage of the National Uniformity Act is on hold for now due to uncertainty surrounding the outcome of the 2008 election.

9

Everything Old
Is New Again

When I started, people hadn't seen a hand cooker in this business for fifty years. They'd all say to me: "It's not done like this any more. You're crazy." But because I didn't have those prejudices, I just tried things. A lot of them worked.

Steve Bernard, Cape Cod Potato Chips

We went back to basics of what potato chips are all about.

Tim Kennedy, Tim's Cascade Style Potato Chips

Not far from Jones Potato Chip Company—some fifty miles east, in the town of Brewster, Ohio—is a different type of Ohio potato chip company. Strictly speaking, it is family owned and uses time-tested methods; but unlike most other Ohio chippers, it is hardly "old time" or "traditional."

The company is Shearer's. In most chip factories, someone at the end of the production line hand-inspects and picks out bad chips; at Shearer's, tiny cameras do the job. The optical sorter has perhaps a hundred little lenses on it, about a fourth-inch in diameter; as potato chips are flung from one speedy conveyor onto another, the cameras photograph each one. If something is wrong with a single chip—too dark perhaps—a tiny air tube next to each camera instantaneously blasts that chip with a small puff of air, knocking it off course and directly onto

Eight modern kettle cookers at Shearer's. (courtesy of Shearer's Foods, Inc.)

another conveyor, where it can be collected to be sold as a second in the company outlet store.

Adjoining the production floor are small laboratory-like rooms. A woman in one room quietly samples chip bags, of every product, every half hour. Shearer's flushes every chip bag with nitrogen, both to vacuum-pack it and to remove oxygen, which causes chips to deteriorate. To inspect oxygen levels, the woman uses a hypodermic needle, about as thick as the needle on a basketball pump but maybe three times as long. She jabs it into the sealed bag—*pfapp!*—and the needle produces a nitrogen readout on a meter.

The woman puts other finished chip bags into an aquarium-like plastic box. A hydraulic press inside the box slowly mashes the bag under water to determine whether it is leaking. If the bag leaves little bubbles in the water, someone has to tell production that there is an unacceptable level of leakage in that batch, and the packaging machinery will be adjusted accordingly.

Another woman grinds chips in a device similar to a Cuisinart and places the sample in a rotary titrator, which measures salt content. She enters the reading for that batch of chips on a chart.

Shearer's has a sludge facility that recovers potato waste and converts it into a powder. The powder is 16 percent protein and ends up in cake form. Once a day, ranchers arrive in trucks, collect cakes, and take them to local cattle pens and pastures for feed. It's said that the cattle come running when they see the trucks. There is also a starch recovery system that utilizes leftover potato starch for a paper producer. A new wastewater treatment plant came online in spring 2004, and they are exploring the feasibility of recycling the water that leaves the plant for use in rinsing incoming potatoes.

When I visited in summer 2004, Shearer's had twelve kettle fryers and six more on order; by spring of 2007, it had grown to twenty-four kettle cookers.

Each kettle at Shearer's—each stainless rectangular tub—is about ten feet square. An axle walks back and forth across the top of every one, with sets of steel paddles, each about the size of a kitchen spatula. The paddle array is like a little Olympic rowing team that hasn't yet learned to dip smoothly, plunking clumsily into the oil on the way to the other side, keeping the chips from clumping together. Through the transparent oil, metal ten-inch cylinders with regularly spaced holes heat the batch, creating undulating ripples in the liquid, much the way the atmosphere is distorted over a campfire. The kettles are lined up in groups of eight, with conveyors from each bringing the chips to a unifying metal trough; in turn, the trough shuffles the aggregate of chips to the packaging equipment far, far away.

Shearer's doesn't just have kettle cookers; Shearer's has harnessed the power of kettle cookers in sequence, like pistons to a crankcase—all part of a superb machine that, perhaps, is the most powerful kettle chip engine in the industry.

Barely more than thirty years old, Shearer's has grown so fast that production has outpaced the ability of the founders to keep up with output; in 2005 an investment group joined to help grow the family business. Significantly, Shearer's "private-labels" special potato chips for Frito-Lay. The item that has made Shearer's blossom—the special chip that Shearer's makes for Frito-Lay—is the industry's oldest product.

The New Kettlers

For most of the twentieth century, starting forty-five years before Shearer's existed, state-of-the-art continuous cookers were the industry rage. Tiny family-run kettle operations like Original Good's of Pennsylvania were the exception, remaining behind in isolated pockets, seemingly unaffected by industry trends. Too small to afford continuous cookers—too set in their ways to change—they stood by their kettles for decades.

Today, their style is in vogue again.

If any one company bridges the old and new, it may be Martin's of York County, Pennsylvania. Located in the heart of the Potato Chip Belt, 1940s-era Martin's was just another chip company until Ken Potter saw the potential for kettle chips in the early '70s. Thirty-one years old and already a veteran in the chip industry, Potter wasn't sure what he had gotten himself into when he first bought the company. "Mr. Martin had one route," Potter says about his predecessor. "Weekly sales were $395. I was kind of petrified. I was hoping that the records were wrong and there was more business."

Late one night in 1973, Potter came home—he was still getting things off the ground, working eighty- and ninety-hour weeks—and caught his wife eating Senft's chips, an old-fashioned kettle chip. "It was a company in York," explains Potter. "My wife was born and raised four doors up from the company, and she was friends of the family. It was her favorite chip. He [Senft's owner] would bring out a package for her, and I would come in, and there she'd be. Eleven o'clock—I tell ya, this is some woman, she's working the [Martin's] books, it's eleven at night. She's eating these chips."

Upset, he asked her why she was eating the Senft's chip instead of his own. "It's a lot better chip than you make," she said. (Martin's then specialized in a waffled barbeque chip.) Potter came around to kettle chips. "It gave me the inspiration to start making that product," he says. "Really, it was the best thing we ever did."

For three nights a week, four hours a night throughout the 1970s, Ken Potter dressed in a clown suit and gave away balloons and bags of Martin's kettle chips in York County supermarkets. Today, Martin's has over fifty routes, with thirty in York and Lancaster counties alone, and its payroll is in the millions. According to Potter, Martin's is the number one chip in the Shenandoah Valley. Martin's has been the potato chip of Air Force One since the Clinton presidency.

Nowadays, kettle chips are considered "gourmet," in vogue; an urban twenty-something might serve them at a party. But thirty years ago, even though they were the original form of the potato chip, people who had not been to Lancaster and York counties had not heard of such a thing. Ken Potter takes no small credit for taking the kettle chip out of Pennsylvania farmers' markets and into national and worldwide presence, where it remains the most expansive segment of today's potato chip business.

"Everybody copied what I did," says Potter today. "I tell you the absolute truth. Everyone said it was a farce and would never sell. I mass-produced it and made it sell, and everyone in the industry followed me."

Boastful words, perhaps, but apparently valid, at least in spirit. Until Martin's under Potter, remnant kettle chippers like Original Good's, Senft's, and Ohio's Gold'n Krisp operated only in localized markets. But as Martin's grew regionally in Pennsylvania and the mid-Atlantic, Potter's aggressive marketing revealed new possibilities for kettle chips. Although Potter's attempts to grow the kettle chip elsewhere met with mixed success—a Martin's of Montana and a Martin's of Tallahassee didn't work out—he tutored others who were curious about the kettle style. In 1980 a young man named Steve Bernard, who had been selling after-market car parts to auto dealers, came to Potter to learn about kettle chips. At about the same time, the Shearer family, also helped by Potter, started their kettle business in Ohio.

Beginning in an eight-hundred-square foot storefront, by the mid-1980s Bernard's Cape Cod soon showed potential for national appeal. Bernard believes the company's prime location in Hyannis, Massachusetts, played a role. Summer tourists shopped at Bernard's storefront location and took the chips home, where they caught on. The novel chips seemed to promote themselves—"I wish I had a dollar for every person who said 'I got you started in St. Louis' or 'I got you started in Minnesota,'" says Bernard.

Eagle's acquisition helped spread the Cape Cod gospel. After the 1985 buyout, Eagle took good care of the chip, keeping the original name, packaging, and recipe intact. Eagle's distribution promoted Cape Cod and, by default, the kettle chip, nationwide. Others saw Cape Cod's experience, and kettle chips became the new industry darling; Snacktime came out with Krunchers, Frito with O'Grady's, and Borden with Cottage Fries. Not all were true kettle chips; but still, they were heavy-duty chips with a similar appeal. By 1990, as overall sales for the industry were rising 5 percent, kettle chip sales soared by 18 percent—a trend for which Cape Cod was receiving industrywide acclaim. Kettle chips were extending the reach of the potato chip and reaching a whole new audience.

By 2000 the few old family companies in Ohio and Pennsylvania weren't the only small chippers hanging around. Despite dire warnings about "barriers to entry" after the failure of the Department of Justice investigation, new chippers, mostly kettle cookers, were springing up all over. For a new generation—one with little or no connection to the family chip traditions of the early twentieth century—it was a flowering season all over again.

Mama Zuma's Revenge

Today no one better epitomizes what the New Kettlers have brought to potato chips than Sarah Cohen of Route 11 Potato Chips. Where young executives employed by snack food companies today are likely to be trained MBAs, Cohen was studying filmmaking at Colorado College and stumbled onto potato chips almost by accident.

"We didn't do any research; it was all luck and intuition," says Cohen about her unanticipated venture into the world of chips. "The fact that we're still in business is amazing."

Her parents, who ran an inn and restaurant in the Washington, D.C., area, had contracted with gourmet food purveyor Williams-Sonoma to produce six thousand tubs of chips to be sold by mail order and needed her help.

"I thought my parents were insane," she recalls. "'Why are you doing this? What are you getting yourselves into?' . . . and I was not even a potato chip eater. I'm more of a pretzel person, actually. . . . It was a three-person operation. It was a big challenge, a big project, it was very intense. And nobody in my family had ever done any manufacturing. . . . Some people said they thought it was like child abuse! [laughs]"

The Cohen family worked night and day to fulfill the Williams-Sonoma contract. Cohen thought she'd do the "chip thing" for a year. Today, from the main highway in Middletown, Virginia, where the company found its name, Sarah Cohen's Route 11 Potato Chip Company continues to make a high-quality product, and its funky-but-chic imagery conveys a hipness that is hard to imitate. Like Ben & Jerry's ice cream or Boulevard Beer, Route 11 has kept big chippers guessing, trying to figure out how they, too, can get a part of this new boutique market. Breaking and marketing a new potato chip—according to traditional chippers, one of the hardest things to do because of the big bucks required for promotion—hasn't been a problem for Route 11, largely because it's too small to play the game.

"We're not trying to get into places where the competition is, because we can't compete pricewise; and we're too small to pay slotting fees, and it's against my principles anyway," she says. "People ask me, 'What do you do in your marketing?' . . . Our marketing is we answer the phone, and that's it. I do one trade show a year in New York." Like Steve Bernard at Cape Cod, Cohen has found that the high-quality chip product sells itself.

"Basically the marketing is built into the product," says Cohen. "We don't cut corners, and try to make a really good potato chip. So that is inherent in the product itself, first of all. Second of all, we don't have a marketing budget. Our best marketing has been word of mouth. What that's led to is a lot of press, and the press wants to feel like they're discovering something."

All the other chippers I have talked with—small, large, old, new, kettle, or continuous—still depend on conventional outlets like supermarkets, gas stations, and convenience stores for sales. Route 11 is distributed by perhaps twenty independents to these sorts of venues, but unlike almost everyone else their principal outlets are gourmet and specialty food shops.

"We're in the Marriott gift shops, and that's a big account for us. . . . I never thought we'd be in Marriott. Some people look at Route 11 as a way to help. . . . They don't want Lay's; Lay's is too common. They want something that's special, that helps their profile."

At Route 11, workers hand-dispense seasoning in metal measuring cups over a fresh, hot chip batch; they then stir the seasoning with a tool that resembles a stainless steel garden rake. For the final mix, a man wearing gloves gets his hands into the batch, heaving the spiced chips like a giant tossed salad. It's hard to imagine an Utz, Shearer's, Herr's,

Route 11 factory and outlet store, summer 2004. (courtesy of Route 11 Potato Chips)

Wise, or Frito-Lay doing what Cohen does: Route 11 produces a literally handmade chip.

"It takes thirty seconds to get a Lay's chip," says Cohen, "but it takes us six or seven minutes. It's a different product."

Cohen's artisan approach differs, too, in bringing out the attributes of the potato. Where most chippers try for a product that is the same year-round, she tries for something else: "With Utz and Herr's and Lay's, consistency is their number one thing. No matter what the potatoes are like when they come in, they kind of try to erase their characteristics. Whereas when we get a load in, it's like we modify our recipe to bring out the best characteristics of the potato."

Part of that approach includes organic chipping potatoes, and Cohen has found good growers for them. When Route 11 can get them, all its chips are organic, but it doesn't boilerplate the "organic" label on the bag because shipments can't be guaranteed year-round.

"Twelve to fifteen years ago," says Cohen, "my parents thought that they could sustain an all-organic potato chip, and when we moved the factory here, I said, 'You know what, we can't do that.' I mean, we were doing insane stuff like flying potatoes from Idaho . . . stupid stuff just to get the organic potatoes. . . . It was just not a sustainable way of doing things."

However, Route 11 does make a special organic line—Yukon Gold—from June through December. Cooked only in sunflower oil, according to Cohen, it generates perennially strong customer demand.

Cohen's slant on kettle chips is truly a "postmodern" approach; Route 11's product occupies simultaneous niches in both the gourmet and health food worlds, while using packaging and flavors that evoke a whacked-out twist on the mom-and-pop chip paradigm.

But if Cohen's product is just a little too colorful and individualistic to sit alongside whole-grained organic products, other new chip companies have not hesitated to put the natural aspect front and center. In the early 1980s, Kettle Foods, Inc., of Oregon saw an explicit opening for potato chips in organic groceries. Starting out with organic nut butters, Kettle Foods soon added potato chips. Jim Green, "ambassador" of Kettle Foods, says that Kettle's natural food niche is integral to everything about the company and extends to its chips. "Kettle brand was raised in the world of natural foods . . . and that's how we made our niche," he says.

As far as Green knows, Kettle is the only chipper that makes an organic potato chip all year. Today, Kettle products are on the shelves of nearly every health food store in the nation, and as supermarkets have added natural food sections, so has Kettle added clients. While batch kettle chips have been the biggest area of growth within potato chips, natural foods have been a major growth area for supermarkets. Kettle brand appears poised to take advantage of both. "We have our own little corner of the market that's really growing," says Green. "Natural and organic foods are growing way faster than regular food products."

As the experimental approaches of chippers like Route 11 and Kettle brand have taken place, other New Kettlers, similarly unallied with the family-owned chip traditions of the past, have also arisen. With no preconceptions about the business, they continue to invent new angles—products and approaches they think are "cool"—and in so doing have found an enthusiastic audience. In 1986 Tim Kennedy introduced Tim's Cascade Style Potato Chips in Seattle, to become one of less than a handful of chippers remaining west of the Rockies. Also out West, Poore Brothers, a publicly traded company on the NASDAQ, has built business with high-end kettle chips and licensing agreements for products like T.G.I. Friday's Potato Skins. In the Midwest, Art's and Mary's has found a new market for strongly flavored kettle chips. On Long Island, third-generation potato farmers Martin and Carol Sidor saw their neighbors resorting to "agri-entertainment"—corn mazes and vineyard tours—and started North Fork Potato Chips using their own chipping potatoes. In the South, Zapp's makes an extra-thick kettle chip cooked in peanut oil.

Like Cohen, Zapp owner Ron Zappe's outsider background—a self-described "refugee from the energy business"—has given him a fresh perspective on potato chips. Zapp's has peppered its line with experimental flavors such as Cajun Crawtator and Hotter 'N Hot Jalapeno. "Our regular flavor is our fourth or fifth best seller," says Zappe. "For most companies it's their top seller."

"Our strong point is our use of bold flavors—jalapeño, dill, barbeque, parmesan," says Brett Albers of Art's and Mary's of Cheney, Kansas, another boutique chipper found in gourmet stores. "Everybody wants new flavors all the time," says Sarah Cohen. "It does cost money, but it helps our marketing, because at the shows everyone's, like, 'What's new, what's new?' We get attention for the new flavors. Like our Mama Zuma's."

On the Mama Zuma's Revenge package, a beautiful Hispanic femme fatale cracks a whip made of jalapeños as a man in a Mexican hat cowers behind a rock. It is a ridiculously hot chip—some would find it hard to eat more than two or three at a sitting. As much as the kettle-cooking process, it is this property—spiciness, especially heat—that is an integral part of the new kettlers' appeal.

Blair's Sauces and Snacks in New Jersey got into potato chips by the back door, as a seller of spicy dips and sauces, soon spinning off its dry rub product as an infusion onto potato chips. Blair's Death Rain chip bags come with a chili-shaped thermometer indicating heat of the product inside. "Smokin' Joe" Palmisano, Blair's regional manager, seems genuinely impressed with his own products' attributes: "We had some guy from England call. He said, 'You know, bloke, this is the first time I've gotten a bag of chips that said it was hot, and really was hot.'"

Although the packaging of Blair's Death Rain chips embodies a certain post-punk-slacker sensibility, Palmisano says the chip does not try for any particular age demographic. Old and young alike, he says, wolf down the chips at Host Marriott stops along interstate highways in the Northeast. "You have to understand something," says Palmisano, in a hearty northeastern accent. "What is the leading cause of death? Highway fatalities. Yet they take something labeled 'Death' and sell it on the highway."

Consumer interest in flavors has not gone unnoticed by big chip companies. Where the appeal of kettle chips with way-out flavors and novel packaging was intuitive for Zapp's and Route 11, for bigger companies these angles are now a conscious marketing approach. Frito-Lay's Jared Dougherty believes that interest in flavors even trumps chip style, cutting across product lines—whether the chips are continuously cooked, kettle, or baked. To Dougherty, potato chips open a door for cautious consumers, providing a context for offbeat flavors in a familiar companion. "Chips provide an opening for people who have not been adventurous in the past," says Dougherty. "It gives them an opportunity to try new flavors, but in a safe way."

Now, with the advent of offbeat flavors and interest in oils—especially in the context of kettle chips—big chip companies are running to catch up. "Things have come full circle," said Herr's Daryl Thomas in 2004. "Fifty-eight years later, we're back to kettle chips."

Today, large chip makers—Herr's, Utz, Frito-Lay—are cashing in on the expanding kettle chip market with multiple product lines. Utz's five kettle lines are based on different types of oil: peanut oil for Kettle Classics; cottonseed oil for Mystic Kettle, with packaging reminiscent of Cape Cod's seaside imagery; partially hydrogenated soybean oil for Homestyle; lard for Grandma Utz, a Lancaster County–style chip; and trans-fat-free sunflower oil for a new line called Utz Natural, sold in matte brown bags. Cohen even met with Utz at its invitation, sitting and talking with executives in suits as they passed her chips around the room. Shearer's, which makes chips for Frito-Lay's kettle line, as well as its own kettle chips, has also shown interest in her approach.

Like stripped-down punk rockers in the 1970s era of stodgy arena rock, do-it-yourself chippers like Route 11, Zapp's, Poore Brothers, Tim's, Cape Cod, and Art's & Mary's have jostled the chip establishment into new worlds of chip styles, textures, and flavors—at the same time recharging the corporate diversity that seemingly had diminished through the chip wars. On the way, a new tool has arisen, one that almost all chippers have made use of . . . though its full potential has yet to be realized.

Webs of Possibility

In the mid-1990s, as Eagle and Borden were trying to become number two against Frito-Lay, a young newspaper editor named Jeremy Selwyn was taking his work breaks at a nearby convenience store in Fitchburg, Massachusetts, home of Wachusett Potato Chip Company and near the historic home of Leominster (Tri-Sum) Potato Chip Company. Selwyn and his coworkers got into sampling new and different chips as something fun to do and came across some unusual finds in the process. They became competitive, trying to outdo each other with "weirder and weirder" chips at the office each day, says Selwyn, who, like a birder, soon accumulated a list of some hundred chips. Then Selwyn got the idea to start a Web site

Today, Taquitos.net hosts reviews and information about more than thirty-four hundred snacks—chocolate, popcorn, pretzels, candy bars. The largest category is potato chips, with three times the number of reviews as the next largest. At the time of this writing, Taquitos.net has reviews of 1,016 potato chip varieties. Selwyn estimates that the Web site averages seven to eight thousand visits with more than fifteen to twenty thousand page views daily. "I would never have believed when I started how interested people are in chips," says Selwyn.

And the number of chip varieties he discovers continues to rise. "It's astounding, the number I can find," Selwyn observes. "I sometimes have to hold myself back. There's only so much I can eat, only so much I have room for."

In addition to finding new chips on his travels, snack companies provide Selwyn with new material to review for the site. "Some days," he says, "I'm just deluged with flavors." Chip flavors, he adds, got him started to begin with—and he "continues to be impressed."

Although the site does pay for itself through advertising, Taquitos .net is not Selwyn's sole means of financial support. Selwyn now works a day job as a software engineer, but with a chip bowl on his desk—"chip of the day"—to keep coworkers updated about his latest discoveries. He believes as many as two thousand different chip varieties may have passed through the workplace chip bowl. He sends daily e-mail messages to update the office about his newest finds.

"I'm not shy about bringing in some fairly disgusting things," says Selwyn, who adds that some coworkers have never sampled the chip bowl, especially during the Atkins craze a couple of years back. Otherwise, it's one of the gathering spots in the office.

I asked Selwyn's to name his favorite nonflavored potato chip.

"Kettle [brand] chips," he replied. "I've been more and more impressed with their stuff over the years. Tim's Cascade Style—they're thick cut and cooked in peanut oil. My absolute favorite is their hot jalapeño chip. I like Wachussett's plain chip."

In addition to product reviews, Taquitos.net has an online message board, "Chip Talk," where chip aficionados can express their enthusiasm about their favorite chips or float questions to the larger fan community. Often, posters are asking about a hard-to-find chip. What follows is a typical exchange:

> *Jason:* I live in Michigan so where can i buy old dutch products from. I will travel to windsor if they have them.
>
> *Chiplover:* You can order Old Dutch products online from www .olddutchfoods.com then click on "contact" link and then there is a link you can click to order any of their products online. Although I noticed they don't have their ketchup chips to order . . . weird.
>
> *Jaydes:* you can find old dutch products anywhere in Canada. Every gas station and grocery store will have them. Make your way to Canada and you will find them.

"People have real attachments to regional companies they grew up with," says Selwyn, "and can be very opinionated about it." People who grew up with lard chips, he says, won't think much of a cottonseed oil chip, for instance. One Web patron sent Selwyn a handwritten letter that "went on for ten or so pages," complaining that "no one ever writes me back" regarding his inquiry about a chip he had been tracking for more than twenty-five years, a chip he'd spotted once in Denver.

Selwyn believes that the loss of regionality in chips has to do with changes in transportation, food technology, and distribution, allowing large manufacturers to operate in ever-widening circles. Still, of diversity he says, "I don't think you've lost it completely. Certain parts of the country are pretty boring, but if I go to Chicago, there's flavors—like hot vinegar—that you can't get anywhere else." Selwyn thinks his record occurred on a trip to London, when he came back with sixty-some bags of chips after stopping himself from buying more.

What does a junk-food junkie like Selwyn do after eating chips? "It's a good thing I run," says Selwyn, who regularly hits the road race and half-marathon circuit.

While most chip companies today have Web sites, Selwyn acknowledges a general consensus within the chip community that no one has quite hit the mark on the Internet . . . yet. Selwyn thinks the direction of a Doritos.com promotion wherein site visitors can vote a new flavor in or out has possibilities. In the meantime, Selwyn gets a lot of "where can I get this chip in my area" questions.

"When someone can't find a particular chip in their area," he says, "it's usually because the chip is just not distributed there. The majority of those kinds of questions are e-mailed to me in the form of: 'Where can I find chip X in area code X?' I don't have information to answer those kinds of questions, and a lot of the chip companies probably don't either.

"But," he adds, "even if I did know, usually the answer would still be, 'They're not sold anywhere near there' anyway, because for some reason some snackers expect that all chips are sold in their own area, when it's definitely not the case." Although many people could find the chips they're looking for by visiting chip company Web sites, people often don't want to pay the cost of shipping. "When you're Fed-Exing chips," says Selwyn, "shipping is expensive. They don't travel well. There's a fairly short shelf-life. There might be some bungling by UPS. You'll get some broken bags. Ordering over the Internet may double the cost." Selwyn himself has actually bought very few chips online, although today even tiny chippers like Good's and Jones have Web sites with ordering options.

When it comes to ordering chips on the Internet, Anchor O'Reilly at anchorsfoodfinds.com may represent the kind of possibility Selwyn hints at: a mail-order chip-of-the-month club, where subscriptions ranging between twenty-seven and three hundred dollars allow patrons to sample everything from Tim's Cascade to Gold'n Krisp of Ohio—apparently shipping costs are no obstacle to some. Web sites like those of Conn's, Herr's, Utz, and Jones give customers an opportunity to become reacquainted with a favorite childhood chip or to ship something to loved ones overseas. As Taquitos.net's Selwyn suggests, most executives believe the Internet does not account for a large portion of business . . . yet. Among chippers, Ron Zappe is unusual in crediting business to the Internet. He believes Zapp's does more mail order business than any other chip company and attributes roughly 50 percent of Zapp's to the Internet.

In the meantime, chippers of all ages go about peddling their product, now over 150 years old, mostly the old-fashioned way: in stores. You can talk to a dozen different potato chippers, new or traditional, and get a dozen different insights about why their companies have persisted, what their struggles have been, and why they are special.

> *Doug Roudebush, Gold'n Krisp Potato Chips, Massillon, Ohio:* People get used to buying our chips, and it doesn't matter if the other companies give 'em away—they're still going to buy ours. Meanwhile, we just try to do our own thing, mind our own business, and stay out of everybody else's way.

> *Dale Backer, Backer's Potato Chips, Fulton, Missouri:* Stay small—that's how we like it. We stay small, don't take on debt, and deliver a good product.

> *Julie Strauss, Golden Flake Foods, Birmingham, Alabama:* Our niche is to appeal to southern tastes. We don't have to appeal to a national audience.

> *Jared Dougherty, Frito-Lay, Dallas, Texas:* We look at flavor trends from the restaurant industry, to what people are preparing in homes, to general food and culinary interests—we look at trends in those areas for inspiration about what flavors to bring to the market in potato chips.

> *Anonymous kettle chipper (about competitors):* We're so close we piss on each other's shoes. We are in the same markets—our chips are right next to each other on the shelves.

> *Sarah Cohen, Route 11 Potato Chips, Middletown, Virginia:* The beautiful thing about Route 11 is that people, if they're used to buying it at a store, will start to complain if it's not there.

> *Jay Poore, Poore Brothers Snacks, Goodyear, Arizona:* I tell retailers, "I don't want to take away from your current sales. I won't cannibalize

your other chips. But customers who don't usually buy potato chips will
buy them now."

The basic human appeal of the potato chip comes naturally and ef-
fortlessly for new chippers like Route 11 and Zapp's. It's evidenced in
their quirky packaging and outlandish flavor profiles. Traditional chippers, who have taken on the family business either willingly or through
the departure of an ancestor, also understand their product's appeal—
they've grown up with it. Even the MBAs who now populate the offices
of large snack companies must eventually come to grips with what potato chips are all about. And if they don't soon get it, renegades like
Route 11 and Zapp's will rise to take their shelf space, trust and antitrust
be damned.

In the end, despite the messy accompanying issues—shelf space,
slotting fees, antitrust, trans fats, low carbs, and acrylamides—potato
chips are all about fun.

Bob Jones, Jones Potato Chip Company, Mansfield, Ohio: I can't think of
too many situations when you're not having fun when you're eating a
snack. . . . You're either watching a ballgame, or with the family at a
picnic, or together with friends . . . and I think almost every occasion
that generates positive feeling is when people are eating the types of
foods that we make. . . . There's a cute commercial on right now about
Bush's Baked Beans, but are you really gonna become emotionally attached to vegetables, or salads, or croutons?

Alan Klein, Mister Bee's Potato Chips, Parkersburg, West Virginia: I still
believe there is a market for potato chips. It's a comfort food. You go to
watch a football game on the television, I don't care who you are—you
want a snack.

Daryl Thomas, Herr Foods, Nottingham, Pennsylvania: When you're
running and stressed and want a quick boost of energy—want a little
reward—our snacks fit that bill. Our category is a fun category.

Keith Ver Vaet, Shearer Foods, Brewster, Ohio: This isn't serious food, this
is fun food. If you're eating this, you're celebrating something—life, a
wedding, birthday, family, friends.

Joe Palmisano: It's fun. It's all about fun.

Notes

Notes to the text are keyed, by page number, to several words of a quotation or passage. Most works are cited by their author's last name and (if needed) a short title. The book *50 Years* is cited by its title rather than its publisher, the Snack Food Association (SFA). The abbreviation *SFBB* stands for *Snack Food Blue Book*, edited by Jerry L. Hess. Full references to books appear in Books Cited. Full names and dates of interviews appear in Interviews. Unless otherwise noted, all interviews were conducted by the author.

Chapter 1. The Great American Vegetable

3   "The houses were all stocked": Quoted in Hawkes, *The Potato*, 22.

4   Russets, Katahdins, Irish Cobblers: Ira Rider interview.

4   twenty-two pounds of chips: *SFBB* relates how K. T. Salem started his Akron, Ohio, chip business in the 1920s after noting brisk sales of potato chips in nearby stores. Salem calculated "a bushel of potatoes has 60 lbs. Each pound has 16 oz. So a bushel of potatoes would make 960 bags. Retail price is 5 cents. This would bring $48. If I make them, I don't want to sell retail. I want to sell wholesale. So 25 percent to the storekeeper. This leaves $36. I thought: 'Ohheeeeee!!! You're going to make too much money'"(78). But as Salem processed the first batch, he soon found his sixty pounds of potatoes reduced to fifteen pounds of chips, because water in the potatoes had boiled off during frying.

4   "A problem we have": Don Ramseyer interview.

4   If the temperature is too low: O. Smith, 387–89.

6   Frito-Lay spokesman Jared Dougherty says: Dougherty interview.

7   "There was a year": Sarah Cohen interview, July 14, 2004.

7   "In the late '80s and early '90s": Interview with anonymous Florida potato grower.

8   "I carried a load": Ira Rider interview.

8   His daughter-in-law, Betty: Betty Rider interview.

8   "If you bruise them up": Ed Rider interview, July 7, 2004.

9   Dakota Pearl and Glacier Chips: Ed Rider interview, June 27, 2006.

10   Within the nightshade family: Hawkes, *The Potato*, 62. Earlier, in a chapter in Harris's *Potato Crop*, Hawkes stated that the genus *Solanum* contained "over 2,000 species" (15).

10   While most tuberous *Solanum* species: Salaman, 1; Hawkes, *The Potato*, 7.

10   temperate climates like Maine and Ireland: Hawkes, *The Potato*, 11.

11   Some tuber-bearing members of *Solanum:* Salaman, 5.

11   as high as fifteen thousand feet: Ibid., 10.

11   hospitable altitudes around eleven thousand feet: Richardson, 14.

11   cultivated in the Andes: Hawkes, *The Potato*, 57–58.

11   domesticated between seven and ten thousand years ago: Ibid., 58.

11   obtained their potatoes by trade: Ibid., 13, 20.

11   are thought to date to about 5000 BC: Ibid., 16–20.

11   may date to about 10,000 to 11,000 BC: B. Smith, 179; Hawkes, *The Potato*, 18.

11   According to Salaman's 1949 book: Salaman says that chuño-destined potatoes are spread on the ground and left to freeze. Depending on the type of potato used or the type of chuño desired, they may or may not be covered with straw; then "women and children turn out the next day and 'tread' the tubers with their bare feet in order to squeeze the water out of them" (40). The process is repeated for four or five days—an ongoing cycle of freezing and drying.

12   In 1532 the cultural trajectory of South America: Richardson, 163.

12   use of chuño to maintain the slave miners: Salaman, 40–41; Richardson, 164.

12   No one seems to know: Hawkes, *The Potato*, 30–31.

12   reached most of the rest of western Europe by 1600: Zuckerman, 10–12.

12   potatoes were suspect: Ibid., 14.

13   "lazy" potatoes: Ibid., 45, 50.

13   Antoine Parmentier of France survived: Salaman, 572; Burton, 26, Zuckerman, 82.

13   even persuading the court of Louis XVI: Salaman, 599.

13   Parmentier persuaded the king: Zuckerman, 83.

13   Continuous warfare and conflict: Salaman, 204-15; Burton, 16–17.

13   Absentee landowners sublet small tracts: Burton, 17; Zuckerman, 38.

13   "rendered the cultivation": Burton, 18.

13   Irish famines between 1800-1801 and 1817: Zuckerman, 139.

13   In August 1845: Salaman, 289–316.

13   Fields could be ruined within a day: Zuckerman, 188.

14   accompanying diseases like typhus and dysentery: Salaman, 301, 304; Zuckerman, 226–27.

14   Accounts of Ireland: Salaman, 300-301, 308-9; Zuckerman, 192–93.

14   Ireland's population fell: Zuckerman, 194.

14   William Penn described potatoes: Ibid., 88.

14   Zuckerman, the potato historian: Ibid., 89–93.

Chapter 2. Creation Myths

15 "Hm hm, that's good": The text appeared in Jean McGregor, "Now It Can be Told: The Authentic Story of Crum and His Saratoga Chips," *Saratogian*, August 30, 1940. Jean McGregor was likely a pseudonym Evelyn Barrett Britten used when writing for the *Saratogian* (Linda Gorham, personal communication to author). Britten repeated the Crum statement almost word for word in *Chronicles of Saratoga*.

15 perhaps as many as five: Waller, 98. The text of a 1992 presentation by David Mitchell, then director of Brookside Museum, home of the Saratoga County Historical Society, indicates Crum was married at least twice. An earlier account says, "George Crum's first wife came from an Indian reservation in Wisconsin" and "Crum reportedly abused and mistreated her so badly that she went back to Wisconsin. Her brother is supposed to have come on and threatened to kill Crum. They must have settled their differences, since a sister, Esther, came on and married Crum" (Earl F. Gates, unpublished typescript, "Chapter 18, George Crum," 46, from *The Town of Malta: Developed by People*, Brookside Museum, Saratoga County Historical Society, Ballston Spa, NY, 1976). Crum's 1912 will bequeaths all of his belongings to Nancy Hagemore, "who now lives with me and has lived with me for so many years" (Brookside Museum).

15 William Vanderbilt and Jay Gould: Jean McGregor, "'Too Thick' Cried Critic: Result—Spa Potato Chips," *Saratogian*, May 3, 1946; Bradley, 123.

16 "the most indigestible substitutes": Waller, 95, 98.

16 Crum's 1914 obituary: Photocopy of newspaper clipping, source unknown, July 27, 1914, Brookside Museum.

16 an obituary in a yearbook: Photocopy of clipping, "Famous Hunter Guide and Cook Dies at 96 Years," attributed to 1907 yearbook, Brookside Museum.

16 other printed records until the 1940s: Bradley, 121–24. Bradley cites the *Hotel Gazette*, August 22, 1885, as supporting the Crum version. William S. Fox and Mae G. Banner could not find the *Hotel Gazette* despite extensive searching ("Social and Economic Contexts of Folklore Variants: The Case of Potato Chip Legends," *Western Folklore* 42 [1983]: 115).

17 described as from Kentucky: Bradley, 121; 1907 yearbook, photocopy, Brookside Museum; McGregor, "Now It Can Be Told."

17 "Stockbridge Indian": Waller, 95.

17 "the St. Regis tribe": Gates, "Chapter 18," 45.

17 confused the concepts *crumb* and *speck:* Britten, 176.

17 Crum's appreciative customers: Bradley, 123; McGregor, "'Too Thick."

17 until "the blood followed the knife": McGregor cites the story as related to her by Cornelius Durkee, a guest at Moon's Lakehouse. McGregor, "Now It Can Be Told," "Too Thick."

17 An entertaining and enlightening analysis: Fox and Banner, "Potato Chip Legends," 114–26.

19 "In Ireland, during the famine of 1845–46": Stelk and colcannon are dishes using potatoes rather than potato varieties; *The American Heritage Dictionary of the English Language,* fourth edition, defines *colcannon* as "an Irish dish of mashed potatoes and cabbage seasoned with butter."

19 Katie Wicks, his sister: Cited in Jennifer Pruden, "It's a Chip of a Mystery," *Saratogian,* February 3, 1992.

19 David Mitchell, former director: Yancey Roy, "The Chip behind the Myth: Historian Clarifies Discovery Shrouded in Grease," *Albany Times Union,* January 30, 1992. Text of Mitchell's 1992 Brookside Museum presentation (as well as Crum's will and other early sources) spells *Crum* with a single *m,* whereas the Roy article spells the name *Crumm* throughout.

20 First-person interviews: Fox and Banner, "Potato Chip Legends," 115.

20 An 1893 history of Saratoga County: Sylvester, Wiley, and Garner, 535–36.

20 The most credible version: Pruden, "It's a Chip of a Mystery," citing David Mitchell. *SFBB* also suggests the Wicks version is the more plausible story (72).

20 Wick's obituary of 1917: Photocopy of clipping, source unknown, May 27, 1917, Brookside Museum. Jean McGregor said the story about Wicks and Crum was told to her by Albert J. Stewart, a great-nephew of Crum's (McGregor, "Now It Can Be Told").

20 brother-in-law Peter Francis: Bradley mentions Francis not by name but only as "a French chef employed at the Sans Souci" (121). The text of the Mitchell presentation suggests that Francis was the unnamed Sans Souci chef.

20 Cary Moon . . . or his wife: Bradley, 121; "Two Famous Saratoga Dishes," *New York Times,* August 13, 1893.

21 when newspaper and book accounts can't even agree: *Chum* appeared in a 1978 SFA advertisement in a Saratoga Springs newspaper (Fox and Banner, "Potato Chip Legends"). *Crumb* was the spelling in Kathleen Dooley, "Spa History Seen in Times Square," *Albany Times Union,* September 8, 1992.

21 likely invented and reinvented independently: John E. Harmon, "The Atlas of Popular Culture in the Northeastern United States," http://www.geography.ccsu.edu/harmonj/atlas/atlasf.html; *SFBB,* 70–72.

Chapter 3. Bursting the Seams

22 "Such periods of expansion": Simpson, 45.

22 "paper cornucopias": Bradley, 122.

22 a caterer named Fleeper: The story about Fleeper was attributed to Frank Dodd, formerly of the John E. Cain Company of Cambridge, Massachusetts (photocopy, Sondrah Marsh; *St. Petersburg Times,* no

date, Brookside Museum). Dodd recalls that the information about Fleeper came to light during a Snack Food Association meeting in Saratoga Springs in the 1970s (Dodd interview).

22 Stores of the time: *SFBB*, 74, 80, 82.

22 "Each summer, the family would pack up": Leslie C. Mapp, "A Common Thing Done Uncommonly Well: The Story of 'Mike-sell's' Potato Chip Company," *Newcomen Publication Society* no. 1236 (1985): 10.

23 "old beer joints": Mesre interview, May 14, 2001.

23 William Tappenden of Cleveland, Ohio: *50 Years*, 10, 13.

23 united as the Ohio Chip Association: Ibid., 30. *SFBB* refers to the organization as the "Ohio Potato Chip Assn" (83).

23 The legend is that Anna Good: Lewis Good interview, July 13, 2004.

24 "Backer's Potato Chip Company was founded": Backer's Potato Chip Co. package, Fulton, Missouri.

24 "The [Ralph] Good's Potato Chip family": Carole Good, customer service letter to students, no date.

24 "Wise Snacks came to exist": Wise Foods, "Too Many Potatoes," www.wisesnacks.com/company_history.html.

25 resisted the snack food business: Noss interviews.

25 Noss was a journalist: Noss interviews; *SFBB*, 84.

25 to become general manager in 1922: Typescript, Don Noss, "Did You Know?" June 1998.

25 The stuffy name of the business: Noss interviews.

25 Harvey Noss set about: *SFBB* credits a Dixico representative in Cleveland named Harry Morgan as the initiator of the Ohio Potato Chip Association (83); *50 Years* indicates that Noss started the organization "with the help of Harry Morgan" in 1931 (30). Noss was president of the National Potato Chip Institute from 1938, shortly after its creation in 1937, to 1940 (SFA, *1996 Who's Who*, 8). Noss also held other offices in the organization. It seems generally accepted that Noss's enthusiasm and promotional talents provided leadership and inspiration, even while others were president, until his retirement in 1972 (*50 Years*, 229).

25 soon added other Ohio chippers: *SFBB*, 83.

26 changed the name to the National Potato Chip Institute: *50 Years*, 30.

26 Don Noss remembers: Noss interviews.

26 It's hard to believe now: *50 Years*, 30.

27 "The bootleg joints": *SFBB*, 74.

27 Leonard Japp Sr.: Jim Mueller, "Still Chipper at 92: Meet Leonard Japp Sr., the Man Who Dreamed Up Jay's [*sic*] Potato Chips," *Chicago Tribune*, October 13, 1996.

27 "he went to doing nothing": William Backer interviews.

27 "Mrs. Flossie Howard and her family": http://www.kitchencooked.net/information.php?info_id=6

27 Charles Seyfert . . . and Herman Lay: *SFBB*, 80.

28 In 1951 the Herr plant: Bellury and Guterl, 8.
28 Early fires also destroyed: *SFBB*, 95, 102; Mapp, "Story of 'Mike-sell's,'" 13.
28 "Vince Flaherty was coming home": Noss interview, February 3, 2005.
29 "driving to Akron with my dad": Bob Jones, e-mail message to author, January 5, 2002.
29 Arthur Ross . . . had a problem: *SFBB*, 82.
29 "kettles" were rectangular cookers: *50 Years*, 144.
29 designed by an engineer named McBeth: McBeth founded MacBeth Engineering Corp—with the *MacBeth* spelling (*SFBB*, 82).
30 hundreds of pounds per hour: *50 Years*, 145.
30 Ferry continuous cookers were bought by: *SFBB*, 82.
30 physically large and prohibitively expensive: *50 Years*, 18.
30 bricked onsite at the chip factory: *SFBB*, 82.
30 heating chambers made an integral part: *50 Years*, 145; *SFBB*, 82–83.
30 "a dehydrated, salted product": *SFBB*, 72.
30 Mrs. Conn "made the chips": Mesre interview, May 14, 2001.
30 "The way you'd close 'em": William Backer interview, March 15, 2001.
31 Betty Rider . . . recalls: Betty Rider interview.
31 Laura Scudder was trained: Blackstock, 2, 4.
31 A determined and decisive lady: After interviewing more than fifty of Scudder's associates, Blackstock says the words most commonly used to describe her were "hard-working," "energetic," determined," "loyal," "ethical," "resourceful," "thorough," and "decisive" (ibid., 12). He adds, "To people who saw her only at a distance, she often appeared aloof, re-served, sometimes abrupt. Those who knew her well mention only the warmth and kindness of Laura Scudder" (13).
31 Chips were bought by the ounce or by the pound: Ibid., 6.
31 Scudder used female employees: Ibid., 7. In the industry before 1945 "women employees usually did the tedious weighing, packaging, and sealing operations" (*SFBB*, 86).
31 iron slips of wax paper: Blackstock, 7.
31 Scudder's business took off: Ibid., 8–12.
33 experimenting with cellophane: *50 Years*, 14. Cellophane had a "less-than-5-percent" wax surface which was "easily damaged by printing." The glassine bag used a different process, was "dipped in molten wax," and could be preprinted. Further improvements in cellophane-printing tech-nology enabled glassine and cellophane to be used contemporaneously, until such processes gave way to early versions of the complex laminates of plastics and foils used in snack-food packaging today (*50 Years*, 191–201).
33 piercing the waxy coating: *SFBB*, 83.
33 Opaque printing inks: *50 Years*, 18.
33 "just burst out of their seams": *SFBB*, 83.

33 Don Noss has what may be: Noss interview, July 9, 2004.

34 Dan Woodman . . . solved the problem: *50 Years*, 93.

34 "My opinion, when I started": Kelley interview.

37 wartime sanctions took hold: *50 Years*, 75, 77.

37 Noss went to Washington, D.C.: Ibid., 77, 79; *SFBB*, 84.

37 National Potato Chip Institute's membership roll: *50 Years*, 80, 82.

37 "never fear when Harvey's near": Interview with Don Noss and conversation with Lois Noss, July 9, 2004; *SFBB*, 83.

38 "The manufacturers worked all the time": Klein interview, May 11, 2006.

38 "The entrepreneurs worked eight days a week": Dodd interview.

38 "My dad had this great big box": Noss interview, December 7, 2005. Noss mentions that someone lent the mongoose box to Ernie Anderson, "who never returned it." Anderson hosted Cleveland television's *Shock Theater* and was a popular kiddie-show host named Ghoulardi in the 1960s; he later became famous as the announcer for *Love Boat, America's Funniest Home Videos*, and many other national television shows and advertisements.

40 Photos in a 1949 *Life* magazine article: "Potato Chippers Have a Convention," *Life*, February 28, 1949, 19–23.

40 After-hours parties: Several interviewees mentioned that because only the larger members could afford to entertain this way, after-hours parties were eventually formalized so that no one would feel left out.

40 Alan Klein remembers hanging out: Klein interview, May 11, 2006.

40 "There's Jerry Husman right there": Noss interview, July 9, 2004.

40 When the Depression put Lay out of work: *SFBB*, 80.

Chapter 4. Storm Warning

43 "We are very optimistic": "Lessons of Leadership, Part 52: Herman W. Lay of PepsiCo," *Nation's Business*, September 1969, 95.

43 eleven-year-old Herman Lay: "Legacy of Leadership, Herman Warden Lay," http://www.knowitall.org/legacy/laureates/Herman%20Warden%20Lay.html. In an interview, Lay answered yes when asked if he "started in the soft drink business" when he was ten ("Lessons of Leadership," 89).

43 "their investment melted away": "Legacy of Leadership."

43 Herman Warden Lay was born June 3, 1909: Ibid.

43 becoming a professional ballplayer was likely unattainable: "Lessons of Leadership," 92.

43 he had been a salesman: "Legacy of Leadership"; "Lessons of Leadership, 92–93.

44 he turned it down at first: "Legacy of Leadership."

44 from Lay's Model A: Ibid.

44 one of the first prospective buyers: Ibid.; SFA's 1987 history, *50 Years* indicates that Lay bought Barrett in 1937 (93); *SFBB* states that Barrett contacted Lay in 1939 (80).

44 Lay borrowed over half: *SFBB*, 80; *50 Years*, 93; "Legacy of Leadership."

44 Next, Lay bought: *SFBB*, 82. Red Dot was a large regional with eight plants, territories in twelve states, and a professionally produced employee newsletter called *Chip Chat* (http://www.wisconsinhistory.org/museum/exhibits/chip.asp). Within days of Lay's purchase of the company in May 1961, Red Dot founder Frederick J. Meyer committed suicide. According to Leslie Bellais, curator of costume and textiles at the Wisconsin Historical Society, Meyer believed that the sale was best for the company, but apparently became despondent upon realizing that he had sold away his life's work (Bellais interview, May 21, 2004). Red Dot bags made after the sale and after the September 1961 Frito-Lay merger had "FRITO-LAY, INC." printed on the back. The chip continued to be sold as Red Dot until Frito-Lay sold the company to H. H. Evon of Little Rock, Arkansas, in 1970. Evon closed the Madison factory and discontinued the brand in 1973. Bellais says that there was a perception at the time that Red Dot lost touch with the Madison community after Meyer sold the company.

44 "More of a builder than a buyer": *SFBB*, 82.

44 Lay built plants in Jackson: *SFBB*, 82; "Legacy of Leadership."

44 Elmer Doolin was living in San Antonio: *SFBB*, 115–16; *50 Years*, 28–29.

45 Doolin even developed: *SFBB*, 116.

45 Frito was adding potato chips: *50 Years*, 173.

45 "Lay's [actually Frito] bought out Num Num": Noss interviews. SFA's *50 Years* lists the date as 1958 (173); whatever the date, the labels initially would have specified the owner as Frito rather than Frito-Lay, because Frito-Lay was not formed until the merger in 1961.

45 Frito entered into agreement with H. W. Lay & Co: *SFBB*, 116.

45 "We set out with one objective": "Lessons of Leadership," 93. Frito-Lay's own materials indicate the year was 1961 (http://www.fritolay.com/fl/flstore/cgi-bin/comp_hist.htm), as do other sources (*SFBB*, 116; *50 Years*, 171; "Frito-Lay May Find Itself in a Competition Crunch," *Business Week*, July 19, 1982, 186; "Who Acquired Who?" *Forbes*, April 1, 1967, 69; "Legacy of Leadership"). An article in *Advertising Age* gives the year as 1960 (Elisa Kaplan, "Frito-Lay: Still King of the Hill," April 30, 1979, S-48).

46 "Lay Co. manpower marrying": Kaplan, "Frito-Lay Still King," S-48.

46 Lay organized his company to canvass: *SFBB*, 82.

46 The merger of Frito and Lay resulted: *50 Years*, 174.

47 "biggest beneficiary of this trend": Ibid., 132.

47 But the Snack Food Association's: Ibid., 343.

47 "Chesty, the first to produce": Ibid., 273.

47   In *Hi There, Boys and Girls!:* Hollis, 129.

48   The SFA's list of food companies: *50 Years,* 132.

48   recipe for tuna and potato chip casserole: Andrea Brown, letter to author, October 12, 1999; Mueller, "Still Chipper at 92."

48   Lipton sponsored Arthur Godfrey's: *50 Years,* 134.

50   Sam Slater on Parkersburg, West Virginia's WTAP: http://electricearl .com/parkersburg/WTAP. Alan Klein and several Web sites mention that Sam's brother Bill Slater was the host of *Twenty Questions* (en.wikipedia .org/wiki/twenty_questions).

50   "The thing I used to love about Sam Slater": Klein interview, November 9, 2006.

50   Mister Bee's motto: Klein interviews.

51   As Mesre recalls: Mesre interview, May 14, 2001.

51   Red Dot's clown, Ta-To: Bellais interviews.

52   Ho-Ho-ho: Leslie Bellais, e-mail message to author, November 30, 2006.

52   In the South, Golden Flake's clown, Goldie: Strauss interview, November 17, 2006.

54   Broski recalls the time: "Whizzo, Ol' Gus, and Me," documentary, KCPT-TV, 1996.

54   Nancy Kulp . . . played a chip inspector: "The Great Potato Chip War," *Newsweek,* July 26, 1975.

54   Jonathan Winters made a commercial: White interview; Bellury and Guterl, 21.

55   "Betcha can't eat just one": "Frito-Lay company," *International Directory of Company Histories,* 206.

55   "His laughter was meant for people, not merchandise": Lahr, 284.

56   Until the early 1970s: Although individuals in America such as Linus Pauling and Adelle Davis had raised concerns about nutrition, the snack industry didn't have to defend itself widely against "junk food" accusations until the 1970s (*50 Years,* 252).

56   "The arrival of Pringles": Ibid., 234.

56   "At least 40 prefabricated chips and snacks": Colin Warwick, "The In's and Out's of Fabricated Chips," *SFBB,* 107–12.

57   General Mills succeeded with Chipos: *50 Years,* 232; *SFBB,* 88–89.

57   The Weaver Potato Chip company: *50 Years,* 232; *SFBB,* 89.

57   "Chippers were especially dismayed": *SFBB,* 88.

57   "A potato chip is a thin raw slice": Noss quoted in "Consumer Goods. Party Gets Rough for Potato Chippers," *BusinessWeek,* November 8, 1969, 36.

57   "Our contention was": Mel Ehrlich quoted in *50 Years,* 232.

57   In the 1971 trial: Ibid., 232.

57   PCII pleaded with the government: Ibid., 241–42.

58   Joseph Seyfert . . . today recalls: Seyfert interview.

58 "My fellow Americans": Russell quoted in *50 Years,* 260–61.

58 Once again, it was ruled: Ibid., 242–60.

58 Terrified, some traditional chippers rushed: "Who Makes the Best Chip?" *Consumer Reports,* June 1991, 379–83; *50 Years,* 256; Warwick, "In's and Out's of Fabricated Chips," 107–8, 110.

58 but this "novelty" was hardly anything new: Warwick, "In's and Out's of Fabricated Chips," 108.

59 PCII president Verl A. Walker: Ibid.

59 "These newfangled potato chips": Ibid.; *50 Years,* 248.

59 sales of Pringles appeared to boost: *SFBB,* 89; *50 Years,* 259.

60 the Federal Trade Commission began to focus: Federal Trade Commission, "Agreement containing consent order, Docket No. 8606, in the matter of Frito-Lay, Inc., and File No. 651 0644, Pepsi Cola Co. acquisition of Frito-Lay, Inc.," May 31, 1968.

60 But in 1965 Frito-Lay merged with Pepsi-Cola: "Frito-Lay History," http://www.fritolay.com/fl/flstore/cgi-bin/comp_hist.htm.

60 but the FTC didn't approve of such language: *International Directory of Company Histories,* 207. A 1995 article in *Brandweek* about Eagle Snacks, owned by Anheuser-Busch, suggests that antitrust sensitivity to advertisement of product combinations had diminished since the 1960s. It mentions the possible legal complications of advertising snacks with alcohol at the state level, but does not address the more general antitrust implications of creating product tie-ins: "Eagle joined Budweiser and Sea World for a July Fourth promotion in Southern California markets. And while some states prohibit sales efforts that pitch food and alcohol together, 'we're trying to take advantage of the fact that we're all one company,' said Eagle President David Poldoian. 'Beer and snacks are a great combination . . . and you're going to see a lot more of it'" (Karen Benezra, "Can Poldoian Fly Eagle," September 18, 1995).

60 "barred from acquiring any snack": *International Directory of Company Histories,* 207.

60 In 1968 the FTC ordered Frito-Lay: Federal Trade Commission, "In the matter of Frito-Lay, Inc., a corporation, Docket No. 8606, Agreement containing consent order, United States of America before Federal Trade Commission," April 15, 1968; *50 Years,* 226.

60 One estimate had it that: Federal Trade Commission, "Agreement containing consent order, Docket No. 8606," May 31, 1968, 7.

60 Frito-Lay was to buy a significant portion: Ibid., 9–10.

60 Victor Sabatino . . . remembers that this strategy: Sabatino interview, May 9, 2006.

61 "I must say that I can't": "Lessons of Leadership," 94.

61 Frito-Lay's "store-door" distribution: Joseph B. Morris, "Frito-Lay/McKinsey Document Snack Profits," *Chipper/Snacker,* June 1981, 22. Jared Dougherty says that the store-door "entrepreneurial spirit" of Herman

Lay—the fact that he brought fresh product to stores in the back of his car and "guaranteed quality freshness, no matter what"—continues to "drive the front line of [Frito-Lay's] sales today" (interview).

61 Where most companies were content: "Frito-Lay May Find Itself in a Competition Crunch," *BusinessWeek*, 186; Morris, "Frito-Lay/McKinsey Document Snack Profits," 24; Kaplan, "Frito-Lay: Still King," S-48.

61 Frito replaced smaller stepvans: Peter Samuel, "Chipping Away at the Champ," *Forbes*, April 25, 1994.

61 In 1960 Sunshine Biscuits: *50 Years*, 172, 181.

61 It got serious in 1977: Ibid., 273; "Acton: a Switch to Snack Foods Has Turned It Profitable," *BusinessWeek*, September 25, 1978.

62 a company called Culbro . . . acquired: Leonard Sloane, "Business People: Culbro Corporation Names President," *New York Times*, May 18, 1981; *50 Years*, 273–74.

62 By the end of the 1970s: *50 Years*, 314.

62 Borden had been in chips since 1964: Ibid., 315.

62 By the late 1970s: Ibid., 314.

62 In 1979 Borden acquired: Paul Bush, "Hyperplants: The Next Phase in Food Processing—Borden's Guy's Foods Div—1989 Processor of the Year—Company Profile," *Prepared Foods*, September 1989; Alison Otto, "Anatomy of a Corporate Culture—Borden Inc.—1989 Processor of the Year—Company Profile," *Prepared Foods*, October 1989.

Chapter 5. Full Combat

63 "The snack aisle is littered": Quoted in Benezra, "Can Poldoian Fly Eagle."

63 In 1982 Borden made only one purchase: *50 Years*, 324.

63 Borden next acquired: Ibid., 329.

63 Jays . . . was added to the Borden stable: Ibid., 341.

63 In 1987 Culbro sold: PR Newswire, "Borden Agrees to Acquire Culbro Unit for $55 Million," July 2, 1987.

63 "Guy Caldwell spent 50 years": Bush, "Hyperplants."

63 In addition to salty snacks: Alison Otto, "Elsie's Heyday: How Borden Has Taken the Bull by the Horns—1989 Processor of the Year—Company Profile." *Prepared Foods*, September 1989; Matthew Schiffrin, "Last Legs?" *Forbes*, September 12, 1994.

64 Borden's expansion was accomplished: Schiffrin, "Last Legs?"

64 The hyperplant doctrine: Bush, "Hyperplants."

64 "At that time I compared our sizes": Waydo interview.

65 The redesigned Guy's potato chip plant: Bush, "Hyperplants."

65 When it finally closed: Dan Margolies, "Judge Oks Plan to Fund Guy's Payroll; Order Authorizes Lender to Advance Company $528,455," *Kansas City Star*, February 16, 2000.

65 By 1989 Borden had salty snacks: PR Newswire Association, "Borden, No. Two U.S. Snack Company, Purchases," September 22, 1987; Otto, "Elsie's Heyday"; John Greenwald, "Frito-Lay under Snack Attack," *Time*, June 10, 1996.

65 Flush with cash: Richard A. Melcher and Greg Burns, "How Eagle Became Extinct," *BusinessWeek*, March 4, 1996.

65 Although many states prohibited advertising: Benezra, "Can Poldoian Fly Eagle"; Richard Gibson, "Anheuser-Busch Will Sell Snacks Unit, Cardinals and the Club's Home Stadium," *Wall Street Journal*, October 26, 1995.

65 Initially, Eagle snacks . . . gave away snacks: *50 Years*, 324; Kevin Bowler, e-mail message to author, June 2, 2006.

66 Vitner's of Chicago produced: Cepa interview.

66 slotting fees: The term *slotting fee* or *slotting allowance* has expanded to include payments for shelf space in general, and is so used in this book; but the original meaning of *slotting* pertained specifically to obtaining a spot in a retailer's warehouse. The term *placement fee* has also been used to describe fees paid for free-standing displays or endcaps in stores (Keith ver Vaet and Gregory Gundlach, personal communications to author; Gregory T. Gundlach, statement on "Slotting Fees: Are Family Farmers Battling to Stay on the Farm and in the Grocery Store?" U.S. Senate Committee on Small Business and Entrepreneurship, September 14, 2000).

66 allegedly started by Coke and Pepsi: Carr interview; letter to the Honorable Janet Reno, March 12, 1995, source redacted; memo, "Telephone interview with [redacted]," William P. Jones to Nina B. Hale, May 7, 1996. The last two items are from materials provided at the author's FOIA request (ATFY01-109), U.S. Department of Justice, Antitrust Division, "investigation concerning anti-competitive practices in the snack food industry," 60-2096-0002. Hereafter, 60-2096-0002 refers to that DOJ investigation.

66 pay-to-stay or pay-to-play: Gregory T. Gundlach, statement on "Slotting Fees—Fees Charged by Grocery Retailers for Shelf Space: Are They Stifling Competition?" before the California State Senate Standing Committee on Business, Professions and Economic Development, February 9, 2005; David Moore, statement on "Slotting Fees," U.S. Senate Committee, September 14, 2000.

66 but not so impulse buyers: Confidential Memorandum: "Anticompetitive practices of Frito-Lay, Inc.," to U.S. Department of Justice, Antitrust Division, June 22, 1995 (60-2096-0002).

66 fresh produce as well: Donna L. Goodson, "Fear of Slotting Fees Gives Chills to Produce Vendors," *Boston Business Journal*, February 25, 2000. Slotting may affect farmers even more than food manufacturers. Produce growers moving into the sale of prepackaged salads have been surprised to find that they had to buy shelf space, rather than "simply offer your

best price and the best quality" and take it from there (Thomas E. Stenzel, statement on "Slotting Fees," U.S. Senate Committee, September 14, 2000). Representatives of produce associations have complained about the lack of relationship between wholesale and retail prices and drops in wholesale produce prices during surpluses that were never passed on to consumers (Moore, statement on "Slotting Fees"). Implicated was increasing consolidation among retail supermarkets, giving them greater bargaining power over farmers. Small family farmers paid a particularly high price by having to add slotting expenses to already small profit margins. Both grocers and farmers have been reluctant to talk about the practice. At a U.S. Senate hearing on slotting, committee chair Christopher Bond said that for a previous hearing only six out of eighty or more "people" they talked to agreed to testify; three of these later backed out, and two of the three remaining showed up with hoods and disguised voices ("Slotting Fees," U.S. Senate Committee, September 14, 2000; Goodson, "Fear of Slotting Fees").

66 "When Eagle entered the market": interview transcript, no date, U.S. Department of Justice, Antitrust Division (60-2096-0002).

66 more and more a real estate business: Robert Frank, "Frito-Lay Devours Snack-Food Business," *Wall Street Journal*, October 27, 1995.

67 Prices ranged from $150 per foot: Memo, William P. Jones to Nina B. Hale, May 7, 1996; memo, Tara Sweeney to "Files," May 31, 1996 (60-2096-0002).

67 could amount to a million dollars a year: Rider family interviews.

67 "It seems that these fees": Bond, committee chair, statement on "Slotting Fees," September 14, 2000.

67 Eagle bought Cape Cod: Glen Macnow, "A Taste of Old Cape Cod," *Nation's Business*, February 1990.

67 by 1988 Eagle chips were available: "Eagle Snacks Up, Though Still Down—Eagle Snacks Inc.'s Share of the Potato Chip Market," *Modern Brewery Age*, November 4, 1991.

67 featuring television's Odd Couple: Margaret Littman, "Chips Down, Snack Makers Play Rough Hand," *Prepared Foods*, October 1991.

68 By 1994 Eagle's sales: Benezra, "Can Poldoian Fly Eagle."

68 market share that never rose above 5 to 6.5 percent: Gibson, "Anheuser-Busch Will Sell Snacks Unit"; Melcher and Burns, "How Eagle Became Extinct." Two articles reported a 9.4 percent share of the potato chip market by Eagle ("Eagle Snacks Up," *Modern Brewery Age*; Philip Robinson, "PepsiCo Peppers Snack Market," *London Times*, December 10, 1991).

68 Even in the small but crucial: Samuel, "Chipping Away."

68 "It was astonishing the money they spent": Carr interview.

68 "more diversion than delight": Melcher and Burns, "How Eagle Became Extinct."

68 To add to the confusion: Kevin Bowler, e-mail message to author, June 2, 2006; *50 Years,* 324; Melcher and Burns, "How Eagle Became Extinct."

68 "They kept changing what they would do": Interview with anonymous individual.

68 "I think the answer you have": Kevin Bowler, e-mail message to author, June 5, 2006.

69 "I think that what happened": Interview with anonymous individual. A remark from Pepsico CEO Roger Enrico supports this view: "Eagle is a concern, not for what they are now but for what they have the potential to become" (Stephanie Anderson Forest, "Chipping Away at Frito-Lay," *BusinessWeek,* July 22, 1991).

69 Frito-Lay's snack products: Dan McGraw, "Salting Away Big Profits," *U.S. News & World Report,* September 16, 1996; Skip Hollandsworth, "Hot Potatoes," *Texas Monthly,* January 1, 1996.

69 Keebler was marketing several chip brands: "Mother's Cookies, O'Boise Corporation Sign Distribution Agreement," *Business Wire,* May 13, 1996; "Who Makes the Best Chip?" *Consumer Reports,* June 1991, 379–83; "Anticompetitive practices of Frito-Lay, Inc.," June 22, 1995 (60-2096-0002).

69 both Keebler and Nabisco garnered a place: Benezra, "Can Poldoian Fly Eagle"; Robinson, "PepsiCo Peppers."

69 Frito watched its market share erode: Greenwald, "Frito-Lay under Snack Attack."

70 Coca-Cola's 1985 "New Coke" debacle: Pendergrast, 351; Cotten Timberlake, "Pepsi-Cola USA's Roger Enrico Grabs Opportunity Unabashedly," *Associated Press,* April 16, 1986.

70 a shy demeanor: Timberlake, "Pepsi-Cola USA's."

70 call in Enrico to take charge: Wendy Zellner, "Frito-Lay Is Munching on the Competition," *BusinessWeek,* August 24, 1992.

70 "We're going to make a major change": Forest, "Chipping Away at Frito-Lay."

70 Characterizing Frito-Lay: Zellner, "Frito-Lay Is Munching"; Forest, "Chipping Away at Frito-Lay"; Hollandsworth, "Hot Potatoes."

70 Eagle priced its products: Robinson, "PepsiCo Peppers"; Zellner, "Frito-Lay Is Munching"; Waydo interview.

70 In 1991 it introduced: "Eagle Snacks Up," *Modern Brewery Age;* Gipson interviews.

70 changing from soy to cottonseed oil: Zellner, "Frito-Lay Is Munching."

71 Frito's profits grew by 15 percent: Ibid.

71 chances were 94 percent: McGraw, "Salting Away Big Profits."

71 Despite Borden's having double: Greenwald, "Frito-Lay under Snack Attack."

71 "It is not unusual": Otto, "Elsie's Heyday."

71 100 pounds of corn meal: Klein interview, May 11, 2006; "Anticompetitive practices of Frito-Lay, Inc.," June 22, 1995 (60-2096-0002).

71 Frito-Lay had come up with Doritos: Hollandsworth, "Hot Potatoes."

72 "Borden's production was almost as efficient": Sabatino interview, May 9, 2006.

72 "generate a series of national products": Seyfert interview.

73 "Part of Borden's problem": Strauss interview, May 28, 2004.

73 "Borden could never make a decision": Interview with anonymous individual.

73 George Waydo says that: Waydo interview.

73 "The problems at Borden": Sabatino interview.

74 "it became a matter of 'who's king of the mountain'": Seyfert interview.

74 a high of 12 percent to 5 percent by 1996: Greenwald, "Frito-Lay under Snack Attack."

74 "inefficient patchwork of declining brands": Schiffrin, "Last Legs?"

74 "I remember one night": Sabatino interview.

74 "I fought vigorously": Waydo interview.

74 Borden announced in January of 1994: "Borden Sells Clover Club Foods Snack Business," *Business Wire*, December 19, 1994.

75 "They fought tooth and nail": Klein interview, May 11, 2006. An event in 2003, the year of the 150th anniversary of Katie Wicks's invention, indicates that a spirit of camaraderie among chippers is still present, at least in Ohio. That August, five Ohio chippers—Mike-sell's, Jones, Conn's, Ballreich, and Shearer's—united to produce the "World's Largest Bag of Potato Chips" at the Ohio State Fair. The giant bag weighed in at 1,082.5 pounds and used 4,250 pounds of Ohio potatoes and 700 pounds of soybean oil (the previous record was 450 pounds). The chips were displayed for over a week and were not distributed for eating, but chippers used the opportunity to distribute bags of their own chips (Leo Shane III, "All That and a Bag of Chips," *Fremont News-Messenger*, August 9, 2003; Kelly Jordan, "Ballreich Potato Chips Part of Guinness World Challenge," *Open Market*, August 30, 2003).

75 "before the chip wars": Memo, Neeli Ben-David to "Frito File," May 15, 1996 (60-2096-0002).

75 "A lot of regionals were hurt": Interview with anonymous individual.

75 Once considered the West's dominant snack company: *SFBB*, 99.

75 But in April 1995, press releases: "Blue Bell Pressured by Industry Giants," "Granny Goose Pressured by Industry Giants," "Bell Brand Pressured by Industry Giants," *Business Wire*, April 12, 1995.

76 Clover Club Foods of Utah: Steven Oberbeck, "California Firm Buys Utah's Clover Club Snack-Food Maker," *Knight Ridder/Tribune Business News*, July 7, 1997.

76 Lance cut five hundred jobs: "Snack Food Company Lance Inc. to Trim

507 Jobs," *New York Times,* December 14, 1995; Edward Martin, "The Snack Attack," *Business North Carolina,* July 1996.

76   "You're talking about 'slotting allowances'": Martin, "Snack Attack."

76   Gibble's and Charles Chips both filed: Kevin G. DeMarrais, "All Charles Chips on Table—Company Faces Auction," *Bergen County Record,* February 1, 1994; Samuel, "Chipping Away." Shortly after the end of the Great Potato Chip Wars, Stehman's and Groff's of Pennsylvania also went out of business (Bob Fernandez, "Pa. Tops in Chips? It's in the Bag," *Philadelphia Inquirer,* June 6, 1999).

76   In December 1996, Bon Ton Foods: Neal G. Goulet, "More Local Jobs at Risk; Bon Ton Foods Plans to Cut 70 Jobs." *York Daily Record,* December 6, 1996.

76   "That's a story in and of itself": Hoover interview, June 14, 2004.

76   Years earlier, Utz employees: Tim McCook, "Thirty Years Ago This Summer," *Snack Food & Wholesale Bakery,* September 1, 2002.

76   Over twenty years later: Goulet, "More Local Jobs."

77   "Going back to the '30s and '40s": Jones interview, July 8, 2004.

77   "If you can't stay on the shelves": Carr interview.

77   After going in to Chapter 11 bankruptcy: Samuel, "Chipping Away."

77   The 1996 Snack Food Association's Membership Directory: SFA, *1987–88 Who's Who;* SFA, *1996 Who's Who.*

77   Gibble's continuously cooked lard chip: To the best of my knowledge, only Gibble's and Ralph Good's of Adamstown, Pennsylvania, make a thin lard chip that is continuously cooked; King's makes a thicker continuously cooked lard chip to mimic the kettle style (Weber interview, July 13, 2004).

77   an attempt to come up with a baked chip: Samuel, "Chipping Away."

78   "The Gibble's plant wasn't necessarily geared": Carr interview.

78   In late 1996 Gibble's was sold: Charles Thompson, "A Newville-Area Potato Chip Business Has Been Sold and Relocated," *Knight Ridder/Tribune Business News,* December 31, 1996.

78   Gibble's today continues to make: "Hot Potatoes," *Town and County,* March 1, 2002; Francine Maroukian, "The Best Potato Chips You've Never Tasted," *Esquire,* February 1, 2003.

78   Hiland too was struggling: Rick Lingle, "Hiland Potato Chips: Small Advantages," *Prepared Foods,* April 1991.

78   Hiland needed work: Blough interview.

78   added corn oil to suit "midwestern tastes": Lingle, "Hiland Potato Chips."

78   "The flavor of America's Heartland": Sherry Gupta, "Touting Heartland Virtues," *Des Moines Buisness Record,* September 24, 1990; Lingle, "Hiland Potato Chips." John Blough relates that Curtice-Burns acquired the Heartland trademark from Northwest Missouri State University in Marysville, Missouri, in exchange for a research grant.

78   seven form-fill-seal machines: Gupta, "Touting Heartland Virtues";
       Lingle, "Hiland Potato Chips."
78   "an unusual orientation": "Hiland Bags a Winner," *Packaging Digest,* No-
       vember 1, 1992.
79   Unfortunately, the sideways labeling: Robert McMath, "What a Differ-
       ence a Purpose Makes," *Brand Packaging,* March 2005.
79   Frito-Lay reintroduced the concept: Ibid.
79   According to Blough, bigger problems at Hiland: Blough interview.
79   Rob Hess of the E. K. Bare potato brokerage: Hess interview.
80   In the late 1920s, Helen Friedman: "Golden Flake History," http://www
       .goldenflake.com/Ourhistory.html.
80   Some of the attrition in the chip industry: Thomas interview, May 6,
       2004.
80   "There was, it should be noted": *SFBB,* 89.
80   In New England, Frank Dodd . . . recalls: Dodd interview.
81   The SFA's chipper membership: Klein interview, May 11, 2006; *50 Years,*
       82; SFA, *1976–77 Who's Who;* SFA, *1987–88 Who's Who;* SFA, *1996 Who's
       Who.*
81   Eagle . . . had yet to post a profit: Benezra, "Can Poldoian Fly Eagle";
       Greenwald, "Frito-Lay under Snack Attack"; Anheuser-Busch press
       release, "Anheuser-Busch Closes Eagle Snacks Subsidiary, Sells Four
       Plants to Frito-Lay," February 7, 1996.
81   "To be sure, Eagle appears focused": Benezra, "Can Poldoian Fly Eagle."
81   newspapers around the country: Gibson, "Anheuser-Busch Will Sell
       Snacks Unit"; Michael Quint, "Cardinals and Snack Unit Are Put on
       Block by Busch," *New York Times,* October 26, 1995.
82   The division was said to have lost: Quint, "Cardinals and Snack Unit."
82   an "infusion of capital": Gibson, "Anheuser-Busch Will Sell Snacks
       Unit."
82   "in '95 the clarion call in boardrooms": Kevin Bowler, e-mail message to
       author, June 5, 2006. A statement by Eagle president David Poldoian in
       January 2007 supports this view: "I don't know whether one would say
       something went wrong. I'd like to think that other priorities came into
       play (Jeremiah McWilliams, "Eagle Snacks Quietly Returns to Area's
       Store Shelves," *St. Louis Post-Dispatch,* January 19, 2007).
82   Eagle would carry existing business: Gibson, "Anheuser-Busch Will Sell
       Snacks Unit."
82   "As you may have already learned": Steven S. Reinemund to "Frito-Lay
       Associates," obtained under ATFY01-109, October 26, 1995.
82   It was reported that Nabisco: George Lazarus, "Eagle's Plants Have
       Landed in the Lap of Frito-Lay," *Chicago Tribune,* February 8, 1996.
82   seven "financial groups" of investors: Melcher and Burns, "How Eagle
       Became Extinct." A motion for a temporary restraining order from

Ronald M. Vincent and others mentions that "two major investment groups" had submitted proposals to acquire Eagle ("Memorandum of plaintiffs in support of motion for temporary restraining order and preliminary injunction," April 18, 1996, *Ronald M. Vincent et al., v. Eagle Snacks, Inc., et al.*, [E.D. Calif.]).

82 "here was a company with poor market position": Melcher and Burns, "How Eagle Became Extinct."

82 Four Eagle plants: Anheuser-Busch press release, "Anheuser-Busch Closes Eagle Snacks."

82 Overall Eagle reportedly took: Melcher and Burns, "How Eagle Became Extinct." In 2007 Eagle quietly made a comeback in its hometown of St. Louis. The brand is sold in about half of Schnuck's supermarkets in the region by Reserve Brands Inc. of Chicago, which hopes to "capitalize on historical goodwill for the snacks" (McWilliams, "Eagle Snacks Quietly Returns").

83 Borden still had Wise: Greenwald, "Frito-Lay under Snack Attack."

83 Keebler had announced plans to quit: Quint, "Cardinals and Snack Unit."

83 Frito-Lay's portion of the salty snack market: Greenwald, "Frito-Lay under Snack Attack."

83 In potato chips, Lay's and Ruffles: Benezra, "Can Poldoian Fly Eagle."

Chapter 6. Trust and Antitrust

84 "There is a paradox at the center of antitrust": Lovett interview.

84 When Frito agreed to buy: Neal G. Goulet, "Eagle Makes Its Last Snacks," *York Daily Record*, March 1, 1996.

85 In the next few months Frito announced: "Frito-Lay's New Factory to Create Up to 300 Jobs," *Nashville Banner*, May 31, 1996; "Frito-Lay Completes Visalia Plant Purchase," *Fresno Bee*, June 1, 1996; "Snack Times Frito-Lay Chips In," *York Daily Record*, February 27, 1997.

86 "If Frito Lay acquires": "Memorandum of plaintiffs in support of motion for temporary restraining order and preliminary injunction," April 18, 1996, *Vincent v. Eagle Snacks* (E.D. Calif.).

86 They claimed the proposed transaction: Ibid.

86 The accompanying complaint for damages: "Complaint for damages and injunctive relief," April 18, 1996, *Vincent v. Eagle Snacks* (E.D. Calif.).

86 "This is a purely bricks-and-mortar transaction": "Memorandum of defendants Pepsico, Inc. and Frito-Lay, Inc. in opposition to plaintiffs' motion for Temporary Restraining Order," April 25, 1996, *Vincent v. Eagle Snacks* (E.D. Calif.).

87 "As a result of its commitment": Ibid.

87 David Poldoian, the Eagle president: Fred Faust, "A-B Sued over Sale of Eagle Snacks," *St. Louis Post-Dispatch*, April 24, 1996.

87   In a paper dated April 25 1996: "Order denying motion for temporary re-
      straining order," *Vincent v. Eagle Snacks* (E.D. Calif.).

87   In late April the Department of Justice closed: Memo, "Frito-Lay's pro-
      posed acquisition of assets of Eagle Snacks, Inc.: Recommendation to
      close investigation," Patricia G. Chick and Joel A. Christie to J. Robert
      Kramer II and Willie Hudgins, April 21, 1996. Approval was given on
      May 3, 1996, according to Robert Frank, "U.S. Questions Sales Practices
      at Frito-Lay," *Wall Street Journal*, May 24, 1996.

88   two commentators: "Justice Department Investigates Frito-Lay for Pos-
      sible Antitrust Violations," May 24, 1996.

88   The new Justice investigation was separate: Frank, "U.S. Questions Sales
      Practices." The request to open a preliminary investigation was made
      March 5, 1996 (memo, "Request to open preliminary investigation:
      Frito-Lay, Inc.," Nina B. Hale to Roger W. Fones, March 5, 1996).

88   Frito-Lay spokesperson Lynn Markley: Janet Kidd Stewart, "U.S. Prob-
      ing Snack Firms, *Chicago Sun-Times*, May 25, 1996.

88   Two weeks later: John Greenwald, "Frito-Lay under Snack Attack,"
      Time, June 10, 1996.

88   Bemused food industry experts: Gary M. Galles, "Guest Editorial: Frito
      Banditos?" *Investor's Business Daily*, June 21, 1996.

88   "Don't blame Frito-Lay": Bob Messenger, "Frito-Lay Probe Asks Ques-
      tions about Shelf-Space Crunch," *Food Processing*, July 1996.

89   A seventeen-page "confidential memorandum": "Anticompetitive prac-
      tices of Frito-Lay, Inc.," June 22, 1995 (60-2096-0002).

89   Withheld from my request entirely: Letter, "Re: Freedom of information
      act request No. ATFY01-109," Ann Lea Harding to author, May 1, 2001.
      Of the documents withheld, fifty-three contained identities of confi-
      dential sources, thirty-four contained responses to a Civil Investigative
      Demand, two were withheld for potential invasion of personal privacy,
      and ten contained confidential business information. Nine documents
      (seventy-nine pages) reflected "the deliberative process of the Antitrust
      Division staff, withheld pursuant to 5 U.S.C. § 552(b)(5)."

90   On the basis of such complaints: Civil Investigative Demand No. 15327.

90   The Department of Justice demanded a surfeit of information: Ibid.

91   "prefer not to pay for shelf space": Memo, "Meeting with Frito Lay,"
      Tara Sweeney to "Files," July 29, 1996 (60-2096-0002).

91   a workbook titled "Customer Focused Selling": Frito-Lay, Inc., "Cus-
      tomer Focused Selling Workbook," no date, 3-10, 4-6.

92   Topic 7 in the workbook: Ibid., 7-5, 7-6.

93   Frito-Lay data about the Atlanta market: undated table and chart on
      page with Frito-Lay logo, "YTD Supplier Performance Atlanta Mar-
      ket," obtained under ATFY01-109.

93   "the highest impulse categories": undated graphic image and text on page
      with Frito-Lay logo, "The Right Fit," obtained under ATFY01-109.

93 "Despite their use of salty snacks": Ibid., emphasis added, citing source as "1995 Salty Snacks Purchase Observation Study/Meyers Research Center."

93 Kroger Customer-Management Agreement: Memo, "Subject: 1997 CMA/Reset schedule," Ken Hall to Kroger Delta Distribution.

94 On DOJ stationery, dated April 23, 1998: "Memorandum: Recommendation to Close Investigation: Frito-Lay, Inc.," Nina Hale, Jill Ptacek, and Dick Doidge to Roger W. Fones.

94 Pages 4 to 14 . . . were entirely redacted: Exemption 5 U.S.C. § 552(b)(5) allows withholding from public disclosure due to "the deliberative process of Antitrust Division staff." Courts have distinguished between "materials reflecting deliberative or policy-making processes" versus "purely factual, investigative matters," stating that the "privilege applies only to the 'opinion' or 'recommendatory'" part of the document and not to the factual information contained within; facts must be disclosed unless they are "inextricably intertwined" with exempt portions (Hammitt, Sobel, and Stedman, 136). On June 21, 2006, I made a second FOIA request for the April 23, 1998, memo; it was denied on August 15, 2006, and an administrative appeal that I filed for the action was denied on February 27, 2007.

94 "the Justice Department has closed its investigation": Nikhil Deogun, "U.S. Probe into Practices by Frito-Lay Ends without Charges Being Brought," *Wall Street Journal.*

94 "We are very pleased with their decision": Dana Canedy, "Inquiry into Frito-Lay Finds No Wrongdoing in Marketing," *New York Times.*

95 James W. Lovett . . . believes: Lovett interview.

95 "The problem is Frito-Lay": Quoted in Canedy, "Inquiry into Frito-Lay."

95 "The conclusion of the Justice Department review": Jared Dougherty, e-mail message to author, May 3, 2007.

96 "By this standard of thinking": Gundlach interview.

Chapter 7. The Heartland

97 "Stable climates with muted seasons": Wilson, 201.

97 "You've never seen anything like it": Ken Potter interview, July 11, 2004.

97 In 1999 Cape Cod . . . was bought by Lance: Steven Wilmsen, "Cape Cod Potato Chip of Hyannis to Be Sold a Second Time; Charlotte, N.C., Snack Company Is Buyer; Price Is Not Disclosed," *Boston Globe,* April 17, 1999.

97 Guy's Foods . . . sought bankruptcy protection: Dan Margolies, "Judge Oks Plan to Fund Guy's Payroll: Order Authorizes Lender to Advance Company $528,455," *Kansas City Star,* February 16, 2000. Today, Guy's chips are produced under that name by Heartland Snacks of Kansas City, Missouri.

97 In 2000 Borden sold Wise: Jim Weiker, "Borden Sells Wise Snack-Food Line," *Columbus Dispatch,* September 7, 2000.

97 Seyfert's . . . ended up with Troyer Farms: Dan Margolies, "Snack Company Investors Sign Letter of Intent to Sell Operation," *Kansas City Star,* March 10, 2000.

98 it employs 350 people: Holinger interview. The 110,000 square feet includes warehouse space.

98 "Lancaster County is the chip capital of the country": Ibid.

98 "This is the potato chip Mecca of the world": Hoover interview, May 6, 2004.

98 "We're in the potato chip area": Hake interview.

99 "People in the rest of the U.S.": Groff interview.

99 Pennsylvania has sixteen independent chip companies: Bickel's, Bon Ton, Dieffenbach's, Gibble's, Herr's, Kay & Ray's, King's, Martin's, Middleswarth, Original Goods, Ralph Good's, Snyder of Berlin, Snyder of Hanover, Troyer, Utz, Zerbe's. The definition of an "independent" chip company is expanded here to include companies having separate corporate histories with distinct products that are now under a single ownership: Bickel's and Bon Ton; Gibble's and Kay & Ray's; and Original and Ralph Good's. Dan Dee, Seyfert's, and O.K. chips all use the same recipe as Troyer's brand chips and are distributed principally in other states (Kane interview).

99 In 2005, market surveys rated Utz fourth: *Redbook, Bakery Production and Marketing,* 42.

100 In 2005, market surveys rated Herr's seventh: Ibid.

100 Like Herr's, Utz has only two potato chip plants: Conversation with Gary Laabs, July 19, 2006.

100 over 500,000 square feet: Ibid.

100 Bob Jones, president of Jones: Jones interview, December 19, 2001.

100 "Unless you've got a really, really super winner": Bob Shearer interview.

100 "There's more to printing a bag": Noss interview, July 9, 2004.

101 "When I was young, there were three flavors": Thomas interview, May 6, 2004.

101 "The trick is to know your market": Interview with anonymous Ohio chipper.

101 "They're doing some 'taste-testing'": Davis interview.

101 "Even the big guys need an enemy": Thomas interview, July 13, 2004.

101 CEO Leonard Japp Jr. died in 1999: Mari Cornell, *Baking & Snack,* November 1, 1999.

101 followed by grandson Leonard Japp III: Sandra Guy, "Still Chipping Away," *Chicago Sun Times,* May 2, 2001.

101 same year founder Leonard Japp Sr. . . . died: Associated Press, "Jays Foods Founder Dead at 96," August 27, 2000.

101   the struggling family-owned company: James B. Arndorfer, "Jays Foods in $30-mil. Buyout Deal," *Chicago Business News*, March 5, 2004.

102   In Chicago, Frito's survey: "Frito-Lay Can't Prove It Tastes Better," *Billings Gazette*, July 25, 2004.

102   After a court ruling in favor of Jays: Matt O'Connor and Jim Kirk, "Frito-Lay Settles Dispute with Jays," *Chicago Tribune*, August 3, 2004.

102   "People often forget": Jared Dougherty, e-mail message to author, May 3, 2007.

102   Original Goods of New Holland: Bon Ton chips, now produced and owned by Hanover Foods, are alleged to have started their operation in 1900. Other old chip companies include Tri-Sum (originally Leominster) of Leominster, Massachusetts (1908), and Mike-sell's of Dayton, Ohio (1910). Wise and Utz both date to 1921. Before 1921, now-defunct companies that mass-produced potato chips early include Toledo's Kuehmann (who later marketed "Q-Man" chips), dating to 1899; Cleveland's Dan Dee from 1913 (now owned by Troyer); and the Noss family's Num Num from 1918 (*SFBB*, 72; *50 Years*, 31, 228; Kuehmann packaging).

103   "Over in Pennsylvania": Mesre interview, May 14, 2001.

103   "The lard taste is pretty particular": Weber interview, July 13, 2004.

103   "In this part of Pennsylvania": Hoover interview, March 30, 2000.

103   "It's like pies": William Backer interview, March 15, 2001.

103   Lewis Good, owner of the company: Lewis and Lynn Good interviews, July 13, 2004.

105   Similar to the Gibble chip: King's also produces a lard chip on a continuous cooker, but it is made to mimic a traditional kettle-style chip (Weber interview, July 13, 2004).

105   Greg Good says they have their hands full: conversation with Good, June 29, 2006.

105   "We just keep it the same": Greg Good interview, July 12, 2004.

105   The Amish population of Lancaster County: Jones, *Religious and Congregational Numbers*.

105   "A lot of our customers come from a distance": Holinger interview.

105   "Further west . . . there's fewer companies": Interview with anonymous individual.

106   The Rider family . . . once supplied potatoes: Rider family interviews, July 7, 2004.

106   "There's no chip plant in Cleveland": Ira Rider interview.

108   "It got to a point where buyers would say": Jones interview, July 8, 2004.

111   "Rap Snacks was a way to create a market": Lindsay interview.

111   At the time of this writing: Conversation with Lindsay, April 5, 2007.

112   "Most of our business is in an area": Jones interview, December 19, 2001.

112   "A lot of people hear *marcelled* and think it's a flavor": Ballreich interview, January 6, 2000.

112   As the story goes . . . Fred Ballreich: "Ballreich History," www.ballreich
.com/history.

112   Cain's Marcelle Potato Chip Company: A company profile in *SFBB*
(103) credits the *marcelled* epithet to Emerson Cain.

112   Mose Mesre, of Conn's: Mesre interview, May 14, 2001.

114   "but it could be the thickness": Jones interview, July 19, 2006.

114   "When a potato gets to our factory": Ballreich, e-mail message to author,
March 1, 2005.

114   Ira Rider . . . recalls: Rider family interviews, July 7, 2004.

115   "That was the greatest thing about O.K. potato chips": Ed Rider inter-
view, June 27, 2006. Today the O.K. chip is made by Troyer Farms of
Waterford, Pennsylvania, using the same recipe that all Troyer's chips use
(Kane interview).

115   Sterzing's . . . makes a thick, robust kettle chip: Blackwood interview.

115   Martin's drops freshly sliced potatoes: Ken Potter interview, July 11, 2004.

115   "When you eat a typical chip": Butch Potter interview.

116   "We fry lower than anyone else": George interview, December 8, 2006.

117   "I knew it would be a dramatic change": Klein interview, November 9,
2006.

Chapter 8. A Few of Our Favorite Things

118   "Now let me tell you something": Mesre interview, May 14, 2001.

118   "The craze on carbohydrates": Weber interview, May 13, 2004.

119   Saturated fats are usually . . . animal fats: Hadley, 2–3. Hadley mentions
coconut, palm, and some "seed oils" as saturated fatty acids (3).

119   cited as having bad effects on health: Onno Korver and Martijn B.
Katan, "The Elimination of Trans Fats from Spreads: How Science
Helped to Turn an Industry Around," *Nutrition Reviews* 64, no. 6
(2006): 275–79.

119   Unsaturated fats . . . are those with one or more double bonds: Hadley,
3–4, 6.

119   "Hardening" of oils: Korver and Katan, "Elimination of Trans Fats," 275.

120   In the process of partial hydrogenation: McDonald and Mossoba mention that quantifying *cis* and *trans* isomers is challenging: "as hydrogenation proceeds, the double bonds of both *cis* and *trans* isomers move up
and down the fatty acid chain. This can produce many isomers in polyunsaturated vegetable oils with the resulting fatty acid isomer mixture so
complex that complete quantification of all fatty acid isomers in partially
hydrogenated oils is very difficult" (Richard E. McDonald and Magdi
M. Mossoba, "Trans Fatty Acids: Labeling, Nutrition, and Analysis," in
McDonald and Min, 161–97).

120   naturally present in animals: Martijn B. Katan, "Regulation of *Trans*

Fats: The Gap, the Polder, and McDonald's French Fries," *Atherosclerosis Supplements* 7, no. 2 (2006): 63–66.

120 trans fats are otherwise rare: Hadley, 4.

120 chips could stay on shelves longer: Klein and Strauss, personal communications with author.

120 trans fats might even be worse: Korver and Katan, "Elimination of Trans Fats."

120 possibly caused inflammation: Katan, "Regulation of *Trans* Fats."

120 "the most dangerous ingredient in our diet": Dariush Mozaffarian, quoted in Ellen Barry, "Proposed Trans-Fat Ban Gains Support," *Seattle Times,* October 31, 2006. For more on the subject, see Mozaffarian et al., "Trans Fats and Cardiovascular Disease," *New England Journal of Medicine* 354 (2006):1601–13.

120 ingredients on Golden Flake bags: Before 2006 chippers were required to state only total fat and saturated fat on package labels. They could volunteer calories for saturated, monounsaturated, and polyunsaturated fat, but trans fat could not be included in the labeling for those fats. Confused consumers sometimes contacted the FDA to inquire why total fats were more than the sum of saturated, monounsaturated, or polyunsaturated fats on some labels (McDonald and Mossoba, "Trans Fatty Acids," 162). By January 1, 2006, labeling of trans fats on food packages was required (Korver and Katan, "Elimination of Trans Fats").

121 "Who knew before that there was bad stuff in it?": Strauss interview, November 17, 2006.

121 Don Markov, director of sales: Markov interview.

122 "We did not and will not change our oil": George interview, November 17, 2006.

122 it isn't "anywhere close to a proven issue": Butch Potter interview.

122 When Mister Bee . . . switched: Klein interview, November 9, 2006.

122 In 1993 Louise's of Kentucky: Hollandsworth, "Hot Potatoes."

122 Frito's scientists tried everything: Ibid.

123 Procter & Gamble . . . developing "sucrose polyesters": "Olean Timeline," http://www.olean.com/default.asp?p=facts&id=t; Zach Schiller, "Consumer Group Takes Chip at Pringles: Procter & Gamble Defends Fat Free Potato," *Newark Star Ledger,* January 2, 1997.

123 By the time olestra was ready: Marian Burros, "No One Can Eat One Bag: Olestra Potato Chips' Flavor Isn't the Problem in Test Markets," *Fort Worth Star Telegram,* May 23, 1996.

123 Frito-Lay became the first: Robert Frank, "Frito-Lay Puts Up More Than Chips in Deal for Olestra," *Wall Street Journal,* May 31, 1996.

123 Frito-Lay sold the chips: Burros, "No One Can Eat One Bag"; Matt Kelley, "Tests Gauge What Sells in Cedar Rapids," *Omaha World-Herald,* September 1, 1996.

124 supposedly costing "in the eight figures": Frank, "Frito-Lay Puts Up."

124 signed the contract for olestra: Dow Jones News Service–Wall Street Journal Stories, "Frito-Lay Inc. Puts up -2: Company Acknowledges Its Risk," May 31, 1996.

124 "It travels through the body unchanged": "Frequently Asked Questions," http://www.olean.com/default.asp?p=faq.

124 olestra . . . "hasn't exactly set the world on fire": Leslie Hillman, "Four-Star Chef Rates Olestra Substitute Highly/Procter & Gamble's Controversial Product Gets Rave Reviews at New York Dinner," *Austin-American Statesman*, February 26, 1997.

124 "I smoke cigarettes": Quoted in Burros, "No One Can Eat One Bag."

124 "if you are the kind of person": Ibid.

124 Defenders of the chip said: Dan McGraw, "Salting Away Big Profits: Frito-Lay Launches a Powerful Snack Attack and Crunches the Competition," *U.S. News & World Report*, September 16, 1996.

124 choosing olestra over fat reduced: "Frequently Asked Questions," http://www.olean.com/default.asp?p=faq.

125 still required to announce: Burros, "No One Can Eat One Bag."

125 Center for Science in the Public Interest: Schiller, "Consumer Group Takes Chip."

125 P&G announced that twelve other "marketers": *Advertising Age*, December 23, 1996.

125 the name WOW! instead of MAX: Hillman, "Four-Star Chef."

125 At the same time, concerns about fats: Dougherty interview; press release, "Lay's Potato Chips Cuts Saturated Fat by More Than Half," http://www.fritolay.com/fl/flstore/cgi-bin/ProdDetEv_Cat_304_SubCat_445469_NavRoot_303_ProdID_476855.htm.

126 Detractors became pervasive by the early 1970s: *50 Years*, 252.

126 "the nutritional or biological value of protein": C. M. McCay, C. J. B. McCay, and O. Smith, "The Nutritive Value of Potatoes," in Talburt and Smith, 293.

127 "On a national basis": Ibid., 299.

127 Other negative aspects: Ibid., 309.

127 "About 100 mg of solanine": Ibid., 298.

127 In 1950 Dr. Norman Childers: Childers, 17.

128 "I have been on the No-Nightshades diet": Ibid., 86.

128 "I am 50 years": Ibid., 89.

128 Of those who followed the regimen: Ibid., 18.

128 published at least one scientific paper: N. F. Childers and M. S. Margoles, "An Apparent Relation of Nightshades (Solanaceae) to Arthritis," *Journal of Neurological and Orthopedic Medical Surgery* 12 (1993): 227–31.

128 "Livestock people have known about nightshades": Childers interview.

128 "a calcification (hardening) of certain tissues of cattle": Davis, "Degenerative Effects of Nightshades on Livestock," in Childers, 172–81.

129 the case of three schoolchildren who died: A. Zitnak, "Nightshade Foods: Effects on Animals and People," in Childers, 193.

129 "We need research on it": Childers interview.

129 some research and opinions cast doubt: *Consumer Reports*, August 1996, 96; David Schardt, "Take Two Walnuts," *Nutrition Action Health Letter* 21 (March 1994): 8; "Ask Tufts Experts," *Tufts University Health & Nutrition Letter* 21 (September 2003): 7.

129 A 2006 study found: A. Peksa et al., "Changes of Glycoalkaloids and Nitrate Contents in Potatoes during Chip Processing," *Food Chemistry* 97 (2006): 151–56. It is not entirely clear from the article whether the "chips" in the study were french fries, which are often called chips in England and Europe, or true potato chips; but the effects of peeling, slicing, washing, and frying on solanine is presumably similar for both.

130 "tough to work with": Jim Green, e-mail to author, December 4, 2006.

131 "Potatoes get a higher sugar content": Carr interview.

131 it is easily converted into glucose: McCay, McCay, and Smith, "Nutritive Value," 308–10.

132 over two-thirds of adults are overweight: Declan Butler, "Slim Pickings," *Nature* 428 (2004):252–54; Cynthia L. Ogden et al., "Prevalence of Overweight and Obesity in the United States, 1999–2004," *JAMA* 295 (2006): 1549–55.

132 In the early nineteenth century: Timo Strandberg, "Roots of the Atkins Diet," *British Medical Journal* 330 (2005): 132.

132 In the 1960s Dr. Robert C. Atkins: Muha, 15.

132 loss of appetite was attributed: Ibid., 18. Researchers in one study doubted that the small increase in blood ketone levels in a low-carb diet had "anorectic effects," but rather that an associated decrease in insulin levels may have reduced appetite (Geunther Boden et al., "Effect of a Low-Carbohydrate Diet on Appetite, Blood Glucose Levels, and Insulin Resistance in Obese Patients with Type 2 Diabetes," *Annals of Internal Medicine* 142 [2005]:403–11).

132 "It was almost as if the more you ate": Muha, 21.

132 The act of breaking proteins' amino acids: John L. Mego, "The Low-Carb Craze," *American Fitness* 23, no. 6 (2005): 40–41.

133 ketoacidosis, a potentially life-threatening condition: Berkow, Beers, and Fletcher, 718; Tsuh-Yin Chen et al., "A Life-Threatening Complication of the Atkins Diet," *Lancet* 367 (2006): 958.

133 In the early 1970s Atkins promoted: Melinda Hemmelgarn, "Dr. Atkins' New Diet Revolution: Selling like Hotcakes," *Healthy Weight Journal* 10 (1996): 74; Daniel Kadlec, "The Low-Carb Frenzy," *Time*, May 3, 2004, 47–54.

133   While eating high-protein meats: Atkins, 5.

133   "between 45 and 100 grams of net carbs a day": Ibid., 6. Another source mentions "40 to 60 grams of net carbohydrates" per day (Mark A. Moyad, "Fad Diets and Obesity—Part III: A Rapid Review of Some of the More Popular Low-Carbohydrate Diets," *Urologic Nursing* 24 [2004]: 442–45).

133   South Beach Diet was lower in saturated fat: "Weighing In on the South Beach Diet," *Tufts University Health & Nutrition Letter* 22 (May 2004): 1–8.

133   Potatoes (and presumably potato chips) were specifically discouraged: Atkins, 39; Moyad, "Fad Diets."

133   Patients reported losing: Atkins, 18, 30.

133   seventy million limiting carb intake: Kadlec, "Low-Carb Frenzy," 48.

133   Heinz, General Mills, Subway: Ibid., 50–52; Marguerite Higgins, "Demand for Low-Carb Products Falls Off," *Washington Times,* August 2, 2005.

133   Surveys estimated that more than 9 percent: Higgins, "Demand for Low-Carb"; John Miller, "Spud Farmers 'Jumping Up and Down in Their Fields' after Atkins Filing," Associated Press State & Local Wire, August 4, 2005.

133   traditional diet programs . . . were losing members: Kadlec, "Low-Carb Frenzy," 54.

134   By 2005 overall U.S. potato consumption had dropped: Miller, "Spud Farmers."

134   Nutritional scientists, caught unawares: Butler, "Slim Pickings."

134   confounding factors such as high dietary fat: M. E. Fleming, K. M. Sales, and M. C. Winslet, "Diet and Colorectal Cancer: Implications for the Obese and Devotees of the Atkins Diet," *Colorectal Disease* 7 (2005): 128–32.

134   "loved the diet": "Study of Obese Diabetics Explains Why Low-Carb Diets Produce Fast Results," *Healthcare Mergers, Acquisitions & Ventures Week,* April 9, 2005, paraphrasing Boden et al., "Effect of a Low-Carbohydrate Diet."

134   low-carb dieters replaced "bad carb" consumption: Richard D. Feinman, Mary C. Vernon, and Eric C. Westman, "Low Carbohydrate Diets in Family Practice: What Can We Learn from an Internet-based Support Group," *Nutrition Journal* 5 (2006): 26.

134   A study that randomly assigned twenty adults: Carol S. Johnston, Sherrie L. Tjonn, and Pamela D. Swan, "High-Protein, Low-Fat Diets Are Effective for Weight Loss and Favorably Alter Biomarkers in Healthy Adults," *Journal of Nutrition* 134 (2004): 586–91.

134   Nutritionists, long skeptical of the low-carb diets: Lyn M. Steffen and Jennifer A. Nettleton, "Carbohydrates: How Low Can You Go?" *Lancet*

367 (2006): 880–81; University of Colorado nutritionist: Butler, "Slim Pickings."

134   A sports nutritionist complained: Nancy Clark, "Athletes Abandon Atkins!" *American Fitness* 23 (2005): 66–67.

135   A six-month study found: Frederick F. Samaha et al., "A Low-Carbohydrate as Compared with a Low-Fat Diet in Severe Obesity," *New England Journal of Medicine* 348 (2003): 2074–81.

135   but a longer study . . . revealed: Gary D. Foster et al., "A Randomized Trial of a Low-Carbohydrate Diet for Obesity," *New England Journal of Medicine* 348 (2003): 2082–90.

135   One group of researchers . . . found: "Brown University: Low-Fat Diet Better Long-Term," *Health Insurance Week,* December 12, 2004.

135   The carb bubble burst in 2005: Higgins, "Demand for Low-Carb"; Miller, "Spud Farmers." Atkins came out of Chapter 11 bankruptcy protection in January 2006 (*London Times,* "Atkins Emerges," January 11, 2006).

135   "come back to common sense": "Brown University."

135   The president of the Idaho Potato Commission: Miller, "Spud Farmers."

135   "Five or six months ago": Bob Shearer interview.

135   "Every time they come up with something different": George interview, November 17, 2006.

135   "It's a different journey for different people": Dougherty interview.

136   In early 2002 researchers in Sweden: Richard H. Stadler and Gabriele Scholz, "Acrylamide: An Update on Current Knowledge in Analysis, Levels in Food, Mechanisms of Formation, and Potential Strategies of Control," *Nutrition Reviews* 62 (2004): 449–67.

136   It is a precursor to a polymer: Center for Food Safety and Applied Nutrition, FDA, "Acrylamide Questions & Answers," February 25, 2003, http://www.cfsan.fda.gov/~dms/acryfaq.html.

136   "cause genetic, neurological and reproductive damage": "Acrylamide: Initial Worry Blunted by New Research, but Still a Concern," *Environmental Nutrition,* October 2003.

136   "probable human carcinogen": Stadler and Scholz, "Acrylamide"; Andy Coghlan, "The Food Scare the World Forgot," *New Scientist* 189 (2006): 8–10.

136   "stagger, collapse, and die": Coglan, "The Food Scare."

136   breads (especially crusts), cereals, coffee, biscuits: Stadler and Scholz, "Acrylamide"; Center for Food Safety and Applied Nutrition, FDA, "Survey Data on Acrylamide in Food: Individual Food Products," December 2002; updated March 2003, March 2004, June 2005, and July 2006, http://www.cfsan.fda.gov/~dms/acrydata.html.

136   Even home-cooked foods were not immune: Coghlan, "The Food Scare."

136   a USDA database of foods tested: "Survey Data on Acrylamide in Food."

137   Utz's Home Style Kettle-Cooked Potato Chips: Fritz Livelsberger, personal communication to author, March 15, 2007.

137 Meanwhile, other products . . . had appreciable acrylamide levels: "Survey Data on Acrylamide in Food."

137 Tests with lab animals were done: Center for Food Safety, "Acrylamide Questions & Answers."

137 data from a long-term sample of nurses: Nigel Hawkes, "Girls Who Eat Chips More Likely to Get Breast Cancer," *London Times*, August 19, 2005. "Chips" in the title appears to refer to french fries.

137 a study of Swedish women found no association: "Acrylamide: Initial Worry," *Environmental Nutrition;* Harvard School of Public Health, "Study Shows Acrylamide in Baked and Fried Foods Does Not Increase Risk of Breast Cancer in Women," March 15, 2005, http://www.hsph .harvard.edu/press/releases/press03152005.html.

137 Research to date suggests that lowering sugars: Stadler and Scholz, "Acrylamide"; Franco Pedreschi et al., "Color Development and Acrylamide Content of Pre-Dried Potato Chips," *Journal of Food Engineering* 79 (2007): 786–93.

137 California's attorney general filed suit: Melanie Warner, "California Wants to Serve a Health Warning with That Order," *New York Times,* September 21, 2005.

138 "when Congress established uniform requirements": National Uniformity for Food Coalition, "About the Legislation," http://www.uniformity for food.org/legislation.htm.

138 In March 2006 SFA announced: "In SFA Victory, House Passes National Uniformity Bill," *Snack Food & Wholesale Bakery,* March 2006.

138 California withdrew rules: "The State of California Has Withdrawn Proposed Rules That Would Have Required Food Manufacturers to Place Acrylamide Warning Labels on Certain Products," *Frozen Food Age,* April 2006.

138 "I love potato chips. Doesn't everyone?": Robert L. Wolke, "Chicken over Chips," *Washington Post,* August 30, 2006.

139 "Katic said that if he is going to stop": "Chicken over Chips?" *Snack Food & Wholesale Bakery,* October 2006.

139 consumers who worried about acrylamide: "Acrylamide: Initial Worry," *Environmental Nutrition;* Linda Bren, "Turning Up the Heat on Acrylamide," *FDA Consumer,* January/February 2003.

139 "election-year politics": Bob Gatty, "Key Legislative Victories Are within Reach," *Snack Food & Wholesale Bakery,* August 2006.

139 Although the U.S. House of Representatives: Clark interview.

Chapter 9. Everything Old Is New Again

140 "When I started": Quoted in Macnow, "Taste of Old Cape Cod."

140 "We went back to basics": Kennedy interview.

141 Shearer's has a sludge recovery facility: Melissa Shearer interview, July 8, 2004.

142 it had grown to twenty-four kettle cookers: Melissa Shearer, e-mail message to author, April 17, 2007.

143 "Mr. Martin had one route": "WHP Legends of Success series by John Resnick; interview of Ken Potter" (audiocassette).

143 For three nights a week: interviews with Ken Potter.

144 "Everybody copied what I did": Ken Potter interview, July 11, 2004.

144 "I wish I had a dollar": Bernard interview.

144 After the 1985 buyout: Jerry Ackerman, "Cape Cod Chip's Plan Is Simple: Get Back on the Shelves," *Boston Globe,* February 19, 1997.

144 Snacktime came out with Krunchers: *50 years,* 330; PR Newswire Association, "Borden Agrees to Acquire Culbro Unit for $55 Million," July 2, 1987.

145 By 1990, as overall sales: Macnow, "Taste of Old Cape Cod."

145 "We didn't do any research": Cohen interviews.

148 "Kettle brand was raised": Green interview.

148 In 1986 Tim Kennedy introduced: Kennedy interview.

149 In the Midwest, Art's & Mary's: Albers interview.

149 On Long Island: Sidor interview. Sidor related an incident in which the bright foil of the North Fork package set off burglar alarms two nights in a row at a Manhattan gourmet food shop. Apparently, headlights from turning cars reflecting off the silvery bags aroused the alarm system, prompting the shop owner to move the North Fork display away from the corner window.

149 "refugee from the energy business": Zappe interview.

149 "We had some guy from England call": Palmisano interview.

150 "Chips provide an opening for people": Dougherty interview.

150 "Things have come full circle": Thomas interview, July 13, 2004.

151 "I would never have believed": Selwyn interview. One category listed on the site as "Snacks that rhyme with (Justice Sam) Alito" is dominated by reviews of Cheetos. According to Selwyn, the category was originally called "Snacks that rhyme with taquito" and later "Snacks that rhyme with Judge Ito."

154 "People get used to buying our chips": Roudebush interview.

154 "Stay small—that's how we like it": Dale Backer interview.

154 "Our niche is to appeal to southern tastes": Strauss interview, May 28, 2004.

154 "We look at flavor trends from the restaurant industry": Dougherty interview.

154 "We're so close we piss on each other's shoes": Interview with anonymous kettle chipper.

154 "The beautiful thing about Route 11": Cohen interview, July 14, 2004.

154 "I tell retailers, 'I don't want to take away from your current sales'": Poore interview.

155 "I can't think of too many situations": Jones interview, July 8, 2004.

155 "I still believe there is a market for potato chips": Klein interview, May 11, 2006.

155 "When you're running and stressed and want a quick boost of energy": Thomas interview, May 6, 2004.

155 "This isn't serious food, this is fun food": Ver Vaet interview.

155 "It's all about fun": Palmisano interview.

Books Cited

Atkins, Robert C. *Atkins for Life*. New York: St. Martin's Press, 2003.

Bellury, Phillip R., and Gail Guterl. *The History of Herr's*. Nottingham, PA: Herr Foods, 1995.

Berkow, Robert, Mark H. Beers, and Andrew J. Fletcher, eds. *The Merck Manual of Medical Information*. Whitehouse Station, NJ: Merck Research Laboratories, 1997.

Blackstock, Joseph R. *Report on Laura Scudder*. Monterey Park, CA: Historical Society of Monterey Park, 1974.

Bradley, Hugh. *Such Was Saratoga*. New York: Doubleday, 1940.

Britten, Evelyn Barrett. *Chronicles of Saratoga*. Saratoga Springs, NY: privately printed, 1959.

Burton, W. G. *The Potato: A Survey of Its History and of Factors Influencing Its Yield, Nutritive Value, Quality and Storage*. Wageningen, Holland: H. Veenman & Zonen, 1966.

Childers, Norman F. *Arthritis—Childers' Diet That Stops It!* Gainesville, FL: Dr. Norman F. Childers Publications, 2006.

Hadley, Neil F. *The Adaptive Role of Lipids in Biological Systems*. New York: John Wiley & Sons, 1985.

Hammitt, Harry, David L. Sobel, and Tiffany A. Stedman. *Litigation under the Federal Open Government Laws (FOIA) 2004: Covering the Freedom of Information Act, the Privacy Act, the Government in the Sunshine Act, and the Federal Advisory Committee Act*. Washington, DC: Epic Publications; Lynchburg, VA: Access Reports, 2004.

Harris, P. M., ed. *The Potato Crop: The Scientific Basis for Improvement*. London: Chapman & Hall, 1978.

Hawkes, J. G. *The Potato: Evolution, Biodiversity and Genetic Resources*. Washington, DC: Smithsonian Institution Press, 1990.

———. "History of the Potato." In Harris, *Potato Crop*, 1–14.

———. "Biosystematics of the Potato." In Harris, *Potato Crop*, 15–69.

Hess, Jerry L., ed. *Snack Food Blue Book: A Bicentennial History, Market Facts Book and International Directory for Manufacturers, Distributors and Suppliers*. New York: Snack Food Magazine and Harcourt Brace Jovanovich, 1976.

Hollis, Tim. *Hi There, Boys and Girls! America's Local Children's TV Programs*. Jackson: University Press of Mississippi, 2001.

International Directory of Company Histories. "Frito-Lay Company." Vol. 32. Detroit: St. James Press, 2000.

Jones, Dale E. *Religious and Congregational Numbers in the United States.* Nashville, TN: Glenmary Research Center, 2000.

Lahr, John. *Notes on a Cowardly Lion: The Biography of Bert Lahr.* New York: Alfred A. Knopf, 1969.

McDonald, Richard E., and David B. Min, eds. 1996. *Food Lipids and Health.* New York: Marcel Dekker, 1996

Muha, Laura. *Killer Diets: Are Low-Carb Diets High Risk?* New York: Chamberlain Bros., 2005.

Pendergrast, Mark. *For God, Country, and Coca-Cola: The Definitive History of the Great American Soft Drink and the Company That Makes It.* New York: Basic Books, 2000.

Redbook, Bakery Production and Marketing. Kansas City: Sosland Publications, 2005.

Richardson, James B. *People of the Andes.* Montreal: St. Remy Press; Washington, DC: Smithsonian Institution, 1994.

Salaman, Redcliffe N. *The History and Social Influence of the Potato.* London: Cambridge University Press, 1949.

Simpson, George Gaylord. *Tempo and Mode in Evolution.* New York: Hafner, 1965.

Smith, Bruce D. *The Emergence of Agriculture.* New York: Scientific American Library, 1995.

Smith, O. "Potato Chips." In Talburt and Smith, *Potato Processing,* 371–489.

Snack Food Association. *50 years: A Foundation for the Future.* Alexandria, VA: Snack Food Association, 1987.

———. *1976–77 Who's Who in the Snack Food Industry.* Euclid, OH: Snack Food Industry, 1977.

———. *1987–88 Who's Who in the Snack Food Industry.* Alexandria, VA: Snack Food Industry, 1988.

———. *1996 Who's Who in the Snack Food Industry.* Alexandria, VA: Snack Food Industry, 1996.

Sylvester, Nathaniel Bartlett, Samuel T. Wiley, and W. Scott Garner. *History of Saratoga County, New York, with Historical Notes on Its Various Towns.* Richmond, IN: Gresham, 1893.

Talburt, William F., and Ora Smith, eds. *Potato Processing.* New York: Van Nostrand Reinhold, 1987.

Waller, George. *Saratoga: Saga of an Impious Era.* Englewood Cliffs, NJ: Prentice-Hall, 1966.

Warwick, Colin. "The In's and Out's of Fabricated Chips." In Hess, *Snack Food Blue Book,* 107–12.

Whitney, Mrs. Cornelius Vanderbilt. *The Potato Chip Cookbook.* Lexington, KY: Maple Hill Press, 1977.

Wilson, Edward O. *The Diversity of Life*. Cambridge, MA: Belknap Press, 1992.

Zuckerman, Larry. *The Potato: How the Humble Spud Rescued the Western World*. New York: North Point Press, 1998.

Interviews

Albers, Brett, April 29, 2004
Anonymous Florida potato grower, May 18, 2006
Anonymous individual, flexible packaging industry, April 26, 2006
Arrigo, Jennifer, July 13, 2004
Backer, Dale, March 15, 2001
Backer, William, March 1, 2000; March 15, 2001
Ballreich, Sue, January 6, 2000; April 13, 2004
Bare, Bob, July 13, 2004
Bellais, Leslie, May 21, 2004; December 1, 2006
Bernard, Steve, June 28, 2006
Blackwood, Tom, May 6, 2004
Blough, John, May 24–25, 2006
Carr, Don, May 31, 2006
Cepa, Ed, April 26, 2006
Childers, Norman F., November 7, 2006
Clark, Chris, April 15, 2008
Cohen, Sarah, April 29, 2004; July 14, 2004
Davis, John, July 12, 2004
Dodd, Frank, July 21, 2006
Dougherty, Jared, April 20, 2007
Ferre, Jordi, May 25, 2004
George, Thomas, November 17, 2006; December 8, 2006
Gipson, Larry, July 9, 2001; September 12, 2002; January 23, 2004; March 28,
    2004
Good, Greg, July 12, 2004
Good, Lewis, May 6, 2004; July 13, 2004
Good, Lynn, July 13, 2004
Green, Jim, July 10, 2006
Groff, Terry, June 28, 2006
Gundlach, Gregory, June 26, 2006
Hake, Greg, July 11, 2004
Hawk, Jerry, July 3, 2001
Herbst, Rebecca, May 21, 2004
Hess, Rob, May 18, 2006
Holinger, Dan, June 27, 2006

Hoover, Herb, March 30, 2000; May 6, 2004; June 14, 2004; July 12, 2004
Izer, Kim, May 20, 2004
Jones, Bob, December 19, 2001; July 8, 2004; September 20, 2004; July 19, 2006
Kane, Linda, December 21, 2001
Keeney, Mitch, July 12, 2004
Kelley, John, May 20, 2004
Kennedy, Tim, May 14, 2004
Klein, Alan, May 11, 2006; November 9, 2006
Laabs, Gary, April 29, 2004; July 12, 2004
Leopard, Marilyn, July 3, 2001
Lindsay, James, June 30, 2006
Livelsberger, Fritz, July 12, 2004
Lovett, James W., June 26, 2006
Markov, Don, November 9, 2006
McDaniel, Vicki Backer, March 15, 2001; December 11, 2006
Meenan, Dan, December 18, 2001
Mesre, Mose, December 18, 2001; May 14, 2001
Murillo, Bob, September 18, 2002
Noss, Don, April 23, 2004; May 16, 2004; July 9, 2004; February 3, 2005; February 5, 2005; December 7, 2005
Palmisano, Joe, June 28, 2006
Pennekamp, Leroy, June 2001; May 19, 2006
Poore, Jay, April 30, 2004
Potter, Butch, March 7, 2007
Potter, Ken, May 20, 2004; July 11–12, 2004; April 26, 2005
Potter, Kevin, July 12, 2004
Ramseyer, Al, July 7, 2004
Ramseyer, Don, July 7, 2004
Rider, Betty, July 7, 2004
Rider, Ed, December 19, 2001; July 7, 2004; June 27, 2006
Rider, Ira, July 7, 2004
Roudebush, Doug, December 19, 2001
Sabatino, Vic, May 9, 2006; December 4, 2006
Selwyn, Jeremy, March 16, 2007
Seyfert, Joseph, May 3, 2007
Shearer, Bob, July 8, 2004
Shearer, Melissa, June 6, 2004; July 8, 2004
Sidor, Martin and Carol, August 15, 2007
Strauss, Julie, May 28, 2004; November 17, 2006
Thomas, Daryl, May 6, 2004; July 13, 2004
Tousey, Anne, May 13, 2004
Ver Vaet, Keith, July 8, 2004
Waydo, George, May 4, 2006

Weber, Glenn, May 13, 2004; July 13, 2004
White, Dick, December 8, 2006
Zappe, Ron, April 30, 2004

Index